Game Design

Game Design
From Blue Sky to Green Light

Deborah Todd

A K Peters, Ltd.
Wellesley, Massachusetts

Editorial, Sales, and Customer Service Office

A K Peters, Ltd.
888 Worcester Street, Suite 230
Wellesley, MA 02482
www.akpeters.com

Library of Congress Cataloging-in-Publication Data

Todd, Deborah
    Game design : from blue sky to green light / Deborah Todd.
        p. cm.
    ISBN 978-1-56881-318-9 (alk. paper)
  1. Computer games—Design. 2. Computer games—Programming. I. Title.
    QA76.76.C672T63 2007
    794.8'1536—dc22
                                                  2007000488

Cover images:

Front cover, clockwise from top left:

Image © 2006 Backbone Entertainment. Death Jr., the Death Jr. characters and logo are trademarks of Backbone Entertainment.

Image © 2006 Backbone Entertainment. Death Jr., the Death Jr. characters and logo are trademarks of Backbone Entertainment.

Image courtesy of id Software, Inc.

Image provided by Harmonix Music Systems, Inc.

Image © 2006 Eidos Interactive Ltd. *Lara Croft Tomb Raider: Legend*, Lara Croft, *Tomb Raider*, and the Tomb Raider logo are all trademarks of Eidos Interactive Ltd.

Image © 2006 Backbone Entertainment. Death Jr., the Death Jr. characters and logo are trademarks of Backbone Entertainment.

Image provided by Harmonix Music Systems, Inc.

Image © 2006 Backbone Entertainment. Death Jr., the Death Jr. characters and logo are trademarks of Backbone Entertainment.

Image © 2006 Eidos Interactive Ltd. *Lara Croft Tomb Raider: Legend*, Lara Croft, *Tomb Raider*, and the Tomb Raider logo are all trademarks of Eidos Interactive Ltd.

Background: Image © 2006 Eidos Interactive Ltd. *Lara Croft Tomb Raider: Legend*, Lara Croft, *Tomb Raider*, and the Tomb Raider logo are all trademarks of Eidos Interactive Ltd.

Back cover:

Top: Image © 2006 Eidos Interactive Ltd. *Lara Croft Tomb Raider: Legend*, Lara Croft, *Tomb Raider*, and the Tomb Raider logo are all trademarks of Eidos Interactive Ltd.

Author photo by Lori Eanes

Printed in the United States of America

11 10 09 08 07   10 9 8 7 6 5 4 3 2 1

Contents

For **Jason**

Acknowledgments

A book, like a game, is a collaborative process. It is only possible because of the stellar efforts of many. I owe a great deal of thanks, and have a very deep sense of gratitude, to the following people for their contributions to this book. To each of you, you know what you did, and I thank you immensely for it. It was great fun!

Jason Todd • Mike Hernacki • Corey Bridges • Jon Landau • Danielle Cane • Jill Marsal • Elisabeth James • Sandra Dijkstra • Kevin Jackson-Mead • Deanna Novak • Alice Peters • Rob Swigart • Danielle Trudeau • Jennifer Omholt • Ty Roberts • Ellen French • Paul Kreider • Karen Johnston • Lavelle Jones • Victoria Naramore • Tony Cox • Carlos Garcia • Richard Teel • Tom Disher • Chris Van Buren • Susan Maunders • Jenna Walden • Noah Walden • Justin Hayward • Charles Balas • Dennis Wixon • Curtis Wong • Ardice Faoro • Rudy Geronimo • Rob Huebner • Clyde Grossman • Bob Jacob • Matthew Karch • Denis Dyack • Noaka Feth • Noah Falstein • Hal Barwood • Annie Fox • David Fox • Ron Gilbert • Ken Goldstein • Roger Holzberg • Susan Cordell • Terry Borst • Susan Gerakaris • Sally Richards • Mark Mishkind • Conall Ryan • Madeline DiMaggio • Kathy Fong-Yoneda • Pamela Wallace • Mark Young • John Vorhaus • James Brightman • Lori Dolginoff • Matt Costello • Tim Willits • Wendy Zaas • Mark Lamia • Mike Mantarro • Adrian Wright • Mike Sellers • Riley Cooper • Tracy Fullerton • Dave Grossman • Dan Conners • Greg Land • Mary DeMarle • Tom Grega • Alex Rigopulos • Greg LoPiccolo • Jason Arnone • Sandra Lim • Chris Ferriter • Joe Morrissey • Mike Mika • Chris Charla • Elizabeth Eggleston • Roger Eggleston • Drena Large • Sydney • Chan

A very special thank you with my deepest gratitude to all of the companies that provided confidential design documents, sketches, concept art, screen-shots, and other images for *Game Design*.

To the individuals within these companies who made this happen, you know who you are—you rock.

Backbone Entertainment
Crystal Dynamics
Eidos Interactive
Foundation 9 Entertainment
Harmonix Music Systems
id Software
Multiverse
Nihilistic Software
Splash Damage
Telltale Games
Treyarch
Ubisoft
Wardog Studios

Foreword
The Century of the **Video Game**

It's been said that the motion picture was the quintessential twentieth-century form of entertainment. It is very possible that it will be said that the twenty-first century belonged to the video game.

Both art forms strive to deliver an immersive experience that breaks down the barrier between the medium and the audience. But the result of this immersion is very different for each medium. With film, greater immersion makes the experience *voyeuristic* because you're always in third-person mode, watching. It's critical that you identify with someone or something on screen, but you don't control them. In games, though, greater immersion makes the experience *personal*. You control the action, you become a participant. It's arguably a more powerful personal experience.

For both games and movies, technology is a critical component of creating an immersive experience. Working with James Cameron, I have a healthy respect for the role of technology in entertainment. In our case, we constantly challenge ourselves to find technologies that we can apply to stories, e.g., *Titanic* and *Avatar*, that could not otherwise have been told.

But the danger, in both movies and games, lies in confusing technology with content. For all the attention you can grab with special effects, if the movie is poorly written, or the game is poorly designed, all you'll end up with is a good-looking (and expensive) flop. Let the technology enable you, but use it in service of the theme. I've learned that a successful movie must have a theme that's bigger than the genre. You leave the plot and the effects in the theatre, but the theme you take with you. You think about it as you walk to your car. You talk with your friends about it the next day. And just maybe it opens up a new avenue of self-discovery. The same is true for a successful game: the theme is bigger than the game. That only happens with great game design.

Hence this book and Deborah Todd. Deb is uniquely qualified to guide you through this topic. She's not just an entertainment-industry veteran—she's a veteran of *two* entertainment industries: Hollywood and video games. Throughout her career, Deb's constantly innovated new ways to deliver entertainment through gameplay. Along the way, she's targeted almost every conceivable demographic with almost every kind of property: from preschoolers to teens to CAD engineers, with original concepts and licensed franchises, from engaging educational content to pure entertainment. And from the start, she's spoken and written about the right ways to marry technology and entertainment to create great games.

As you immerse yourself in this industry, you'll find it both challenging and rewarding. It's a wide-open frontier, but Deb can guide you only so far; so always be thinking of new ways to create engaging, cutting-edge entertainment that makes a lasting impression on your audience. This is where hard work meets heady fun. It's where your collaboration with a team results in something that's far greater than the sum of its parts. Keep your wits and your will, and you'll be able to tell your grandkids that you were there at the start, helping make this the century of the video game.

—Jon Landau

Jon Landau is an Academy Award®-winning producer and COO of Lightstorm Entertainment, Inc. In addition to producing James Cameron's Titanic, *Landau is the former Executive Vice President of Feature Film Production at Twentieth Century Fox. Landau and James Cameron are on the board of advisors for The Multiverse Network, Inc., which is building the world's leading network of massively multiplayer online games (MMOGs) and 3D virtual worlds.*

Chapter 1

The **Games Industry** in All Its Glory

"I can't find Joe anywhere, but you guys have to come look at this thing in the kitchen!"

—Chris Charla, Executive Producer, Development, Foundation 9
Searching for lead designer Joe Morrissey and instead finding a giant Snickers bar

So you want to be a game designer? Well, the good news for you is that it takes a *lot* of people to make a game. And the even better news is that this industry is *huge*—it surpassed Hollywood in terms of megabucks years ago,[1] and depending on whom you ask, it is now a $40 billion-a-year industry[2] (or at the very least will be by 2008[3], 2009[4], or 2010[5]). So things are good. And they're looking up!

Why? Console games. PC games. Online games. Casual games. Serious games. Portable games. Mobile games. New platforms. New markets.

More and more the industry is looking at designing games that will hook people who have never played before and are now suddenly hot to try them. Adult people. Business people. Professional people. Then there are the little people—children, who constitute an evergreen market that sees new game players getting into the mix every year and new potential game players being born every year. All in all, there is a whole lot of gaming going on.

---

[1] In 2003, *Compiler*, "A monthly magazine for technologists worldwide," ran the headline "Global Gaming Industry Now a Whopping $35 Billion Market," and declared "gaming is now a mass-market form of entertainment, and no longer something that is enjoyed solely by computer 'geeks'…" This by the magazine written for, uh, what was that again? Oh yeah, *technologists* world wide, a.k.a. computer geeks.

[2] In September 2004, an article about the conditions of working in the industry was published online by Builder AU, and declared this a $40 billion industry. The *Sydney Morning Herald* tells us on September 7, 2006, that this is a $40 billion industry. The Aussies at least are consistent.

[3] BBC News Worldwide.

[4] According to Western Knight Center for Specialized Journalism.

[5] That would be the prediction of Slate Magazine. By 2011, according to a GameSpot article on the analyst predictions from DFC Intelligence, the industry will be at $44 billion.

And so it is. Big industry. Growing market. Increased need for content. That's where you come in.

Do What You Love...

Switch gears with me for a moment to May 7, 2006, when an article appeared in the *New York Times* entitled "A Star is Made: The Birth-Month Soccer Anomaly." A Florida State University psychology professor named Anders Ericsson revealed his marvelous discovery, namely why the world's best soccer players are born in the first three to six months of the year.

Stick with me. It's pertinent to you.

More specifically, he and his colleagues discovered the magic secret to what makes someone really good at what they do. By running an experiment on memory with a person of only "average" memory, i.e., the ability to repeat a pattern of seven digits, Ericsson was able to increase their memory capacity to 20 numbers after 20 hours of training, and to more than 80 numbers after 200 hours of training.[6]

What Ericsson and his team ultimately discovered was that excellence on the soccer field comes not from birth date, but from the result of what the kids with those earlier birth dates were getting from their coaches. Since they were a little bit older, and had an edge on motor function, they had the inherent ability to play slightly better. This showed up looking like natural talent. And because they *appeared* more gifted, their coaches paid more attention to them and gave them more constant and directed feedback.

What Ericsson discovered was the concept of "deliberate practice," which he defined as setting specific goals and getting *immediate* feedback on both *technique* and *results*.

And *this* is what you do when you play video games.

You have a goal. You start playing. You're singularly focused on accomplishing your goal, and you keep playing no matter how many times you're annihilated—you come back again and again, sharpening your skills and refining your gameplay, getting better and better until you're killer at your game.

It's now scientifically official, thanks to Ericsson's work: practice *does* make perfect, if it's deliberate practice and includes immediate feedback. This technique works extremely well for musicians, surgeons, and the aforementioned soccer players, to name a few. And it also works well for gamers. Obviously.

---

6 How much time have *you* spent playing video games?

So how does that relate to you and your love of games and your burning desire to become a game designer? Ericsson's research says it best. According to the article, Ericsson confirms that "When it comes to choosing a life path, you should do what you love—because if you don't love it, you are unlikely to work hard enough to get very good."

Understand what I am telling you. "When it comes to choosing a life path, you should do what you love…"

Play as Work

So you've just been given scientific backing to become a game designer. And now you want to know what it takes to actually do it.

There are some common skills that everyone I interviewed agreed are necessities. But first, let's start with the trait that is universally cited as the most important if you want to get into game design: you have to love games.

Nice how that coincides with Ericsson's findings.

Riley Cooper, lead developer at Crystal Dynamics in Menlo Park, California, shares this sentiment: "Most of us go into the industry because we love games."

True love and passion for games are the *essential building blocks* for your career in the industry, akin to the kind of foundation you'd want for your house—solid and strong and able to withstand a 6.2 on the Richter scale. And I do mean the *essential* components. Because things can get pretty shaky when you're trying to put together a title and get it out on time.

Remember, the good Dr. Ericsson said if you don't love it, you're not going to get very good at it. I'm here to tell you that if you're not very good at it, the job *and* your teammates will eat you alive.

Or, to put it in the words of Mike Mika, studio head for Backbone Entertainment, "…shipping a game can break people."

Crunch Happens

We've all heard stories of the companies that work their teams 15- to 20-hour days during "crunch." And, yes, you're on salary so, no, you don't get more pay. You live like a sequestered juror, only you don't get regular meal breaks, and you never know when your day is going to end.

Or, if you have a really good attitude about the whole thing, you can think of it as if you're living in a Vegas casino—you're stuck inside, you're having fun, and you have absolutely no idea what time it is or what's going on in the world at large.

Here's a sample crunch routine:

You start out for work early in the morning when it's still dark outside. Once you arrive at work you don't get to leave the building during daylight hours, which means you are deprived of the natural elements and you never know if there's been any sort of catastrophe in the real world.

I once worked on such a team, and after nearly three weeks straight of this craziness, a few of us decided we needed to take a walk in honest-to-god sunshine. We got about five blocks away when, literally from out of the blue, dark clouds descended and the skies opened up and drenched us. We had no idea that freaky weather involving spontaneous rainstorms was predicted. We did the only thing we could do—went back to work, wet clothes, soggy shoes, dripping hair and all. That'll teach us not to appreciate fluorescent lighting.

And yet there's more! In this surreal sequestered Vegas-esque day-for-night-and-night-for-day atmosphere, people you've never seen before (people who are free to come and go as they please) bring you food and drinks at seemingly random times throughout your sojourn so you'll stay put and keep throwing your assets on the table. This can go on for weeks or, dread, months (in the above-mentioned case, we did it for six weeks).

But at some point every day, after hours of sun deprivation, natural-air deprivation, and being denied of the basic instinct to hunt down and buy your own food, you finally have to stop and sleep. If you're lucky, you'll get to leave the building and go home (or to your hotel) for a few hours (as opposed to collapsing on the floor in the corner to catch 40 winks, which is about all you'll get on cement floors no matter how well they're carpeted), only to discover that just as REM is starting to kick in it's time once again to get up and go back into the abyss of artificial lighting, recycled climate-controlled air, and no contact with normal people. Just like in Vegas.

In the games industry, we all either (a) know someone who has lived/worked through this or (b) have lived/worked through it ourselves.

"Probably the most esoteric thing, or potentially the least practical advice I can give is to make sure that you have a wide range of life experience and skills before getting into the games business, because the games business tends to be very confining, and defining of your lifestyle.

"The amount of hours that are required always makes people gasp when I tell them how many hours I work at certain periods in the project. During those periods, there's what you would assume about the social life of anybody who works 90 hours plus-or-minus a week. That's what I mean by defining. In this industry the time required can restrict other portions of your life, so as such you need to have a good sense for life outside of that line of work.

"There are a lot of folks who come in and work all hours of the night and come in on weekends. In the short term that might seem good for the project. But immediately I think that any project really benefits in the longer term from people going out on the weekends and not letting the project take over their entire life.

"It's a tough one. I have a tough time with it, because I'm often wanting to come back in and do those tweaks and make something look just how I'd like. I'm always wanting to give it that extra little bit. But that means an extra hour. Or two. Or three."

—Justin Hayward, Level Designer and Artist, *Halo 3*

Now for the Good News

Fortunately, companies are growing up. It's no longer considered all that much fun to go through crunch after you've done it, oh, *once*. And game design is much more of a systematic process than it was in the early days of the industry, when companies were making it up as they went along and everybody had a wild enthusiasm for rolling up their sleeves and doing *anything and everything* it took to get the game out on time. It was great fun. And then enough was enough.

"The practical advice I would give, if you have absolutely no experience in the games industry, is to work on mods. That's a great way to get an idea if this is really something you want to do for a living, because many mod groups can be just as organized, with similar timetables, schedules, and politics as an actual production team. You get a real feeling for the structure that's required to work in this business."

—Justin Hayward

Today, game design is in large part becoming more of a well-tuned engine. Processes are in place. Teams are bigger. People have lives and they demand to live them. And budgets and schedules are much more thought out, precisely measured, and adhered to during development. Crunch still happens, but I hear it repeatedly—for the most part, as an industry, we're getting better at making it manageable.

Beyond love and passion, there are other elements that surpass the initial enamored stage of "Wow, this is so cool and fun that I could spend the rest of my life doing it." Because the truth of the matter is, if you want to work in the games industry the key word to keep in mind is "work."

Riley Cooper discloses what he calls "a weird ironic truth about the industry." You get into the business because of your passion for games, "but you work so much that it's difficult to find time for other games. A lot of people will tell you they used to play games like crazy, and then when they got in the industry it stopped."

And yet, he sees this trend as somewhat dissipating. "As the industry evolves, this is changing," he says. "We crunch less and less because we develop smarter."

Better systems mean less craziness around shipping.

What I Really Want to Do Is Design

Nearly every conversation with every game designer I've ever had about "when" they started working in the biz began like this: "I got into the industry in (pick a date), but really I was designing games all my life, from the time I was a little kid…"

Take, for instance, Hal Barwood, whose background in the movie business gave him a strong foundation for his career as a designer and writer, when he was lured to the games side by LucasArts in 1990.

"Before I became interested in games and went to work in this business, I had been building video games for nearly ten years, and building paper games for myself for amusement since I was a kid." Barwood's first professional gig in games was on *Indiana Jones and the Fate of Atlantis*. "It was my first game at LucasArts, but by no means my first game," says Barwood.

"I'm a self-taught assembly language programmer, and I did some games for the Apple II. My background is not in engineering or computer science. In particular, I had cut my teeth on doing long, elaborate adventure games. I built a game called *Space Snatchers* that was a tile-based action-adventure game where you're a tiny character kidnapped by UFOs and held prisoner in a zoo and you have to get home by co-opting the aliens to help you. It was a one-man project, and it was really elaborate."

"To be a senior, responsible, creative leader, anyone with any ambition, you ought to think very hard about building your own games. There is no substitute and no way of telling you how much you will learn after you've done one game, and then again how much you'll learn after you do a second one. And when you learn something by that way, you learn it in your bones. You never forget."

—Hal Barwood

So when Barwood went into the business professionally, he was primed for the adventures of Indy. He went on to do *Indiana Jones and the Infernal Machine*, *Rebel Assault II*, and many other games during his nearly 14-year tenure at Lucas.

And then there's Noah Falstein, who started in the business in 1980 right out of college and has had a stellar career ever since. "It's easy to point at when I started in the business professionally, but to some extent I was making games as a child, so it was a smooth transition to get paid to do it.

"One of the first ones I remember—a lot were war-inspired, liked military strategy games—one of the early ones I did was because I had seen the movie *Sink the Bismarck*. Because of this movie, I made a cardboard ship profile and sat it on the linoleum floor in the kitchen, and a cardboard airplane model with a slot cut into it, and I put coins in the slot and that would be the torpedo bombers, and there were different scores for hitting different parts of the ship.

"I'd play this with a friend of mine and we would get tired of taking turns, so I decided I would make an interceptor with marbles, and while one person tried to sink the ship the other got to try to defend it. Other games I made were pretty traditional board games. I made a really elaborate game once, much like *Empire* or one of my favorites, *Advance Wars* on DS, with simple rules to keep track of fuel and ammunition and stuff."

Matt Costello also began creating games well before he achieved rock-star status for his breakout CD-ROM game *The 7th Guest*. "I really got started in college when I decided to more or less stop going to classes and stay up all night playing board games. We played things like Monopoly and Risk, but we invented rules and changed things. I'd stay up till dawn, until the bread man came, playing Psycho Monopoly and Bizarre Risk."

Chances are, everyone who designs games for a living started out making up their own games as a child. The difference is that we've seemed to keep this trait alive into adulthood.

Our industry "want ad" could read: *Creativity required. Apply outside the box.*

As a relatively new industry, I think we're all relieved that we now have *many* people who have been in the biz for over a decade, and some masters who have more than 20 years under their belt. It's our first glimpse at longevity. Finally. And it's a very, very good thing.

We also now have people coming into game design who have been playing games almost their entire lives. It's second nature to them now. There's no learning curve. No fear of technology. They know what good games are. And they know it on a nearly cellular level.

So we now have a winning combination:

Instinct + Intuition + Experience + Skill

The next generation in game design is you. And according to the pros who are in the thick of it, a fundamental understanding of all of the elements discussed in this book is important to your game-design success.

All of the people on the team are also important to your career. And yes, I do mean all.[7]

The Team

When Rob Huebner, CEO of Nihilistic, started his company, it was with a group of 11 other guys who had all worked together on a little project at Lucas called *Star Wars Jedi Knight: Dark Forces II*. A blockbuster game. This team of superstars decided to form their own company to see if they could sell an idea for a game they wanted to make on their own.

"We had a couple of pages of design on paper, and it was primarily the strength of the team we had assembled from LucasArts that sold it," says Huebner. "It was much easier, then, to start a team with no demo or tangible assets. We were lucky as far as that goes."

Gone are the days when a handful of people can get together, jot down some ideas, and get a major publisher to back them. Now it takes a village

---

7 And yes, that includes marketing.

Concept art for a new intellectual property (IP). Image courtesy of Ron Kee for Nihilistic Software.

to create a game. And some villages are bigger than others. Here are a couple of examples of what you can expect to work with in a "small" and "large" developer studio.

Nihilistic Software

Today, Huebner is head of a 60-person company (and growing) in Marin County, California. They're expanding their offices and claiming adjacent space to accommodate their need for more of everything. They release one AAA[8] title every two years.

Their current project, just past the middle of its two-year development cycle, has 43 characters and 21 missions and is supported by a team of 12 programmers, 30 artists, two full-time producers, a half dozen designers, two full-time testers, and a variety of other employees and contractors. Huebner's development process is one of the most impressive I've ever seen. Precise, focused, clean, state-of-the-art game development. They all look like they love their work. And even the office dogs seem to be having a good time. Budget on current title: $10 million.

---

8 AAA (Triple A) refers to the success, or anticipated success if in development, of a title. Sometimes AAA is defined by the amount of money it costs to develop the game. A $10–20 million budget qualifies as a AAA title in development. If during alpha and beta the publisher feels the title will be a smash hit, they might invest a similarly-sized marketing budget with a big marketing push on the game, believing it will be a AAA title. Generally speaking, at the end of the day, regardless of how much money was spent in development and marketing, if the title comes out and is a blockbuster, selling over a million titles, it's considered a AAA title.

Foundation 9 Entertainment

Across the bay in Emeryville, California, is Backbone Entertainment, owned by Foundation 9, which supports studios in Newport Beach, California; Eugene, Oregon; Vancouver, British Columbia; Boston, Massachusetts; and Charlottetown, PEI, Canada. That's pre-merger with Amaze Entertainment.

According to James Brightman, lead business editor of *GameDaily Biz*, "With the merger with Amaze, Foundation 9 will be the largest independent developer in the world."

Of its 450+ employees pre-merger, approximately 30% are engineers, 35% are artists, 20% are designers, and the remaining 15% are producers, admin, and execs. Many people cross-pollinate; in other words, some programmers can be designers, some designers can be producers, so they have flexibility on who-works-on-what from title to title. The average development cycle at Foundation 9 is 14 months. Budgets range from $1.5 to $12 million or more per title. They ship between 20 and 30 games a year and are some of the nicest people you'll ever meet.

Sketch of lead character for Backbone Entertainment's original intellectual property (IP) *Death Jr.* Image © 2006 Backbone Entertainment. Death Jr., the Death Jr. characters and logo are trademarks of Backbone Entertainment. (See color plates.)

Bottom Line

Teams are huge. Budgets are in the millions. A lot of work goes into games, and you can't find a more fun industry in which to work in the entire universe, known or unknown.[9]

What Makes a Great Game?

Ask anyone on the team, "What makes a great game?" and they'll tell you. They know. Of course, they'll each tell you something different depending on their job title. But that's not necessarily a bad thing.

So, really, what makes a great game? It goes something like this:

---

9 "In the entire universe, known or unknown," is a common phrase you can expect to see if you're ever lucky enough to negotiate a contract with a big publisher. This is where they have the rights to your game. I kid you not.

Artist: You have to have killer graphics. Look at the number of artists working on a project. It's definitely the art, art direction, cinematics, the overall look that is key to making a great game.

Sound Engineer: Art is really important, it's true, but you can have cool graphics and if your music and sound effects are lousy you'll have a game nobody wants to play. Music is far more important than people might think. So, definitely, the music and quality of the sound recording are what I think make a great game.

Designer: It all starts with really solid game design. If you don't have a good design, good structure, integrating good mechanics and gameplay, all fitting together, the whole thing falls apart. You can't even get it off the ground.

Writer: You have to have characters that people will want to play, and of course you need a story wrapped around the game that makes sense. There's a lot that goes into it. Who are your characters? How do they relate to other characters? Where and how do they fit in this environment and in the story? What *is* the story? The dialog has to be tight. It all has to be engaging. The story has to be compelling. The cut scenes have to be figured out and well delivered. Why is the player playing the game? Why are they here? Why do they care? It has to support all of these elements of the game. So, definitely it's story and characters that will engage the player.

Programmer: The technology. The mechanics. What can we do that nobody's ever done before? How do we take this great mechanic and make a hot new game? Definitely the technology.

Producer: Teamwork. Communication.

Tester: Getting the games in front of the users as early as possible, listening to what they say, finding out where you get held up, where the problems are, where things are working and where they aren't, and incorporating what you learn into the game so that when you deliver, it works.

Marketing: I don't care how good your game is, if you don't have marketing behind it you'll have a flop.

Who's right? Absolutely all of them. But sometimes, some of them are more right than others.

I saved marketing for last because there is a perception in this industry, in all industries actually, as far as I can tell, that marketing people are a pain to work with, and when they step into the mix they really mess things up. Well, it's true marketing people *can be* a pain to work with, but if you look at them that way you are truly undermining your success.

"I used to view them as enemies when I was a PD[10] person, but now I embrace those people," says Clyde Grossman, former vice president of product development for Sony Computer Entertainment of America. Grossman and Bob Jacob are co-founders of the agency Interactive Studio Management (ISM) and have been helping developers turn the corner to becoming major players in the industry for more than ten years.

"The fact is that marketing and finance *are* viewed as the enemy by product-development people," says Jacob. But, he points out, "there are cases in the industry where titles were very, very good but did not sell because marketing and sales didn't believe in them. They had no buy-in, and they died. That's what a developer wants to avoid."

"My clients need those people on their side, and looking at them as the enemy sets up a wrong dynamic," adds Grossman. "I can still remember feeling that way about them, but my attitude has changed 180 degrees. We try to communicate that to our clients. You need to embrace them as part of the team. Our best developers insist on marketing and finance as part of the team because their success is dependent on those people and those departments working supportively. You don't get support from people if you call them the enemy."

It's Business

So, it's business. It's the business of making great games, and of selling them. And now, developers are becoming more and more aware of the *business* of making their games a hit.

"Marketing gets involved really early," confirms Huebner. "They'll focus test the concept before they green light *any* money for it." And the reality is, if marketing says no, the publisher says no.

Keep this in mind throughout your game-design career, and you will be an invaluable member of the team.

Breaking in with Mike Mika and Chris Charla

Mike Mika, studio head at Backbone Entertainment, and Chris Charla, executive producer of development at Foundation 9, discuss the key components

---

10 Product development.

they see to having a successful start and career as a game designer. Foundation 9 has produced more than 360 games, including the original IP[11] *Death Jr.* and *Death Jr. II: Root of Evil.*

Mika: Breaking into the industry, there is a belief that comes up all the time: once you're in, you're in, but you gotta *get* in. But nobody knows how to get in. What's the best path into the industry?

It's tough to break in because, as someone who's hiring, if I'm given a choice between somebody who has shipped a game and somebody who hasn't, well, shipping a game can break people.

So where does that leave students? I've had mixed experience with kids coming out of school. For example, computer-science degrees tend to be very general, so students would know learning systems, but they wouldn't get a lot of things that are part of this particular industry, like working on simulations, for example. It can be too theory heavy, too scientific. This is changing with new schools focusing specifically on games. We're starting to see students who have a better understanding of the industry and what goes into making games.

In the past, we have mostly promoted designers who started out in other disciplines, like artists and engineers. And we've hired out of other studios.

Charla: One thing that's often overlooked is a lot of associate producers or assistant producers do a ton of design work. A lot of times, they come out of school and get hired as an associate producer and they do design work in level placement, for example. They don't get a "designer" credit, but they do a lot of design work.

Mika: The other thing I'll say is we've hired designers out of every single discipline, including testing.

Charla: As far as the skills go, communication is the number-one skill for a designer because a lot of frustration comes from not being able to communicate what's in your head with the rest of the team. I've seen people get really frustrated by that. You have to know how to do flow-charting, and describe things in a technical manner, the behaviors of a character broken down into states, and flowchart that, instead of "Oh, he shoots a lot."

11 Intellectual property.

On the opposite side is not over-designing. A mistake I see a lot is people spending too much time poring over details—they're doing just *too much* detail work. You need to have compromise between designing enough and not designing too much, because the artists and programmers can add a lot and you need to give them the space to do that.

It's hard work. So people have to be able to see the reality. Designers are the first on the offensive on the project because they have to scope out everything about the game so the engineers and artists can start building and iterating right away.

Mika: You have to be flexible and roll with the punches. The designer isn't the end-all for the video game, because it really takes compromise and flexibility to build a good game. Sometimes, from a PR aspect, you see a designer presented as the author of a game, but reality is 99.9% of the time it's a team effort.

Game Designers: Advice and Traits

Noah Falstein is the president of The Inspiracy and is a well-known, deeply admired, and highly accessible icon in the games biz. Here, he shares his advice to new designers and the most important traits he feels designers can have.

"My two biggest pieces of advice for new designers are this:

(1) Be willing to do other things, and be interested in other things, not just game design.

(2) Persistence is a key quality to being successful. I know a number of people who are not particularly talented but were very persistent and consequently very successful. But I also know a lot of people who were very talented who were not persistent and not successful. If there is one quality that I would say you have to have to be successful, this is it. It doesn't hurt to be talented, too, but persistence will get you farther.

"The biggest error I see in aspiring designers is an impatience to start designing right away. I don't mean it's a bad thing to do design work. In fact, just like that old adage 'writers write,' if you want to be a designer and you aren't already finding yourself doing game design on your own, that's a red flag. It may be just jotting notes about game ideas on napkins when you're out at dinner, or staying up late talking with friends about why in your opinion the latest *Halo* isn't very good and how you would make it better. But unless you're thinking in those terms already, it's going to be a huge uphill battle for you.

"The impatience part comes in for a lot of people when they come up from college—they've been to Full Sail or DigiPen or some game school, and they want to get hired as a designer, and not *just* a designer but as the *lead* designer. Well, that happens rarely, and here's why: As any good gamer knows, you make mistakes the first few times you try things, like when you try learning a new game. In design, the same thing happens. It is much better to make mistakes under the radar, as a level designer or an associate producer or a tester. So, it's much better to learn game design on a project under the radar, and that way when you do get your first credit you can really show yourself off.

"Also, to be a strong designer, you need to be strong in things that complement design. If you have no interest in producing or writing or programming, that's a problem. I've never met a successful designer who didn't have several other fairly strong interests. People my age almost universally started out as programmers, and there's a huge overlap in designer-writers.

"Game designers are universally fascinated by what makes people tick, what makes *everything* tick. For the most part, they are somewhat introverted, although there are some who are extroverts. But that degree of introversion is necessary to sit and noodle out how a design is going to work. In game design that introversion and extroversion tends to balance a bit.

"The personality of game designers is remarkably consistent, and this is an interesting point, specifically with full-time lead-designer types. There's a sense of kinship we have for each other in this industry. In fact, one of the most interesting things is to see who has taken the Myers-Briggs personality test.

"Myers-Briggs breaks people into one of sixteen groups.[12] Patricia Kaiser, an MMO[13] designer, was at a conference one time and we were talking about this, and just out of blue she said, 'How many of you have taken the Myers-Briggs test?' Everybody raised their hands. Almost all of the game designers in the workshop were in two groups,[14] and these two groups total only about 2% of the population.

---

12 The Myers-Briggs Type Indicator® (MBTI) is based on Carl G. Jung's 1920s theories on psychological type and identifies and profiles 16 personalities types, stressing that it "sorts for preferences and does not measure trait, ability, or character," and that all types are equal. It is taken by more than 2,000,000 people a year.

13 Massively multiplayer online game, also called an MMOG, or MMORPG (massively multiplayer online role-playing game) for role-playing MMOs.

14 INTJ and ENTJ.

"Our brains work the same way. For example, all hardcore game designers I know are passionately interested in a bunch of things. Any one of us has at least three areas of expertise that would usually be considered trivia by a normal person, but we're passionately knowledgeable about them. For instance, I can tell you WWII details, Gilbert and Sullivan details, and we are all Star Trek and Star Wars nerds to a pretty disturbing degree. In fact, that mix of high and low culture is very common with us as a group. We can talk about anything from the latest Simpsons episode to Homer's *Odyssey*. We're perfectly comfortable with and capable of going from one Homer to another."

Game-Designer Checklist

- ❏ Do what you love.
- ❏ Love to play games.
- ❏ Be massively creative.
- ❏ Communicate well.
- ❏ Work well with others.
- ❏ Have a broad range of interests.
- ❏ Have areas of expertise outside of game design that are of deep interest.
- ❏ Bonus: Have a good sense of humor—it will keep you sane in this crazy industry.

Chapter 2

In the Beginning, There Was **Blue Sky**

"I really love enabling people to do things that no one's ever done before and no one's ever thought of before, and I wanted to give that wild inspired chaos a place to thrive. Technology, when it enables innovation, is bloody fascinating."

—Corey Bridges, Co-founder, Multiverse

Every person who has ever worked on designing a game will tell you that every project is different, and every company is different. And yet, there are certain parts of the process that are consistent in nature across the board. And first and foremost is that everybody does blue sky.

"For us, when we start on a new game design, it's very top level," says Tim Willits, co-owner and lead designer at id Software, creators of such franchises as *Quake*, *DOOM*, and *Wolfenstein*. "You have John Carmack, Kevin Cloud, Todd Hollenshead, and me, and we kind of point in a direction, it's a very basic vector direction. Do we want to do another version of an older IP, or do we want to start a new game? Then we do broad strokes. Do we want it set in the past or in the future? Where does it take place? Then we talk about technology, new rendering. This is my blue sky."

Image courtesy of id Software, Inc.

Like all other companies, id goes through a very iterative blue-sky process with each new project. The starting point is always the big idea.

There are a couple of things to keep in mind about blue sky that differentiates it from brainstorming:

(1) The blue-sky process really is all about "the sky's the limit." It's the "if I could do any game in the world, this would be it…" phase of development. It's the wild, loose, unencumbered, creative, open-your-mind-to-possibilities step one of game design. And it is one of the coolest parts of the job. It is absolutely where the fun begins.

(2) The only editing or censorship that goes on in the blue-sky process is by the creator of the idea as they put together their "here's the coolest game in the world," concept.[1]

Equally important to keep in mind is this: Blue sky is *not* the same process as brainstorming, which is a much more focused affair. You might have noticed there are two separate chapters on these topics. There's a reason for that. Blue sky is all about "*yes.*"

Methods of Blue Sky

For many companies, like id, blue sky is handled by just a few high-level people. After the field of possibilities is narrowed down with these key players in a subsequent high-level brainstorming session, they bring in additional members of the team and begin to further brainstorm ways to grow the ideas into gameplay.

This is also the process when a publisher, who already has an idea for a game, approaches a developer to execute that game. They know what the basic parameters of the game are: genre, location, general story, and basic characters are all figured out, and the publisher is looking for someone to execute their ideas. Sometimes, they even pretty much already have a contract in hand.[2] In this case, blue sky is skipped by the developer—the publisher has already done it—and the developer goes straight into brainstorming given the constraints the publisher has presented them.

For other companies, the blue-sky process is about coming up with game mechanics that nobody else has done. Here, the resultant blue-sky ideas are captured in descriptive game one-liners, much like Hollywood's loglines[3], to relay those concepts to others. This was the case for a hot concept developed by Saber Interactive.

"That's exactly what happened with us," says Saber's co-founder and CEO Matthew Karch. "We sent some ideas to Clyde (Grossman) and said, 'These are things we're thinking about for our next game.'"

---

[1] The only thing that's censored is censorship.

[2] As Chris Charla of Foundation 9 puts it, "that doesn't happen often, but it's really nice when it does."

[3] A logline is a one-sentence summary of a screenplay or teleplay that captures the essence of the entire show. A good example of loglines can be found as the description of the programs listed in *TV Guide*.

According to Bob Jacob, Grossman's partner at ISM, "Saber came up with a lot of ideas for a first-person shooter, and they shipped them to Clyde for his assessment. He sifted through it all, and buried inside was a gem of an idea that became the whole basis for their next game."

Grossman adds, "I saw this idea about controlling time, where you can slow it down, reverse it, speed it up, and it doesn't affect your character—you live outside of time—and they had devised a way to do that. And I said, 'Now *that* I can sell.' It was a fresh approach that nobody had ever integrated into tactical and strategic gameplay in a first-person shooter."

"It was really unique and hadn't been done before," agrees Jacob, so "we threw out the other 28 ideas, and it became the essence of their game."

That blue-sky idea based on a game mechanic that allows the player to control time became the foundation for the game *TimeShift*, a 2007 title with publisher Vivendi.

Many developers approach the blue-sky process from an entirely different direction—the opposite direction, in fact. In these cases, the companies place a virtual "call to all hands," and everybody gets to give their input on what the next great game should be.

Again, in these situations, there is no limitation to the ideas submitted.

The Way We Were

Back in the day, when companies were relatively small and the whole team consisted of only a few people, here's how the blue sky process worked: if someone had an idea for a game, they'd lean across their desk and start an impromptu conversation, a.k.a. blue-sky session, with the two or three other people sitting in the room.

If they were lucky, they might have a conference room to make it more like a special meeting of "the creative types."

David Fox was the first person hired to work at Lucasfilm Computer Games Group in 1982 by Peter Langston. And the teams at Lucas were small. "Most of the games at Lucas were done with two- to five-person teams," explains Fox. The film and games divisions were designed to run as their own units, so George Lucas did not interfere with the developers.

"Lucas specifically was not looking for hardcore typical game designers. They were looking to break away from what was already done. They could have recruited Atari VCS people to do their first games, but they wanted to start fresh with people who didn't have set ways of doing games for the Atari consoles."

Fox was a natural, having co-founded with his wife, Annie, The Computer Center in 1977, a non-profit located in a 5,000 square foot state-of-the-art facility in Marin County, California. Their mission was to bring people into the computer era and to "be the human face to the computer age." Here, they taught children's classes on programming, took computers to schools to teach teachers how to use them, wrote articles for computer magazines, converted games to run on different types of computers, and introduced a new generation to computer technology and gaming. They also wrote books. Hers was on computer programming, *Armchair BASIC*, and his was *Computer Animation Primer*, showing how to program animations using the Atari 800.

So when Fox was hired to work at Lucas, followed soon thereafter by Dave Levine and Loren Carpenter, among others, it was with a more or less free reign to experiment with game design. In fact, their first two games, *Ballblazer* and *Rescue on Fractalus!*,[4] were done as experiments.

"We said, 'Let's do a couple of throw-away games first to get our feet wet, and if they're any good we'll put them into production,'" says Fox. "There was all this hype around Lucas getting into games, so when we announced that the first games were merely experimental, it took the pressure off of us."

The small team size and low cost of development actually aided in the design team's creativity. "Our game budgets were in the range of $75,000 to $200,000, and we could complete them in 9 months. The huge difference between then and now was, besides the fact that you could take risks, you could do something more creative that wasn't necessarily guaranteed to be a smash hit. Because the budgets were low to start with, you could make your money back. We had huge latitude.

"We couldn't do any *Star Wars* stuff because Lucas wasn't involved with what we were doing, so *Labyrinth*,[5] based on the movie, was our first licensed game. Until *Indy*[6] in the late 80s, the games we did were all original titles. It was very freeing because we didn't have to match a license. Back then the

---

[4] Both released March 1984 for the Atari 800 and 5200, and later for the Commodore 64, Apple II, PC, Amstrad, Sinclair Spectrum, and Atari 7800.

[5] *Labyrinth: The Computer Game*, released in 1986 for the Commodore 64 and Apple II in conjunction with the movie *Labyrinth*, a sci-fi fantasy starring Davie Bowie and Jennifer Connelly, directed by Jim Henson, Peter MacDonald, and Jimmy Devis, and produced by Jim Henson Company, Lucasfilm, Ltd., and Delphi Productions, specifically George Lucas, David Lazer, Eric Rattray, and Martin G. Baker.

[6] *Indiana Jones and the Last Crusade—The Graphic Adventure*, released July 1989 for PC, Amiga, Atari ST, Macintosh, FM Towns, and CDTV in conjunction with the movie of the same name, released in May 1989, an action adventure starring Harrison Ford, Sean Connery, Denholm Elliott, River Phoenix, and John Rhys-Davies, directed by Steven Spielberg, Michael D. Moore, and Frank Marshall, and produced by George Lucas, Frank Marshall, and Robert Watts.

project leaders were all lead programmers. We were really a team. There wasn't that separation there is now. We had to do everything."

But things change.

"That sounds like an ideal environment to design a game in," says Annie Fox. And who could argue with her? "But by the time I got into it in 1990, there was a really big difference. The marketing people had come in, and many of them had preset ideas of what would sell, and that was not necessarily based on what a good game was. Sometimes, they had never even played games." [7]

As CD-ROM and computer games started taking off, it seemed everyone was jumping on the game bandwagon. It was the same phenomenon witnessed again in the late 1990s with dotcoms—everybody wanted to do it whether they had any clue about what "it" was, or what they were actually "doing." It's what I like to call the *Lemming Effect* [8]. But even major companies were making huge mistakes when it came to game design, and it changed the way the industry worked. There was a whole lot of shake up going on. Not all of it good.

"I worked on several projects where animators were forbidden to talk to designers," she continues. "So what would sometimes happen was we'd design the games, and then things would get handed over to the company and we'd get cut out of the rest of the creative process. Big chunks would get cut out of games without us having any input, and as a result the games seemed very fragmented. It was as if they were so eager to cash in on all the money being spent on CD-ROMs for kids that they were not concerned about the product.

"That didn't always happen, and it never happened with Humongous [9] because Ron was first and foremost a game designer. Collaboration with Humongous was great. They would call up and get input from us, and we'd put our heads together and come back with a solution and say, 'Here's the fix.' In other situations, people who were not designers were making those calls. Many companies did things quick and dirty, and it didn't make any sense.

---

7 And people wonder why marketing has earned such a bad reputation?

8 One of my favorite games of all time is *Lemmings*, where all of the characters in the game jumped in line and followed the lead lemming for no apparent reason other than because it was going somewhere. Usually where they ended up going (unless you could figure out the puzzle and save them all) was over the edge.

9 Humongous Entertainment, co-founded in 1992 by Ron Gilbert, became a leading children's interactive edutainment and entertainment game developer and publisher, creating many successful franchises. Series include Big Thinkers, Blue's Clues, Fatty Bear, Pajama Sam, Freddie Fish, Let's Explore with Buzzy, Putt-Putt, SPY Fox, and Backyard Sports.

"You'd get into a meeting where they would hire you because you're enormously creative and they'd say, 'Take it and run with it,' and that was about it for the creative process with the company. You'd have very little interaction with the producer, then you'd hand it off to them when you were all done and they'd say, 'Okay, thanks, bye,' and three to six months later the game would show up in your mailbox. You'd look at it and say, 'What happened to that whole second act?'"

All of this is to give you some perspective on where things have been in the good, the bad, and the ugly of the industry, and juxtapose that with where they are now.

Gone are the days when the producer disappears on you.

And gone are the days where you get to just go off and design a game on your own. Mostly.

The Email-Alias Approach to Blue Sky

The only thing that even closely approximates the "go off and design a game" approach in some companies today is the blue-sky process. In most instances, this freedom to go forth and create starts with an email.

I have found developers, both large and small, who take this path to starting new projects: send an email to everyone in the company and ask them what *they* would do if they could design the next game.

Not only does this harken back to the way things were done in the early days of game design, but for those who weren't in the industry back then it causes a sense of excitement that can only be found at this juncture in the creative process. It's a very cool time. Everyone gets jazzed. And companies have found that this approach speaks volumes to the employees, where people from all job descriptions feel equally valued as creative and contributing members of the team. Truly, people love it.

Nihilistic, for one, takes this collaborative route.

"Normally we have an email alias called 'game concepts' that involves almost everyone in the company," explains Rob Huebner of Nihilistic. "We send out an email inviting everyone to submit their ideas for a new game, and anyone who wants to can send in their pitch. They write a one- or two-page proposal that includes all of the main information about the game—the genre, main character, key gameplay elements, type of gameplay, the setting, all that."

The last time Huebner's company went through this process, they received about 20 pitches. "Everything from hard-core sci-fi, to post-Apocalyptic, to sports. Just about anything goes. And the ideas can come from everyone, art-

Plaza color study for new original IP. Image courtesy of Ron Kee for Nihilistic Software. (See color plates.)

ists, designers, testers—QA testers are really gung-ho about getting into the design process. Then we put all of these ideas into a folder on the network and everyone can make comments on them."

That's the beginning of Nihilistic's blue-sky process. Next, Huebner does his review of the games in the folder and picks five or six games that he thinks have the most potential and calls a company meeting. This is where brainstorming begins at Nihilistic.

Huebner is sold on this approach to starting a new game design.

"We use a system that's philosophical," says Huebner. "Some companies have a Design God, one person who throws out ideas and everyone stands around and collects them. That might work okay for them, but it's not our style. We use a collaborative process."

At Huebner's company, and at many others that use this approach, there is an overseer of the blue-sky process—someone who owns the collection of ideas, and the communication about that collection with the team. That person is also usually responsible for narrowing down the possible choices and getting from a plethora of ideas, some of which seem more viable than others, to a manageable A-list of ideas, the few that have the potential to actually catch the interest and funding commitment from a publisher.

In other companies that go this route, the difference lies in the narrowing-down process. Ideas are voted on by the entire team, and each time the field narrows, the stakes go up for the originator, who has to/gets to keep building out the game concept. He or she is asked for more about story. More about characters. More about gameplay. More about mechanics. And this can go on through several iterations until there's consensus from the overall team and narrowing down to just a few final candidates. Sort of like a *Fight Club* approach to game design. You keep knocking out the opponents until there's only one left.

Then blue sky makes a quantum shift and turns into brainstorming.

Blue-Sky Exercise
Yes—Okay—That Sounds Good to Me

It has been said that by the time a person reaches the age of 18 they will have heard the word "no" 200,000 times. With those kinds of stats at work, it's easy to see why people have such a hard time being creative—they're pretty much scripted to think "no" about everything:

No, I shouldn't say that.
No, I can't do that.
No, that's not possible.

The only antidote to "no" is "yes," and I can tell you that when you start using the word "yes," you will discover an amazing tool to spark your creativity. Which makes sense, when you think about it. By its very nature, "yes" looks at things from the "what *is* possible" point of view. And when you're thinking about what is possible, you're engaged in the act of creating.

The following exercise, based on an improv technique, is one that has had the most profound impact on opening up the flow of creative juices that I have ever seen—both on individuals who participate in it and on the group dynamics of a room full of people doing it. It is a great way to get outside the box, and it really works!

So here's the rub:

It is the easiest thing to do.

And it is really hard to do.

Which, of course, makes it really fun to do.

What to Do:

- Get in a group, ideally two to five people.
- One person speaks at a time, and you take turns. Pick someone to start.
- First person starts: In a sentence, the first person states something they want, *whatever* they want, no matter how ludicrous or preposterous that desire might seem. They say, "I want…" and fill in the rest.

    For example:

Person 1: "I want to snap my fingers and have a million dollars appear at my feet."

- Next person responds with either:

Yes…
Okay…
That sounds good to me…

And then builds on the first person's statement.

Example:

Person 1: "I want to snap my fingers and have a million dollars appear at my feet."

Person 2: "That sounds good to me. *And…* while you're standing there looking at all that money lying at your feet you'll just happen to notice my shoes, and you'll say, 'Damn, those are the most stylin' shoes I've ever seen,' and you'll give me your million dollars in exchange for my Hush Puppies, and everyone agrees that this money is all mine and there's no more trading, and nobody else gets any of it."

Obviously, the first person is now thinking "No, that is *not* what I'm going to do."

And yet, the next response has to be either:

Yes…
Okay…
That sounds good to me…

And then build on the last statement.

Example:

Person 1: "I want to snap my fingers and have a million dollars appear at my feet."

Person 2: "That sounds good to me. And while you're standing there looking at all that money lying at your feet you'll notice my shoes, and you'll say, 'Damn, those are the most stylin' shoes I've ever seen,' and you'll give me your million dollars in exchange for my Hush Puppies, and everyone agrees that this money is all mine and there's no more trading, and nobody else gets any of it."

Next Response: "Yes. And… then it will occur to us, 'Hey, if one person loves those shoes enough to pay a million dollars for them, there's gotta be more people out there who would lay down that kind of money for a pair just like them,' and we suddenly realize that we need to figure out what it is about those shoes that makes them worth that much money, so we start a new business, which of course *you* offer to fund with that million dollars."

Next Response: "Okay. And what we discover is …"

And so on into creative yes-ness.

Here's what's going to happen:

At first, everybody's going to be *really* pushing their luck. Why? Because they know they can ask for whatever they want and you can't say no.

You'll notice nervous laughter.

You'll notice competition.

You'll notice people trying to figure out how to say "no" in a way that sounds like "yes."

And then, something amazing happens.

Almost as if someone flicked a switch, the dynamic changes. After a few rounds of people getting used to saying "yes" to each other, a rhythm kicks in. Competition becomes positive. Everyone starts to like the sound of yes. And everyone starts to think of the possibilities within the "limitation" of having to say yes. It's a great dichotomy that turns into a synergistic freeing of the mind.

Give it five minutes. Open your mind to yes.

Now, start to blue sky your game.

Blue-Sky Checklist

- ❏ The sky's the limit.
- ❏ All ideas are valid—blue sky is all about yes.
- ❏ Present broad strokes of the game.
- ❏ Components include mechanics, genre, environment, characters, story.
- ❏ Bonus: Write it up in a page or two to capture your ideas.

Chapter 3
The Yin and Yang of **Brainstorming**

"Every good brainstorming session starts with a 15-minute discussion of *Star Trek*."

—Noah Falstein, quoting Ron Gilbert

The truth about brainstorming is this: Brainstorming is not blue sky, and blue sky is not brainstorming. They might have elements in common. And in fact one might beget the other. But still, they are decidedly *not* the same.

Blue sky is all about the sky's the limit and imagining all possibilities. But at the end of the day the reality is that you can't have everything you want—you can't have all possibilities, and you can't say yes to everything. You can *start* that way in blue sky. Yet sooner or later, usually sooner, you have to hone in on one idea for your game and turn that concept into a game people will love to play. This is where you start to narrow your focus on what you *really* want, and can have, in the game. And that's where brainstorming comes into play.

Let's use the metaphor of writing. One way to look at this is that blue sky is much like stream-of-consciousness writing. Whatever you think, you write. No holds barred, no rules, no limits. Just get it out there, down on paper. Brainstorming, on the other hand, is more like editing—it's taking that stream-of-consciousness work and molding it into something that can be grokked by others. You organize the thoughts into some semblance of order, make them cohesive, cut things out, add new ideas where needed, and you have something imminently useable—a good first draft.

Noah Falstein looks at brainstorming this way: "There are a lot of rules you read about brainstorming that are available in non-game books, for example, how to teach corporate executives to brainstorm. I consider those to be training-wheel rules that are good if you've never done it before. But if you have any experience, they can actually slow you down.

"One example you hear about all the time is, 'Don't criticize; don't stifle the process by judging; every idea is a good idea.' Under corporate circumstances, that might be useful. But all hardcore game designers criticize each other left and right. The difference is they don't take it personally. It's okay to critique. That way only the strongest elements survive."

Falstein sees a strong correlation between the discerning of ideas that occurs during a good brainstorming session and Darwin's "survival of the fittest" postulate. He adds, "Darwinism is very appropriate to correlate with game design."

Avoid Clichés like the Plague!

The biggest problem inherent in the brainstorming process is that clichés and stereotypes are *always* the first thing to come up as the "best" ideas or solutions in a game. There's a reason for that—television, film, books, and other games are full of them. Daily conversations are full of them. The world is full of them. The problem is that they're not very interesting.

Case in point. We need a non-player character in a game. We're going to make her a little old lady. Describe what she's like.

Stop. Think about that for a second. Describe what a little old lady looks like.

You already have a picture in your head. Maybe she's wearing a frumpy black dress with a little white flower print, knee-high nylon stockings that are sagging around her skinny little legs, and non-descript black shoes. She has wrinkly skin, white hair pulled up in a bun behind her head, glasses slipping off the end of her nose. Maybe she carries a cane.

The trouble is that when people are developing any component of a game, like a character in this case, they usually get as far as the stereotype and then stop.

Your challenge is to go beyond cliché.

How do you do that? Easy. Here are the steps:

(1) Don't fight clichés and stereotypes. They're gonna come out, and the sooner you get them out of the way, the sooner you can start getting beyond them.

(2) After you've exhausted the stereotypes and clichés, go to the *opposite* of them. Let's take granny, for example. Black shoes become genuine alligator cowboy boots. Or bunny slippers. Or bright red Converse sneakers. Each of these changes instantly gives some new dimension to her character, and each gives us a very different sense about who we're dealing with here. Let's change her cane. Maybe it's a broomstick. Or a cue stick. Maybe she pokes people with it. Maybe she whacks people over the head

Hairless Lab Rat concept art. Image © 2006 Backbone Entertainment. Death Jr., the Death Jr. characters and logo are trademarks of Backbone Entertainment. (See color plates.)

with it. Cliché? Okay, maybe it's hollow and she carries her whiskey in it. And maybe she's wandering around hitting people with it, and she takes a slug of whiskey each time she whacks somebody. Now things are getting interesting.

In brainstorming sessions, always be on the lookout for stereotypes. And then take those clichés to the opposite extreme, twist them around, combine them with non-related things, and turn them on their head.

The simple act of going beyond cliché is really easy to do. And by adding unexpected elements to your game, you will delight your player. It's almost like having Easter eggs[1] in your game. You can have wonderful surprises evolve—granny is a pool-playing, whiskey-drinking, Converse sneaker–wearing piece of work. Maybe she still wears that frumpy black dress and those sagging nylons, but there's something there that says "I'm more than meets the eye, and if you're lucky you might find out a thing or two about me when you play this game." Now there's an interesting little old lady.[2]

If you develop some creative outside-the-box components to your game, you're likely to find creative outside-the-box ways to use them. But if all you have is stereotypes and clichés, all you're going to end up with is predictability. And predictability is definitely not very fun.

Limitations Will Set You Free

In game design, you're going to constantly be presented with the need to brainstorm your way into solutions. Whether it's at the beginning and choosing that *one* best game you hope to turn into a AAA title, or further along when you're designing the best characters for the game, the best story, the best environments, the best mechanics, and the best way to tie it all up so you can actually get the game made. While this kind of deletion of all of those other great ideas you came up with in blue sky might sound at the outset like the opposite of brainstorming, it really is the brainstorming process that helps you codify your ideas and get the work under way.

The key, then, is to know what outcome you want when you begin the brainstorming process. Some examples:

---

[1] A hidden message or feature found in a game.

[2] There is a great "little old lady" character in the animated film *Triplets of Belleville*. She is full of lots of believable, fun, unique characteristics and is utterly delightful despite the fact that she *never speaks a word*. She's a perfect example of beyond cliché.

- We need to figure out how to get the character through this encounter with the villain without the character or the villain dying.
- We need to figure out how to put this (*insert product placement*) in the game in a way that doesn't disrupt the flow, that meets the needs of the marketing group, and that helps the player further his or her way through the game.
- We need to figure out how to change the characteristics of this character because legal came back to us and said we had to.
- We need to figure out how to add this mechanic because marketing said we have to have it in.

The point is this: begin with the end in mind, and then get creative in coming up with solutions by going beyond the easy answer and brainstorming possibilities that are focused and purposeful.

You'll find that when you start working *within* constructs and limitations, something really amazing happens—it frees you up to go in directions you never would have gone before.

Case in point. In Hollywood, network animated shows for children are ruled by something called Standards and Practices, which places very specific restrictions on what can and cannot be done in children's animation. It is because of the Standards and Practices rules that you'll never see Saturday-morning network cartoon characters smoking, ingesting magic potions or pills, shooting at each other with handguns, tying anyone up with ropes, or hitting anyone with a commonly available object like a skillet or a baseball bat.[3]

The reason is that children have been known to see things on cartoons and then act them out in real life, often with devastating results. So when writing animation for kids, the challenge is to come up with some fun devices in the story that are organic and true to the show, fit within the rules of the cartooniverse, and affect the story the way you need them to.

These rules by design create very rigid limitations. However, because of these restrictions, you now have to, and get to, think up some really creative ways to get things done. Here's an example. We had an animated script that put the characters in the Wild West, in other words they were cowboys, and they were faced with many of the typical cowboy problems, not the least of which was unruly cows who, wouldn't you know it, ended up in a stampede. Now, if there were a stampede in real life, real cowboys would chase down

---

3 This is why anvils are a favorite cartoon device—they're not typically found around the house, and they're impossibly heavy for a child to throw on somebody's head.

those cows and lasso a few of them and get them under control. But we couldn't do that. Why? Standards and Practices. The last thing you want to do is give kids the idea that it's okay to throw a rope around a cow's neck and pull it into a corral. You can image the results of that play-acting. So, what do you do about the cows?

Time for some brainstorming. In this case, it's pretty easy to see what the restrictions are. You can't change the characters from cows to something else. You can't change the environment. You have to keep things organic. But it's a cartoon, so it doesn't have to be "real," and it should be fun. So, question: how do you corral cows without throwing a rope around them? Easy.

As it turns out, the cowboys are really good at what they do, and this means they're super duper fast at twirling their lassos. They are so fast, in fact, that when they work together twirling their lassos, in unison, aiming them at the same spot on the dusty prairie ground, they create a wind, and that stirs up a dust devil, and that immediately grows into a twister, and the twister goes around and picks up all the cows and conveniently drops them into the corral where they're now safe and sound and the day is saved. And that is a lot more cool than just lassoing a cow. Without the restrictions of Standards and Practices, it is highly doubtful that something that original and fun would have ever made it into the cartoon.

Serious Work Meets Fun and Games

Let's recall once again what should become one of your guiding mantras in game design: every project is different. Also remember that within this truth lies another: while every project is different, all projects have similar components. Brainstorming is one practice that is done consistently throughout the industry.

Tracy Fullerton, assistant professor at USC's School of Cinematic Arts, Interactive Media division, and co-director of the Electronic Arts Game Innovation Lab, has first-hand experience with a variety of brainstorming approaches. "Brainstorming is different for every project I've worked on," says Fullerton. "I've seen anything from having 10 to 11 people, half of whom are clients, sitting in a room, to sitting alone at home and brainstorming ideas. I don't prefer either way. The most important thing is you have a goal, you have enough information to work from, you've done enough research where your research is informed, you have an understanding of those problems before you, and you have a creative understanding of what your needs are."

A major theme that runs through the industry regarding the brainstorming process is keeping the balance between work—hashing out the prob-

The most successful brainstorming sessions usually start with some sort of fun and games.

Sketch of factory interior for *Amplitude*. Image provided by Harmonix Music Systems, Inc.

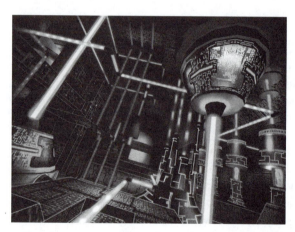

Color sketch labeled Factory Main Conversion Area for *Amplitude*. Image provided by Harmonix Music Systems, Inc.

lems—and inspiring creativity. You need to be sure to allow enough space for the mind to come up with creative solutions to those problems. The good news is that this invariably involves one of the things this industry does best: playing.

Fullerton found that some of the most productive brainstorming sessions she's participated in involved play. In her experience, "Some of the best brainstormers are Imagineers[4]. They often have very large brainstorming sessions, with people from very different backgrounds, and they have physical toys to keep people loose. And somehow, tossing toys around gets the creative ideas flowing, and I find that very successful."

Toys are just one device used to free the mind. "Different facilitators have their different tricks," notes Roger Holzberg, Vice President, Creative, at Walt Disney Parks and Resorts Online. "Typically, blank cards and colored markers get thrown out on the table."

Brainstorming is a critical component of game design to Holzberg and his team. "I have an entire wall of my office that's an erasable whiteboard, and people draw all over it all the time. There's something very freeing about it. And of course there are wonderful icebreakers around, like picking up a toy and describing why it's relevant to you."

Holzberg explains a *pre-brainstorming* experience he participated in that was designed to open up creativity. "We took a piece of paper and folded it into quarters, so we essentially had four pages, and each page was a different page in the story of our life. The first page was the title page, and it was a song—the first song that comes into your head. The next page was the place where you were born, and the number of years you've worked at

---

[4] Disney Imagineering.

the Disney Company, and that was the table of contents. Next we drew a picture of what our job was like. No matter how bad of an artist you are. And then we drew a picture of what life was like when we were retired.

"When we were finished with the books, we shared them along with the reasons why the elements were there, and it was very open and very revealing. And *then* we began the brainstorming after that, and it was one of the most open and facilitating brainstorming sessions I've ever been a part of."

Holzberg is very big on fostering creativity for his team. "One of the things that I desperately try to get creative teams to do is to find whatever that quiet or loud or crazy or calm or scary or exciting place is that allows them to make the synaptic connections that bring out their creative energy, because the corporate environment and working in cubes can kill it."

Great Minds Think Alike?

Falstein's brainstorming advice is based on over 20 years of experience in the industry and working with such creative giants as Steven Spielberg and George Lucas. "A lot of my experience came from eight years at LucasArts, and we had such an amazing group of people. When Ron (Gilbert), David (Fox), and I worked on *Indiana Jones and the Last Crusade*, the three of us were co-designing as equals. There was some concern about having three strong-willed guys collaborate. We frequently disagreed. Sometimes we would come into a meeting and two of us had one opinion, and the other one wanted to do something else. And as often as not the one would convince the other two."

"The ideal size (for a brainstorming group) is between three to seven people. The more experienced the people are, the closer you can get to three."

—Noah Falstein

What Falstein and his co-designers could not have guessed was that based on their success as a team with *Indiana Jones*, they would soon have company brainstorming on a new project.

"Spielberg is a big game player, and he often came by to see what we were doing, and he started calling us for hints when our game came out. So we gave him the name of the three project leaders (Fox, Gilbert, and Falstein), rather than have him go through the hint lines. We spent hours on the phone with him. Sometimes he'd be playing with his son Max on his lap, and I could hear him talking to Max and guiding him through the experience.

"He submitted an idea to us when we were working on *The Dig*,[5] and we worked with him through many brainstorming sessions. One of the high-

---

5 Sci-fi adventure game by LucasArts, released in 1995.

lights of my career was in the first couple of brainstorming meetings. It was not just Steven, but George also wanted to be in on that, and I got to run those meetings.

"I've found that what is helpful is to strike a balance between staying focused and letting conversation wander," says Falstein. "I'm going to quote Ron Gilbert on this; he says, 'Every good brainstorming session begins with a 15-minute discussion of *Star Trek*.' These days it might be *Lost*. For a while it was *Buffy the Vampire Slayer*.

"The thing that's important is that it's some kind of pop-culture thing that everyone has experienced and that has little to do with your session. That's part of the process, and it allows your mind to wander and come back. That's part of the rhythm. I'm really happy that George Lucas and Steven Spielberg are the same way in their brainstorming. Some people don't want to stray at all, and that's a terrible thing to do—there's nothing faster to cutting off creativity."

Brainstorming at Nihilistic

The brainstorming process at Nihilistic begins when Huebner chooses five or six games that seem to be the most promising from the bounty submitted by his employees and calls a company meeting. Here, Huebner conducts the brainstorming sessions, acting as "moderator."

Sample design from original *Zombie* IP at Nihilistic. Image courtesy of Bren Adams for Nihilistic Software.

Sample concept art from original IP—*Zombie* pitch. Image courtesy of Bren Adams for Nihilistic Software. (See color plates.)

"It's a matter of getting all the right people in the room, all the interested parties, and letting them riff off of each other's ideas. As the moderator you get it all gelled. It's like funneled brainstorming, and when it goes well, everyone feels invested, like they had some part in developing or pushing it further."

Huebner says once this process begins, "The scope of brainstorming goes down fast. We describe the ideas to our group in a face-to-face meeting and ask people to make constructive criticism, to point out flaws and make suggestions for improvement. Then we either go to a more thought-out document, or we drop the idea altogether. We winnow it down to three or four IP concepts that go further into development and get additional refinement.

"From that point, we schedule a meeting to talk about each individual pitch. Maybe one's a zombie, one's a role play, one's a sci-fi, and we invite everyone in the company if they're interested to come to the meeting, usually a lunch meeting, and people throw out ideas for the game. We take notes and give them to the original author of the pitch and ask them to take it to the next phase, put in more detail, make a stronger pitch of four to six pages.

"We try to distill the game down to the key features that differentiate it from other games, with a succinct one- to two-line summary, very high level—like *cheesy movie so-and-so* meets *so-and-so*. Then we decide what platform, what about ratings, and the five to ten main selling points. We want to get that information in right up front, for example, *Zombies meets Sim City*—something high level and quick to grasp, and to the point that it is tone setting—and then we describe what the player is doing, tell what the mechanics are, like fighting, shooting, exploring, hiding, what the player's actions are. Those are really the key things we're after."

Brainstorming *CSI*

Brainstorming does not just happen at the beginning of the project—it occurs all the way through. Greg Land, lead designer at Telltale Games on *CSI: 3 Dimensions of Murder* and *CSI: Hard Evidence*, was handed the responsibility of staying true to a major license, which just happens to be the top-rated fictional show on television, bringing in about 25 million viewers a week, according to the Nielsen ratings, and in which 100% of the people who buy the game are fans of the show. But, hey, no pressure. What this boils down to is that authenticity is of the utmost importance to the developers and the publisher, Ubisoft. This often required brainstorming sessions throughout development with people outside of the company.

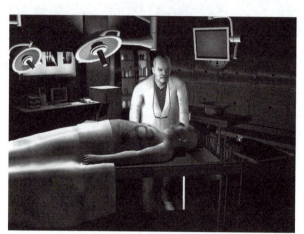

CSI: Hard Evidence morgue screenshot. Image courtesy of Ubisoft.

"During story development, once we had a set of stories with characters that we really liked, we ran the ideas by the *CSI* writers in L.A. to do a little bit of brainstorming with them. Since they were writers from the show, they had some great insight, and they helped us get a couple of cases on track, to really solidify motives and come up with some extra cool reasons people might behave in interesting ways.

"Part of my job is gathering a lot of feedback, so first I take a pass at getting as many people to look at the design as I humanly can, and I listen to what they have to say and address it to the best of my ability. Fortunately I had some really good people around me who had some excellent input, and it helped the story.

"Once we had story ideas—the plot, who's the killer, how they did it, why they did it—I would assign each story to a particular writer for three to four weeks and have them develop a two-page detailed treatment and then a full-length screenplay that lays down all the details of the case, including evidence, when you can get warrants, that type of thing."

Brainstorming *Buzz Lightyear* in Two Different Worlds

"For a very long time, since many years ago at Walt Disney Imagineering, we've dreamed about how we could create gameplay elements that make our product compelling to teens and tweens. And a big part of what we do in our parks and resorts with the advanced projects group is to work on that," explains Roger Holzberg. "There clearly is a generation who grew up with video games, and video games are part of their language. And the *Buzz Lightyear* attraction talks that language like no other; it's a ride through a video game. It became a compelling part of that experience to take this ride out into the virtual world."

The challenge of *Buzz Lightyear Astro Blasters Online* was to figure out how to merge the gameplay online in real time with players riding the attraction in the park. And it had to be launched as part of Disney's 50th anniversary. "It's really the idea of Tomorrowland," notes Holzberg, "where the real world meets the virtual space and these two come together and play. Impacting the attraction during the course of play—well, it's a very interesting phenomenon when you're playing online. The online gameplay is a lot more robust and deeper, even though it's the same length as the attraction gameplay in the ride.

"In the park, they get in a ride vehicle, and each person has two laser blasters. Buzz gives them an assignment to collect batteries, which have been stolen by his evil nemesis, so you can get enough power to defeat him. As you ride through the ride you use your blasters to hit the targets. The targets have a score, and you're playing against one another to get the highest score, and to get the highest score as a team in your vehicle.

"We took that concept and thought how cool it would be to play online where you match one-on-one with the players in the attraction. You're teleported into a game where you are attached to a ride vehicle. So the players online are wedded with the players in real time, with exactly the same pace and speed as a ride vehicle at the park, and you have similar perspectives."

Bringing the online world into a real-time interaction with people riding in the game at the park, Holzberg's team used some solid first-person shooter game strategies.

"There's functionality online where you can rescue little green men, and when you rescue a little green man you turn on a special target in the ride. When these targets are hit by people in the ride, it increases your overall team score and enables your team to do better. People in the ride who don't know about the online play think the specials are randomly turning on, but actually it's the player online who's turning on those specials. It's a really fun, dynamic, cool game."

When you're working in an arena that has never been explored before, that crucial first step is brainstorming. And not just brainstorming, but *effective* brainstorming that goes from "Wouldn't it be cool if we could do this," to "Here's how we're gonna do this." There's not just one way to get there. But there are good examples of how people do it. Holzberg's group has created a new approach to facilitate that process.

"Just recently we developed a process with the creative directors that is twofold—two answers to this question. First we do a 'creative pitch-off,' and then we do a 'creative pitch-in.' The creative pitch-in I open up to the entire organization, and when we as senior managers cast our core team of a project, we like to begin the creative process with a pitch-in. An email is sent to the entire organization inviting them to participate in the pitch-in. They get the topic, and we're all connected online so we can share sketches or whatever.

"The project creative team leads the pitch-in, and everybody within the organization is invited to pitch an idea that will make the creative genesis of the project groundbreaking. Pitch-ins can be prepared ahead of time—they usually get a week or two notice, and I give special credit to partners who work on one together; for example, if a tech director partners with a flash designer or a biz dev person and those two give a pitch-in together, that's rewarded. They get an extremely brief period of time to give their pitch, and they're on the clock. So the first half of the pitch-in is a free-form spanning of ideas.

"Then we clear the room for a few minutes, and the senior directors in the room, along with the senior project leaders, aggregate the ideas into categories: ideas that are similar, ideas that have to be explored further, ideas that are aligned with business objectives of the company. Then we bring everybody back in and the pitchers are put back into those groups and they come up with more ideas. Then the creative team goes away with that supply of fresh, raw, unedited, creative ideas, and they use them to develop the project."

Of all the people I've worked with in the industry, Holzberg has just about the highest regard for fostering creativity that I've encountered. He honors the creative process. And he gives space and time to creatively work.

"The other thing I try to live by as a law in working with creative folks is to enable them to find the space where they can be truly creative and put the right ideas together. When I say creative folks, I include product management, business development, and tech folks. If there's a lesson to be learned from great partnerships, it's that great creative vision doesn't live alone. Walt Disney would not have existed without his brother Roy, the 'business guy.'

"One of my favorite, favorite points that Malcolm Gladwell makes in one of his early chapters of *Blink* is around the reason why the head acquisitions person at the Getty could not see that the Greek statue they were about to pay $10 million for was a fake when several contemporaries saw it immediately. She was overwhelmed with business pressure, and that hampered her ability to see creatively."

Whether you're spending $10 million on a statue or designing a game, the pressure of the business needs can easily seep into the daily realities of the team trying to pull it all off. And there's nothing worse than pressure to squash creativity. But the good news is that you can get away from it and break free of its hold, and I'd venture to say that's more true in this industry than in any other. We know how to play.

Holzberg offers his antidote. "The financial pressures from business development, the product pressure from the product-management team, the financial pressure from the finance folks, can crush the technical creativity or story or gameplay or creative spark out of a person. And for me, one of the smartest things you can do to start brainstorming is send people out to the park to run, send them to a theme park and let them ride rides, get them out of the office and let them get to a different place. For me, I know where the best creative connections come to me when I work, and I encourage everybody to find those spaces for themselves."

Brainstorming Exercise

Choose a topic that relates to a game that you want to either narrow in scope or come up with a fix for. It could be a game you want to do, or a game that's already on the market that you think could be better.

Get two to five people together for a brainstorming session on this topic. You should be clear who's going to be the moderator of this session before you start.

Spend the first 10 to 15 minutes or so playing with toys, filling out Mad Libs, drawing, playing a game, etc., or talking about a new movie, cartoon, TV show, etc.—anything but the topic at hand.

At a natural break in the play time, start the discussion of the topic you've chosen. It's the moderator's job to keep the topic going and to note the creative ideas and solutions proposed by the group.

Brainstorming Checklist

❏ Start your brainstorming sessions with something fun that is *not* about the problem you're trying to solve or the task at hand—play.

❏ Begin with the end in mind—know what you're brainstorming toward and what you want to accomplish.

❏ Go beyond clichés—let the clichés and stereotypes come out, then take them in the opposite direction, and twist things around until you come up with interesting and fun solutions.

❏ Let the conversation ebb and flow throughout the brainstorming session to keep creativity flowing—the mind works in mysterious ways, so let it.

Chapter 4

Story in Game Design—The Thousand-Pound Gorilla

"If games are going to be a true dominant art form in this century, we have to elevate them beyond the simple mechanics of the gameplay or the graphics. All that matters is actually the experience. When we realized this, that's when we started focusing on story."

—Denis Dyack, President, Silicon Knights

Every year at GDC[1], which is arguably one of the most significant must-attend conferences in the industry, there are sessions on the art, craft, and design of creating the story in games. The 2007 conference boasts an all-day *Interactive Storytelling Bootcamp*, an all-day *Learn Better Game Writing* tutorial on story structure, character development and dialog, a two-hour lecture and roundtable on creating *Emotional Characters*, a one-hour *Game Writers' Roundtable* on the craft of game writing and sharing "tips, techniques, and concerns," a 60-minute lecture on *Avatar Psychology* and character creation (the player characters populating the story), and an hour lecture on *Writing for the Hero with a Thousand Faces* and how that relates to the storytelling challenges of *Gears of War*.

Storytelling is the world's second oldest profession. And I would venture to guess that it probably got started by telling tales about the world's first oldest profession. But even if the nugget of a game comes from some great idea other than story, like a cool game mechanic as in *Time Shift*, an amazing environment as in *Myst*, or a character as in *Lara Croft Tomb Raider: Legend*, eventually you're gonna have to face the facts: (1) everything in life has a story, and (2) that includes your game.

Hear me right on this. Not every game has a rich, deep, elaborate story-line. And not every game needs one. Solitaire, for example. But every game

---

1 Game Developers Conference.

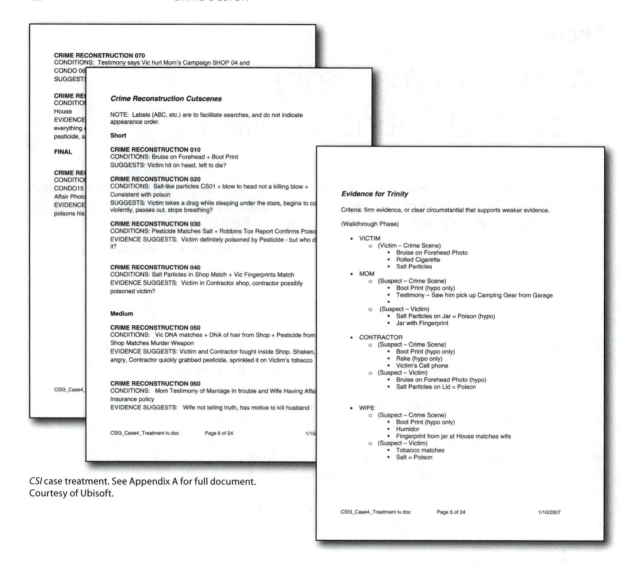

CSI case treatment. See Appendix A for full document.
Courtesy of Ubisoft.

does have a story. As soon as you start to tell any interested party what your game is about, you're telling its story.

Who is the game about? What is the goal? When does the story take place? Where does the story take place? Why is this going on in the story, and why do you as the player care? How are you going to accomplish your goals and interact with the story and the characters?

How do you begin to answer such questions? You might remember these fundamentals of writing from junior high school: who, what, when, where, why, and how. In its simplest form, that's what you need to answer in story and game development. Now, you can probably come up with some rudimentary answers to each of these, but good game design involves a little more than just fill-in-the-blanks for questions like these. And the more thoughtful you are about delving into these areas in some depth, the more reason you'll give players to connect with your game, play it more, tell their friends, and help make it a hit.

CSI: Hard Evidence screenshot with Brass. Image courtesy of Ubisoft. (See color plates.)

"Writing embodies the premise of the story, a cast of characters, a setting, a time, and a place, and probably an inventive plot—a series of incidents that are unusual and carefully thought out that involves the cast, with conflict between the hero and the villain both pushing toward a goal that each desires and only one can have."

—Hal Barwood

Where the Writer Fits In

I was at E3[2] one year with a publisher showing off our new game based on a very high-profile marquee character, which consequently gave us some really nice attendance privileges when it came to a certain hip L.A. party. Okay, we crashed the party. But we felt justified going because it was hosted by an internationally recognized publisher with very close ties to our game's publisher. And besides, our producer hired a couple of limos for us, so at the very least if we got kicked out we'd leave in style.

The said event was held around the pool of the infamous Chateau Marmot,[3] and movie

Brief Timeline of Events Surrounding the Crime

- Mom demands Victim take his belongings out of her garage so the Contractor can hang drywall; camping gear is among the items in question.
- Victim decides he'll take the gear then head out to the desert - alone.
- Victim informs Mom of his plans, "I'll come get that crap tomorrow."
- Mom informs Contractor of his plans, "That stuff will be out of the garage tomorrow so you can finish your work in there."
- Contractor leaves note for Victim.
- Victim informs wife of his plans that morning.
- Wife hurriedly poisons Victim's tobacco.
- Victim arrives at Mom's house, takes gear, finds note.
- Victim heads to Contractor's shop in a rage and gets into an altercation with Contractor.
- Victim heads out to desert.
- Wife demands Contractor get his crap out of their kitchen.
- Contractor stops by condo to retrieve tools and things, including canister of pesticide.
- Wife has lover over for tryst.
- Contractor brings canister of pesticide to Mom's garage. Forgetting lid at shop.
- Victim smokes a cigarette and dies.
- An anonymous hiker discovers the Victim's body and calls the police from a pay phone. Moves victim out of sleeping bag and steals his wallet.

CSI3_Case4_Treatment tv.doc   Page 24 of 24   1/10/2007

CSI case treatment. See Appendix A for full document. Courtesy of Ubisoft.

---

2 Electronic Entertainment Expo.

3 Famed 1982 death place of actor John Belushi.

stars were everywhere,[4] with the women wearing designer gowns and dripping with jewels, while the men looked debonair and dashing in their tuxes. We party crashers blended in perfectly. We were wearing our "booth clothes"—khakis and big blue denim shirts tastefully embroidered in full color with our character's image.

So when about 15 of us poured out of our limos and descended on the crowd, we sort-of looked like we belonged. Everyone knew our game's character, and so conversations were easily started. One of my most memorable conversations of the evening was with a producer from the host's publishing company as he started chatting me up about a new game they were working on. "We're just about ready to hire a writer," he told me. "We have the programming almost all done."

Huh?

That's right. *They were just about done programming the entire game!* Next logical step? Hire a writer to figure out the story, of course.

You can see why that was a memorable conversation. I hope.

So let's just get this straight, to be sure that you are capable of making better decisions during your game-development career: there is a good time to hire a writer, and there is a not-so-good time to hire a writer, and after you've already finished programming the game, well, that falls under the category of the not-so-good time.

So, when *is* the best time to bring a writer into the mix? Honestly, as early in the process as you can possibly imagine, then about two to four weeks before that is ideal. But practically speaking? Well, here are some scenarios:

> *"There is a danger of separating the writer from the process. You can have stories in game. And you can have very good dialog. But without that narrative position, someone who knows the story and the game design, we have to reinvent the story along the way. And the story is not just plot; it's visuals and game mechanics as well, and if they are all working together they will enhance the theme of the game."*
>
> **—Mary DeMarle, Ubisoft**

Scenario 1: We did our brainstorming session already and we have all of the big strokes of the game figured out. When should we hire a writer?

Answer: Now.

---

[4] Martin Landau and I had a lovely discussion about computers and computer games. What a man. And as if I needed any more incentive, now I *really* adore him. And if you don't know who Martin Landau is you are not a true geek.

Scenario 2: It's about time to start brainstorming our next game. When should we hire a writer?

Answer: Now.

Scenario 3: We got our programming all done. When should we hire a writer?

Answer: We've been over this already.

Having a writer involved sooner in the process rather than later helps get a handle on where you're going with your game, whether it's a simple "story wrap" you need for a first-person shooter, a rich story to integrate with a well-known marquee character for an RPG, or a story of unknown dimensions and genre on an original IP you're starting to pull together to create a new franchise. And if a company can have a designer who is also a writer, they have struck gold.

At the very least, it's clearly important for game developers to understand some basics about story, its structure, its purpose, and all the other reasons people pay hundreds of dollars to go to conferences to learn about writing in games from the pros. Because if a game is designed without an understanding of what makes a good story, it takes a lot of resources to recover from the mistakes that are made, and that's assuming they can be fixed. Sometimes, the game is so botched it's beyond repair.

Hal Barwood has seen this first hand, consulting in the industry as a writer-designer. "Everyone understands writing when it comes to a screenplay or a book. But writers in our business generally come in late in development, and this has been done by design."

Often developers think along the lines of, "We'll just throw a story together; how hard can it be?" But this line of thinking can be fatal. Barwood elaborates: "The developer will figure out the heroes and villains and effects and incidents of plot before they even think about bringing in a writer. And if that has not been done well, it's hopeless for the poor sap who comes in with the task of writing the story for them. Maybe they won't have good character relationships and the characters won't have conflicts. Maybe the plot is too crazy in some way so there's no way to bridge the gap and make it believable in terms of suspension of disbelief."

> *"Ideas are very much the easy part. I literally have a file drawer full of game ideas, most of which I'll never get to. Ideas are important, but just really the first step, or the zeroth step. Once you have that seed, you need to go back to how does the player feel, what's their journey, or what's the task, what are they trying to accomplish—the nouns and verbs."*
>
> **—Mike Sellers**

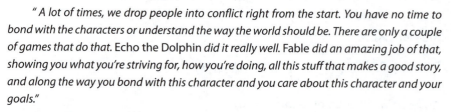

" A lot of times, we drop people into conflict right from the start. You have no time to bond with the characters or understand the way the world should be. There are only a couple of games that do that. Echo the Dolphin did it really well. Fable did an amazing job of that, showing you what you're striving for, how you're doing, all this stuff that makes a good story, and along the way you bond with this character and you care about this character and your goals."

—Chris Ferriter, Producer, Ubisoft

Cinematic sketches for *Death Jr. II*. Images © 2006 Backbone Entertainment. Death Jr., the Death Jr. characters and logo are trademarks of Backbone Entertainment.

Story Structure

Stories are about characters in conflict. This usually manifests as two opposing forces who both want the same thing, or at least want to keep each other from having it. In the story, we'll also have other characters that are pulled into the drama, even if it's a comedy, in some capacity while the hero, a.k.a. the protagonist, fights against the villain, a.k.a. the antagonist. And as Barwood put it so succinctly, with both "pushing toward a goal that each desires and only one can have."

Hollywood has a long history of delivering stories that captivate an audience and take them on that emotional roller-coaster ride of the tug-of-war of desire. Writing is about weaving a good story around this dilemma, presenting interesting characters, making the audience care, and doing it in a way that works time and time again. To that end, there are some basic components of writing a story that are essential for the game designer to know.

Three Acts

Generally speaking, stories occur in three acts. These acts are the beginning, the middle, and the end, a.k.a. Act 1, Act 2, and Act 3.

Rough Cut
Case 4 Treatment

Updates
8/5/05 - Minor Updates mostly to evidence -GL
8/8/05 - Trinity updated - GL
8/9/05 – Rewrote Crime Recons & Added Forensic Recons – GL

Overview
The son of a politically connected real estate developer is found dead in a remote desert area. Poison is the cause of death and everyone in his life has a motive for the killing. Evidence points to a contractor owed a large sum of money and the victim's hard edged mother, who is currently embroiled in a tight primary race for a nomination to the state senate and is upset over negative publicity stemming from her son's public life. Eventually the evidence proves the victim's wife killed her husband to cash in on a life insurance policy and begin life anew with another man.

Characters, Line Counts & Relationships

CSI case treatment. See Appendix A for full document. Courtesy of Ubisoft.

The beginning is the set-up. It's usually short. And it needs to be compelling and draw the audience into the story. In movies, the set-up is just about the first ten pages of a 110-page script. If you miss the first ten minutes of a movie, you miss the entire set-up, and it's very difficult to come in after this point and fully understand where you are, why you're there, and the point of what is happening. It is the set-up that pulls us into the story and makes us care. It establishes the lead characters, and as we go into the second act it's presenting us with what we're up against.

The middle is, obviously, the bulk of the story where all the action takes place. And it's where the roller coaster takes us on the highest highs, around the fastest corners, and down to the lowest levels of the ride. It has to have a good pacing of highs and lows, otherwise you either exhaust your audience from the constant adrenaline rush, or you bore them to tears.

The end is not only the wrap-up of the adventure, but it returns us back to the real world and leaves our character in a different, usually deeper emotional state than when we first began. Maybe they're in familiar territory or maybe looking ahead to facing new challenges.

Organic

Good storytelling is organic in nature. In other words, things happen within the story that are natural occurrences to that time and place and with the characters that populate it.

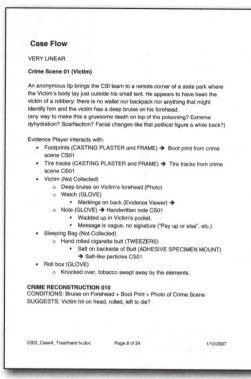

Case Flow

VERY LINEAR

Crime Scene 01 (Victim)

An anonymous tip brings the CSI team to a remote corner of a state park where the Victim's body lay just outside his small tent. He appears to have been the victim of a robbery: there is no wallet nor backpack nor anything that might identify him and the victim has a deep bruise on his forehead.
(any way to make this a gruesome death on top of the poisoning? Extreme dyhydration? Scarfiaction? Facial changes like that political figure a while back?)

Evidence Player interacts with:
- Footprints (CASTING PLASTER and FRAME) ➜ Boot print from crime scene CS01
- Tire tracks (CASTING PLASTER and FRAME) ➜ Tire tracks from crime scene CS01
- Victim (Not Collected)
  - ○ Deep bruise on Victim's forehead (Photo)
  - ○ Watch (GLOVE)
    - ▪ Markings on back (Evidence Viewer) ➜
  - ○ Note (GLOVE) ➜ Handwritten note CS01
    - ▪ Wadded up in Victim's pocket.
    - ▪ Message is vague, no signature ("Pay up or else", etc.)
- Sleeping Bag (Not Collected)
  - ○ Hand rolled cigarette butt (TWEEZERS)
    - ▪ Salt on backside of Butt (ADHESIVE SPECIMEN MOUNT) ➜ Salt-like particles CS01
- Roll box (GLOVE)
  - ○ Knocked over, tobacco swept away by the elements.

CRIME RECONSTRUCTION 010
CONDITIONS: Bruise on Forehead + Boot Print + Photo of Crime Scene
SUGGESTS: Victim hit on head, rolled, left to die?

CSI3_Case4_Treatment tv.doc   Page 8 of 24   1/10/2007

CSI case treatment. See Appendix A for full document. Courtesy of Ubisoft.

"We had product placement in CSI, and the difficulty was nobody wanted criminals using their products. We had a Nokia cell phone, and we were told criminals cannot use a Nokia phone. So, the player finds the cell phone, and he can pick it up and examine it, and it works without being intrusive.

"We also had a marketing company come to us and ask, 'Can you put Mr. Clean Auto Dry Car Wash in the game?' Well, you can't just have it show up without a good reason for being there, so we really had to figure out how to make that appear in the game in a way that made sense. And we did it. In the end, we didn't get the placement, but it was gratifying to know that we were able to work something like that in. We were also able to work in Visa. They were very interested in getting the word out on their product. Visa has fraud protection, so we used their product to help us establish a timeline."

—Greg Land, Lead Designer, *CSI* 3 and 4

This is important for story design and for overall game design and is especially important when you're faced with, for example, including product placement into a game because some corporate PR department thinks it would be cool to have their brand show up in this "new" medium. Well, it can't just show up—it needs to make sense. And where it needs to make sense is within the story.

Episodic

When stories are strung together and one story has little to do with the next, the stories are called episodic. You remember *Batman*. This week, Batman fights the Riddler. Next week, Batman fights the Joker. His fighting the Riddler this week has nothing to do with the episode next week with the Joker. This is episodic.

What's also referred to as episodic in this industry is a story that is really usually considered serial in nature. Think of *The X-Files*, for example. This week something happens, and next week something different happens that doesn't really have anything to do with this week's show, but at some point Scully is going to bring up something from several episodes back that will help her figure out a mystery.

In a perfect world, we'd all be in agreement what to call things. Is this serial or episodic? The truth of the matter is that in game design, as you've already heard, every project is different, and every company is different, and what works within your company is what you go with.

Backstory

Backstory is the information about the characters and the environment and everything that happened *before* the story that your user experiences takes place. It's the story before the story.

All of the backstory information is written in a document called the story bible, usually along with character bios and sketches, and it explains all of the essential elements that get us to the point of where our story begins.

One of the most important functions of the backstory is to give depth and richness to the overall story, so that when you're ready to start making decisions about what happens with your characters or the action, you already have some really relevant history about what got them to this point in time. Creating backstory is a *lot* of fun. And if you do it well, creating backstory will save you a *whole lot* of time. It's also really great to give the story bible to your talent (voice-over actors) because actors like to know who their characters are so they can really get into a role.[5]

Bookending

Bookending is a technique used to tie the whole story together and give it a nice clean wrap-up that audiences really love. This is done a lot in movies. For example, we start in one locale, the hero (lead character) is thrust into a situation that takes the entire movie to figure out, and then ends up back in the same place we saw in the beginning, with new lessons learned and a broader sense of self.

Fish-out-of-Water Story

The best example I can point to of a fish-out-of-water story is figuratively and literally the movie *Splash*. The fish, in this case Daryl Hannah, leaves the water

---

5 It really makes a difference. You don't want actors who don't care about their characters. That leaves you with flat characters. It's gotta be fun for the actors to do their job, and letting them know who they are playing ahead of time (like as soon as you cast them, hand them the story bible) is a huge step taken for getting a good performance out of them.

"Game design is not done in a vacuum. It's all done in stages—all the processes are happening in parallel, and they're all informing each other each step of the way. So while you're prototyping player mechanics you're also prototyping character models and textures and flushing out the bio of the character. While you're starting level design, level locations are being finalized, and concept art is being finalized. Every department is always furthering their understanding of their particular contribution and is informing the other groups, and then story lives in design."

—**Riley Cooper, Lead Designer, *Lara Croft Tomb Raider: Legend***

Scene from *Lara Croft Tomb Raider: Legend.* Image © 2006 Eidos Interactive Ltd. *Lara Croft Tomb Raider: Legend,* Lara Croft, *Tomb Raider,* and the Tomb Raider logo are all trademarks of Eidos Interactive Ltd. (See color plates.)

to find out what life is like on dry land, and in the end returns to her watery world, taking some of her new experiences, and Tom Hanks, with her.

"And then…" versus "And because…"

One of the most important things you can do in storytelling is avoid what I call the *"And then…" Syndrome*. It is one of the most common mistakes I see with inexperienced writers, and it is so easy to fix and to avoid that once you know about it and know what to do about it, your storytelling will be instantly more compelling. Here's how it goes:

> **This happens, and then this happens, and then this happens, and then this happens.**

And you know what? It might be true that in your story this happens and then this happens and then this happens, but it's not very interesting.

What's more engaging is when the story develops as "And because…". It goes like this:

> **This happens, and because this happened then this happens, and because that happened then this happens, and because that happened then this happens!**

Now you've introduced cause and effect. And that's a much more inviting game to play.

Let's compare with a scenario.

And then…

I walked into a dark tunnel, and then two guys started shooting at me, and then I ducked around a corner, and then I jumped on a hover board.

Okay. But so what?

Now let's try it another way.

And because…

I walked into a dark tunnel, and because it was dark I couldn't see where I was going so I tripped, and because I tripped the two guys leaning against the far wall heard me and starting shooting, and because they started shooting I ducked around a corner, and because I ducked around the corner I happened upon the stolen hover board so I jumped on it to get out of here—kills two birds with one stone if you ask me: makes me the hero for finding the prize and gives me a chance to save myself, and because the two guys were in the main part of the tunnel now I had to find another way out of here and that's when I spotted the manhole—now how do I make this thing do more than just hover?

The movements we make are the same in each scenario. But in the second example we now have reason for doing what we're doing. And we have the beginnings of a story with purpose and tone and sense, and that is a whole lot more interesting than just reciting the steps we can take or the moves we can make. It also makes it pretty clear what we could do if we wanted some organic options to the story and, in fact, in the gameplay:

I walked into a dark tunnel and because I had a flashlight I noticed the dead body recently dropped in the middle of my path just about five feet inside the entrance, and because I saw him I knew right away I was not alone so I scanned the perimeter and that's when I noticed two guys leaning against the far wall, and because I saw them before they saw me I was able to take them out with my .357 Magnum, a gun I carry around for sentimental reasons, and because they fell in a split second I felt I had some time to look around and maybe figure out what this little gathering was all about, so I went further into the tunnel with my handy flashlight and my big gun.

Wait a minute; he didn't find the hover board. Yep. Options, as you know, are a good thing.

Another Lesson from Hollywood

Robert McKee is a Hollywood storytelling guru who gives substantial classes on story structure and scriptwriting, at substantial prices, to substantial players and wannabe players in Hollywood. He's been doing it for a substantially long time.

One of the things he's come up with is his own "Ten Commandments" on writing. One of them is something that I repeat to myself over and over again when I design and write any new game: "Know your world as God knows this one."

This is not about religious beliefs. The lesson from McKee is what I believe to be the most important when it comes to story and character development. Be the expert of your world. As the author, exercise your authority.

So when you're creating a game, or the story of a game, if you know that world "as God knows this one," you have the depth necessary to help you with a couple of things: (1) make the game more interesting, and (2) get yourself out of trouble in sticky situations, like when you encounter structural holes and narrative gaps.

And this is where the whole idea and practice of developing backstory comes into play.

Which Came First, the Comic Book or the Game?

"We get asked that all the time, and they both came at the same time," says Mike Mika about Backbone Entertainment's original IP *Death Jr.* "It's such a bizarre world to describe to people that the only way we could pull it off was to show them a sample of it. So we produced a real comic of it and gave it away as part of a focus test at Comic-Con, and it was a huge success. We used that success as part of the pitch to the publisher, with a video of people lined up to play our demo of the game. *Death Jr. II* got greenlit through the publisher before the first game even shipped.

"The way we do it is that we start off with what would be cool this time around for DJ," adds Joe Morrissey, lead designer on *Death Jr. II: Root of Evil.* "So we get one-paragraph pitches that are huge email chains, and they say things like, 'This would be cool; let's have a science fair and the whole town gets turned into demons, and you can use a spitball,' stuff like that. You get a lot of quirky directions. Bad stuff stays at the bottom and good stuff rises to the top. You get a good idea of where things are going in two days or so. And from there, you sit down with the principals and do defined brainstorming.

"You want to have your *über*-story or higher story in place, like, 'DJ is going to fight this nature girl gone evil and in the process travel

 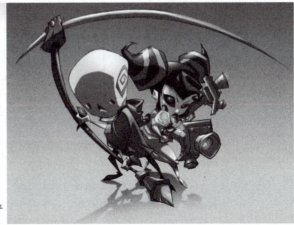

Sketch of action pose for DJ and Pandora, and concept art of same pose, for *Death Jr. II*. Images © 2006 Backbone Entertainment. Death Jr., the Death Jr. characters and logo are trademarks of Backbone Entertainment.

to various places to accomplish different goals and eventually get to the final level where you can fight her.' People on the team come back and say, 'Hey, we can do this really cool technology,' like some cool lighting effect, for example, and then you shoestring it all together.

"You figure out where you want to start the game, you obviously know how you're going to end it, and once you get the visual vibes of that, then it's just a matter of coming up with the mechanics of that—what type of monsters are they going to fight and what kind of platform is the game going to be on—so that when you get through the game, you have gone from the more easy things to learn to the more difficult. Then the player is like, 'Hey, I've learned to do the triple jump hover slide,' and they feel really good about that. You have to make sure that people are having fun.

"You show off your stuff to other designers and listen to their feedback. A lot of junior designers get too attached to what they're working on. You need to be passionate enough about your ideas to fight for them, but professional enough to know when to walk away. We have people who are very professional but they never seem very invested, and then you have guys who are really invested but when you

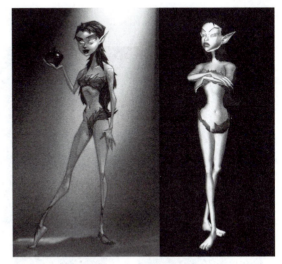

Concept art and render of Furi, DJ's nemesis in *Death Jr. II*. Images © 2006 Backbone Entertainment. Death Jr., the Death Jr. characters and logo are trademarks of Backbone Entertainment.

Cinematic sketch for *Death Jr. II.* Images © 2006 Backbone Entertainment. Death Jr., the Death Jr. characters and logo are trademarks of Backbone Entertainment.

don't use their idea they get destroyed. You need the balance—I think this is really cool and this is why it's cool, and then sit down and find out we can and can't do. Sometimes you hear something you don't want to hear, like that it'll take three code days to develop one cool thing and you say, 'Oh, crap. All right. Well, can we do this instead?'

"A lot of the time you end up with people who get one mindset that this is how it has to be done, and if they can't do it like that they bang their head against the wall. You need to be able to really look at the design you want and come up with other ways to do it. You have to be able to think around corners.

"Once you get the ideas, you have a keeper of all of them; in this case it was me. So, you look at what rings true. Do level ideas organically grow from those story ideas? Do different characters and monsters organically come out of

Concept art of Tree Boss scene for *Death Jr. II.* Image © 2006 Backbone Entertainment. Death Jr., the Death Jr. characters and logo are trademarks of Backbone Entertainment.

this? Then, when you do a couple versions of the one- or two-page story doc, you get a pretty solid idea of what the game could be. Then you go and flesh it out and see different levels you could have. What's the beginning, middle, and end?

"One of the main things you do, especially when working with levels and story as a designer, is that you have things that happen in between levels, usually cinematics, or even in levels. Then you come up with what you need to do and show within the level to push the story forward, and you start getting an idea for what the cinematics would be—not exactly what the dialog is. For example, we might say DJ is hanging out with the gang at the sawmill and they're discussing what they're going to do next. Well, that's going to be a really boring cinematic because they're talking heads, but it's important to move the story forward so you figure out ways to spice it up.

"The top line is you start small, and you keep building. You keep fleshing out more and more elements of it. At some point, art is going to want your scripts for cinematics so they can figure out assets and running time and levels, and code is going to need to know if there's anything bizarre, like DJ goes into death mode where he turns into a ghost and they need to do a shader, or any other technical issues they're going to have to manage. Once we have 15 to 20 pages of full game of each level, and a brief summary of cinematics and storyline, then we do a cinematics doc. In this case we use a standard movie format, and from that we kind of get an estimate of how long it'll take, for example, a minute a page. That works well when you do a two-hour script, and it's not quite exact, but it's close enough when we do cinematics.

"Story elements and mechanics can come together to make memorable elements that are essentially the 'wow' points in the game. It could be like an amazing vista, a big shot over a cliff, or some cool powered attack that DJ gets. Anytime you can get, 'Oh, that's cool!'— and you want to pace those out through your game—those aren't just design elements. One is art. One is code. But still, it's also design. Design can say, 'Here's what we need for our memorable elements,' like maybe platform ramping—what platform elements do you need to have in the game to keep things interesting? Jumps, hover jumps, ledge grabs, wire slides, rafters, hook, chimney jumps, balance beam, those are our basic mechanics, and all of those have different degrees of difficulty to them. So you figure out what's the easiest to introduce to the player at the beginning. And then you let them learn harder elements as they go along. A lot of game design is you're the teacher who teaches the student—as opposed to the 'evil game designer' philosophy in that you're trying to kill the player all along the way."

Sketches for *Death Jr. II* Saw Mill interior. Image © 2006 Backbone Entertainment. Death Jr., the Death Jr. characters and logo are trademarks of Backbone Entertainment.

Portal

In 1977, author Rob Swigart got his first computer. When the Apple II came out, he got computer #73. "I was an early adopter," he says, "and I thought the computer would be an interesting technical medium to tell stories. Then in '84, I got a call from a producer at Activision who wanted me to write a manual for a music program. I did, and I gave him one of my books, and he said to me one day, 'Boy, you would be perfect at telling stories through the computer.' It's as if somebody had said, 'What are you dreaming of?'"

"So we started cooking up *Portal*, and meanwhile I started scripting a game called *Murder on the Mississippi*, a murder mystery set on a riverboat with little characters that ran in and out of the rooms. They gave me a terminal at home attached to their PDP-11, I think it was a DEC, and it was a mini-computer. I guess it was at Activision, so I was basically hooked into their computer. I had a lot of fun with that one. I didn't design the puzzles, but I invented all the characters and did all the dialog. Then I wrote a proposal for *Portal* and pitched it and sold it to Activision.

"*Portal* was the idea that the screen of the computer was the portal, and the concept of it was the user is basically an astronaut who has returned to an Earth that's depopulated and finds a terminal that is barely alive but slightly active.[5] And gradually, by interacting with the AI[7] storytelling algorithm, you begin uncovering the story of what happened to all the people.

"I wanted to do a story that was a real narrative, but not an adventure game. I thought of adventure games as a very wide world but shallow, and I wanted to do a world that was narrower but deeper. There was nothing like it, which shows you that I was out of my time. Not even ahead of it, but out of it. The closet thing was Pinsky's *Mind Wheel*, but even that was more of an adventure game.

"I had a meeting with a guy who was a developer, and his big idea for the game was to have white text on a red screen. He didn't really get it. But Paul Saffo introduced us to Gilman Louie,[8] who had a little company called Nexa, and we had a meeting with him and he got it immediately.

"Gilman had taken over his parents' house in San Francisco. They had the dining room table covered with computers. The whole downstairs was taken over by his company. He had about ten guys in the house working. Then while they were developing *Portal*, they got an office on Bryant Street,

---

6 The terminal's name is Homer.

7 Artificial intelligence.

8 Gilman Louie started Nexa Corporation, then was CEO of a string of successful companies, including Sphere, which merged with Spectrum HoloByte, and MicroProse, which was sold to Hasbro, before going to In-Q-Tel, the IT company funded by the CIA.

and it was 15 programmers, me, the producer, and the VP of Activision. That was great.

"Gilman did a lot of graphics for *Portal*. He'd whip them up on the spot, and I'd whip up the text on the spot. We were a good team. We had lots of discussions on how to design in terms of interactivity. The 'bash the troll, grab the gold' text-parsing algorithms were not very satisfying in terms of interactivity. 'Go north, open the door'—it was very hard to design a robust way of making the computer sound intelligent. It wouldn't pass the Turing test.[9]

"So I thought about it. Computers can do three things: word processing, spreadsheets, and databases. Word processing is how I write, but that didn't seem like an interesting way to do a game on the computer. And I couldn't figure out how to do a game on a spreadsheet. So I thought, 'Let's use a database with seemingly endless storage.' So it's a database story with hundreds of small stories, 400 or some, in 12 databases, and the AI that told the story. There was some encyclopedia-type information that was hidden in some of the databases, but mostly you interacted with Homer, and as you went through the game, more stuff appeared in the databases so that you would feel the network was coming to life.

"The databases were icons, so it was icon-based, but it mostly was a text window that the story appeared in. Homer was an image, a drawing, and the 12 databases were represented as a screen full of icons you could click on. Remember, this was the year the Mac came out, and people didn't think in terms of icons and clicking on the screen yet. Maybe that was ahead of its time, too. It had an impact.

"I discovered that while I was designing it, there were two narratives going on at the same time. One was the story of what happened, and one was the story of Homer, who was waking up and becoming more human. And as I did the book,[10] I realized that there was a third character, the astronaut, so then it was a triple narrative.

"They spent $100,000-plus on it, not counting me, and in those days that was a lot of money. The game came out in '86. We had developed it for six platforms, and it came out on five and on the Mac Plus. The week it was released, the Mac SE came out and it didn't work on that machine, but they refused to spend $200 to have the code tweaked for it.

---

9 Referring to Alan Turing's work on AI. Turing believed that a computer would be deemed "intelligent" if you could interact with it and not be able to tell that it's a computer.

10 *Portal* was released first as a video game and then as a book.

"The prettiest system for it was the Amiga, because it was kind of animated in the sense that it looked like Christmas-tree lights, but not really richly graphic.

"Also, they were charging $1000 *a word* to digitize sound to make sound files. Today anybody could do it for free, but in 1985 it was expensive. So there was music, but no voice. If I were to do it now it would have video and lots of sound.

"*Portal* was nominated for an SPA[11] award, so we went to the awards ceremony, where Douglas Adams was the keynote, and I knew it wasn't going to win because it was way too experimental. And I was right. Print Shop from Broderbund won.

"*Portal* sold 30,000 copies. It wasn't a huge bestseller, but I still get emails from people who say, 'I played *Portal* as a kid, and it was so wonderful,' and now they're all in their forties.

"I was happy the way it came out, especially considering the primitive technology at the time. It looked kind of crude; the graphics were crude. And the text was 80-column block letters, but I had a strong belief you needed to keep the file short because people don't want to read a lot of text on screen.

"As an interactive novel, it was the first of its kind. You had to make an effort to look in likely places for new files. It was context-dependent, so for example, if somebody mentioned science, you had to look in the science database. It wasn't terribly interactive, but it required some effort—it wasn't meant to be puzzle-based. You were meant to be engrossed in the story and that worked.

"It was Frank Catalano[12] who wrote that you just didn't want to stop, you wanted to see what happened next and stay up all night. I had several people write me about that, and that was the intent. It took longer to play than it would take to read the book, but that wasn't a consideration. I don't recall anybody asking, 'How many hours of entertainment do you get from this?' It was a wonderful experiment, and I really don't regret doing it. I still like the story."

---

[11] Software Publishers Association.

[12] Frank Catalano was a well-known technology journalist and author of the popular column *Byte Me*.

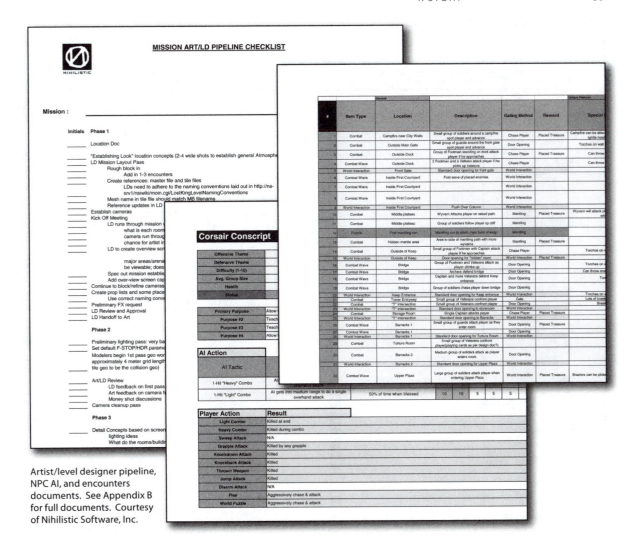

Artist/level designer pipeline, NPC AI, and encounters documents. See Appendix B for full documents. Courtesy of Nihilistic Software, Inc.

Nihilistic

Nihilistic does only T[13] and M[14] rated games. And their games are always story-driven. Rob Huebner explains, "The story drives all the other assets of the game—we have to know where the story is going to go so we know our sets and locations.

---

13 Teen.

14 Mature.

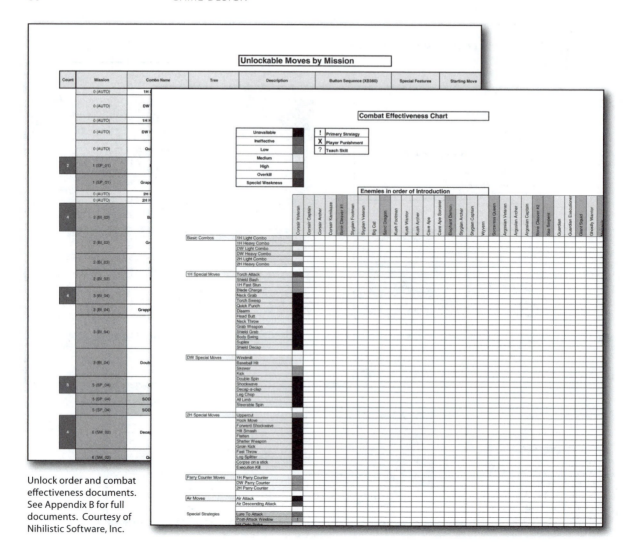

Unlock order and combat effectiveness documents. See Appendix B for full documents. Courtesy of Nihilistic Software, Inc.

"Usually we have the story outline if not the dialog done before we actually sign the contract. We need to know how many missions and how many characters we have in the game, and those metrics are driven largely by the story.

"We don't let the platform affect the story too much. It's more the audience. If we're making a mature-rated game, we assume some sophistication following the concept of the story, so we can make more twists and turns, and more meaningful relationships."

Myst

Mary DeMarle, who works as a narrative designer for Ubisoft, started her career in the games industry as a writer. Her first project was *Myst III: Exile*.

"On *Myst III*, it was interesting—the first *Myst* came out, and then *Riven* came out, and *Riven* closed the storyline. Cyan [Worlds] had written it, and they said they were not going to do another of these. Then we decided to do *Myst III*, and we *had* to do another one, but now we had different parameters. We needed to figure out how to work with the story we had, and we thought about using the sons. But we weren't allowed to use the sons as characters because another company was working on a different game in which they were using the sons.

"So we were looking at, 'What could we do? What could we do?' And I remember coming up with the initial story idea—it was really from looking at the original *Myst* game, and looking at the box cover. And I said how bizarre a world it was that it had such things in it, and how could anybody create such a bizarre world, and who would do that? I thought, 'Well, maybe you would do it if you wanted to teach someone else how to do it.'

"So we came up with teaching; that worked with the gameplay design, and we looked at the story, and we said, 'We can't show the sons, but we can show the effect of what the sons had done, and we can show their storylines through the eyes of a new character.' Then it's a question of what's the game structure that you can do that enables you to do these puzzles, and at the same time what's the story you can put on top of it to give extra depth to it.

"Everybody on the team had played both of the previous games, and Presto preferred the original *Myst*, because *Riven* was a deeper story but it was harder to get unless you could get every single thing in the scene, and that was a problem. If you were not a very visual person, you wouldn't get half the story. But when we started on *Myst IV: Revelation*, everyone said *Riven* was a far better game, so they wanted to have the story drive the worlds.

"When working on *Exile* with Presto [Studios], I felt caught between a rock and a hard place, because I wanted to get more story in it. But because we had such a tight production timeline, the story had to be window dressing, and we did the best we could with that window dressing to make it a great game. But on *Revelation*, the story had to drive everything. And you want to know the story that happens to these people. And you want it to be integrated into the environment and the puzzles themselves. Both of these experiences have really led me into the narrative design position I'm in now.

"As an industry, we haven't really learned the language of story in games yet. In films, they had to devise their own language of editing and close-ups to tell a story. And we as an industry are trying to figure out how story and game work together, and we haven't developed that language yet.

"When I worked as a contractor out-of-house, my frustration had been feeling disconnected with the game-design process. You're told, 'Come up with a story, and we'll figure out how to get it in,' and they'll come back in a few months and they say, 'We had to change it a lot because there was too much,' or it was too big in scope and you weren't involved in that. There is a danger of separating the writer from the process. You can have stories in games, and you can have very good dialog. But without that narrative position, someone who knows the story and the game design, we have to reinvent the story along the way.

"And the story is not just plot, but visuals and game mechanics as well. And if they are all working together, they will enhance the theme of the game."

Splinter Cell 5

DeMarle's role as narrative designer at Ubisoft shows a philosophical shift in the idea of story development in gameplay, especially on a AAA hardcore-gamer title like *Splinter Cell 5*. Story is an integral part of the design process. And she doesn't go anywhere without it.

"What's interesting is that I really was hired by them as a game designer to work with the creative director. He was the same creative director I worked with on *Myst IV*. But really, what's needed in the industry is a position we call a narrative designer, where you're working as the game designer and also bridging the gap between story and game design. What that means is I've come up with the story, and I work closely with all aspects of production to ensure that we're getting the experience that we want across in the game.

"I work with the creative director to plot out what the game experience is going to be, and I work out how to carry out his vision of what experiences and feelings we want the player to have through the game mechanics and make sure the story reflects that. When I define 'story,' I'm talking not just about plot, but what I call the two levels of story in the game. There's the high level, which is the plot, and then there's the low level, which is the player's experience of the game and the story—what he tells his friends of what he did.

"The story needs to be integrated much better in games so that everything is reflecting that experience that's set out from the beginning of what we want for the player. On the project from the beginning, I'm working with the creative director and another game designer, working on the mechanics to get the experience across. And I work on story to get that experience across. And

I work with the level designers and say, 'Here's the story were trying to tell; here's the experience we want the player to have.' Then through the script and events team, we ask, 'What's the best way to convey the story?' I have hired a contract writer who is helping to write it—I'm saying, 'Here's the scene,' and he's giving me input on the story. What I give him is a blueprint of the story and say, 'Here it is,' and then he can go and write it.

Silicon Knights

"If you look at content in entertainment," says Denis Dyack, co-founder of Silicon Knights, "and that's what we are, we're a content-driven industry—if you look at the movie and book industry, they fall into categories of things like horror, science fiction, action. The games industry has been skewed by technology and interactivity, and interactivity really is the new element in the mix.

"We have categories of first-person shooters and role-playing games, and I think the best thing to realize in the industry is that the games that are starting to stand out are the ones that focus on content. We will move away from saying a game is 'first-person shooter' and say, 'This is a military game,' for example, and those other kinds of genres will go away. It will largely be based on content. Content will define the next-generation games.

"The difference between the PS3 and the [Xbox] 360, well, it's very difficult for people to tell the difference. Nintendo right now is saying that hardware doesn't matter. I wouldn't say hardware doesn't matter, but it's becoming less significant, and content is becoming most dominant. To say story doesn't matter, that's old school. When you forget the arts, the science is lost."

What Do *The 7ᵗʰ Guest, Pirates of the Caribbean*, and *Just Cause* Have in Common?

The answer is these games were all written by Matt Costello. As were many others. Costello made game-industry history when he worked with the Trilobyte team writing and designing the first full-motion video CD-ROM game, *The 7ᵗʰ Guest*. And as he puts it, when it hit the market, well, "that changed everything."

"At first when they talked about making a game, computer games were like either Atari cartridges, or Odyssey cartridges, or floppy disks. So they wanted to do a CD-ROM, and they had ambitions to do full-motion video, and Virgin funded them to do that. When they contacted me out of the blue, I didn't know who they were. They were in Jackson, Oregon, and I was in New York.

"I flew out a couple of times, and there were six people, including a secretary and me. It was a very intimate process, very different from what happens now. There were infusions of fresh money that came in from Virgin as time went on. The story was all mine—the way it played out, and the scripting, and they used a lot of puzzles from a book I did called *The Greatest Puzzles of All Time*. They edited my script, gave me feedback, and made changes, and then they made the game. It quickly became apparent to me that they were making history. What they were doing never existed.

"From the moment we started, my primary work was about eight to ten months, from creating the story outline, the synopsis, expanding it, breaking it down, interactively scripting it, revising it off and on. For them, it took years to develop. Virgin gave them the money and didn't want to know about it until it was done.

"I remember going to Chicago CES, and it was like being a rock star because everyone was talking about *The 7th Guest*. No one did full-motion video. In fact, people said it was impossible. Even at CES, people said, 'You're not going to be able to do it; it's not going to happen.' And it did. And that changed everything.

"On *Pirates of the Caribbean*, I did the game design to appear in the summer 2007 game, coming out with the third film. I'm doing two separate scripts—one is current gen and one is next gen. As a true next-gen game; it'll look photorealistic. The mission is pretty big and expansive with a lot of things to do and things to play. There are two full teams working on it, both current gen and next gen, and the producer came to me because I worked with him at Eidos on *Just Cause*, which was a pretty big hit. He brought me in to do story consultant, and eventually he hired me to create the story, the scripts, the dialog—the full monty. The goal was to encompass all three movies and also have its own story—it took a lot of work, two years, and it pretty coherently tells all three movies with its own story and leaves plenty of room for expansion. It has raids, playing cards, duels, and all that fun stuff.

"The *Pirates* characters everyone knows. It has a mythos that has many parts. So you take established stuff and take new stuff and somehow synthesize it so that it's leaner and it will play out in 12 places with new missions. And you have to create a story that won't get in the way. I did a lot of writing back and forth until we all said, 'This is it,' then began breaking it into chunks assigned to different locations.

"We had meetings in England where we talked about the locations—Port Royale, the Flying Dutchman, Hell, using the locations and parsing out the story, then creating cut scenes that need to play out in different locations. And then scripting of the main text before you get to all the incidental stuff, which for the next gen there are tons of things like that to deal with, like, 'Hey you, stop!' 'Stop, don't go there!' 'You there, stop!' 'What are you doing?' And all of the different variations of it. There are 35 ways to say 'hello' and other different things for each character. When it comes to scripting things like this, I do think it's important to have a writer do it—they have a little more power and bite to them.

"Every game project has creative challenges, and from a writer's point of view there are technical challenges, which are, 'How do you do what has to be done here?' and, 'What form is this going to take?' It's not as if you're making a suspense movie and it's like a gazillion other suspense movies. In *Pirates*, the challenge is that it's coming out at the same time as the third film and it needs to encompass the entire mythos of all of the films. But at the time when we started working on it, we only knew the first film. This also gives added value to not just being a rehashing of the film but to make it its own story.

"It's a very creative process. Very challenging. It began with iterations of 'What's the story?' on paper, then back and forth for many months, taking ideas people had and using them or discarding them, and coming up with what seemed to be sound decisions every step of the way. And we had to run everything by the creators of *Pirates of the Caribbean*, the screenwriters. A lot of simplification had to occur. And a lot of clarification. So things are different and yet it still feels the same. The voodoo priestess says, 'Same story, different version.' But we're covered because of the myth and legend, and the facts and truth are forever changing.

"With *Just Cause* the producer saw *Avalanche* from this developer in Sweden that had this amazing technology that lets players go from an airplane to a car to a jet ski to parachuting off a cliff—it was a large environment. And that involved going over and seeing the technology and getting an idea for the kind of story they thought could work. So we did *Just Cause*, a semi-humorous regime change. Doing the cut scenes and dialog was a similar kind of process, as was getting the story hammered out, etc.

"When I started in the industry, game design was my ace in the hole. In my earlier projects, *The 7ᵗʰ Guest*, *The 11ᵗʰ Hour*, *The Cartoon History of the Universe*, *Aladdin*, not only was I doing story and dialog and figuring interactively how it played out, I was also doing game design. But then, as story became more important, even though I could do game design, my value as a writer was much more important. They really needed good writing by someone who could do story and who understood game design. That became my primary role.

"When I did *Just Cause*, that was a case where there was a strong integration of story and missions. A lot of the gameplay, in terms of what you do, was in the design doc I did. The game stuff was there. And they would revise and adjust that.

"I had a meeting recently with a publisher and they were looking for story help for a game, and they had already designed the game. But when you have both from the very beginning, well, that's a good way to go.

"In a project that starts from scratch, which pretty much *Pirates* did and *DOOM 3*[15] did, the initial thing I'll do is a backgrounder on the world—where is this place? where did it come from?—and make it enjoyable. In television terms, it's called a bible, and it covers what's in the world, who the characters are, what the ongoing situations are. If you do that in games, the story for the game and the sequels is inherent in the document, because you see the conflict, and you've built a rich world.

"When they made a film of my book, 110 people were running around, and it's amazing—every single person knows their job and the chain of command and the mission. There should be in every game project a formal title of script editor, to guarantee the uniformity of the script, track the changes in it, do the same thing they do in film. I've never really seen it in the games industry. Usually the producer sort-of does it. But that's absolutely vital.

"In one project I'm aware of, nobody actually knew which was the most current version of script. It was in freefall. Somebody would layer something on, changes would come from the publisher, nobody knew which script was the right script, the producer was running around, and the script editor should be tracking that like a missile."

Quake, DOOM, and id's New Game

Tim Willits, lead designer and co-owner of id Software, explains the story-development process while working through their mega-hit IP franchises *Quake, DOOM,* and the newest title, which we shall refer to simply as the "new game" (working title only).

"For us, because id Software develops original technology at the same time we develop the game, game design is always a challenge because the game has to fit with the technology and the technology has to fit with the game. So as new things are developed and processes start to not work, you need to constantly adjust your game design.

"Game design really comes down to compromises—being practical and realistic about the resources you have and the time you have. Really it comes

---

15 *DOOM 3* is another one of Costello's writing projects.

down to getting it done. I'm one of the practical ones, and game design is working with your team generating ideas together, resolving conflicts, compromises, and working as a team to make it as fun as possible with what you have—that's real game design in my opinion.

"Once we get the direction, we work with a writer, and then we distill that down to rendering and game design and work to create a demo so we can present the game to publishers. Once we create the direction, once we pick the game, like *DOOM* or *Quake*, and the basic story, I'll write it up something like a treatment and will sit down with the lead artist and lead programmer and go over the treatment and discuss ideas and changes, and then we will talk about the team size, and see if this game design will fit with the resources we have.

"If the game is very model-intensive and we don't have a lot of modelers, we either have to hire new modelers or adjust the game. For example, this new game is a lot of driving, and we don't have a driving programmer, so we have to look at that skill set. We see if the game design and resources jibe, and then we make adjustments to the game design. Then, I'll go back to fit it in with the resources. Then we try to work on a rough basic story, maybe only ten pages to distill the information into a story format for the other developers on the team to understand the game we're making.

"Once all the developers understand what's going on, then we start coming up with all the major tasks and systems of the game—AI, physics, rendering, level design. We start separating those up and then we say, 'Okay, we need to write the engine, so we first need to start on the rendering and physics.' So we start creating tasks—a technology task line, concept task line. We expand the story out, put in NPCs,[16] and then we look at individual missions or chapters or episodes—what's the story?

"You always need fun activities in the game, but the fun activities have to jibe with the story. So if you want to have a mission where you ride shotgun and that's fun to do, you need to see how it goes with the story. This industry is famous for doing activities that don't have anything to do with the story, because the missions are fun. So when you come up with a mission that's 'fun' and it doesn't necessarily fit into the story, then you have to make a decision—are you going to keep the mission?

"To expand the story, and match the story with the fun stuff, and making that come together—that's the hard part. We always have these missions that don't work with the story—so do you jury-rig the story or get rid of the fun stuff? In our industry, we tend to jury-rig the story, but that really is a dif-

---

16 Non-player characters.

ficult thing to do. But for the most part, people just don't care that much if it doesn't fit with the story, as long as it's really fun.

"We as game designers stress about the stupidest things. Like in *DOOM 3*, the character was really cool looking, he had a great looking head, but when we added a helmet you couldn't see his expressions. So we said, 'Let's not add a helmet,' but then we were on Mars and you have to have a helmet in that atmosphere—so we really stressed over this. We went back and forth and back and forth. 'Do we *have* to have a helmet?' It was keeping some of us up at night. So finally we said 'no,' and what we came up with is we just ran outside and you could pick up these air canisters and get your oxygen from them. And we as designers were all worried about this. But the players don't care as long as it is fun.

"Let's talk about which order I make games, because that's important. A game has a beginning, a middle, and an end. Lots of people make their game in that order, but I don't actually like to work like that. I do the middle first, then the beginning, then the end. Because the best stuff you make is not going to come out at the beginning of the process, it's going to be in the end. When the player first starts playing your game, you want to put your best foot forward, so you make the beginning later in the game design process. Then, in the end, you're probably going to run out of time anyway, and the reality is that most people don't finish games. Some of the greatest games have crappy endings. Like *Half-Life 2*, *Quake 1*, they're great games, but their endings are crappy. But it doesn't matter. Like in most RPGs[17], at the end you kill the dude and you go back and the king says, 'Hurrah,' and who cares? But that's okay. Nobody cares that it doesn't have a great end. But it has to have a great beginning to hook the player."

Story Exercise

Start with your premise from your brainstorming sessions from Chapter 3.

Your brainstorming sessions should have provided you with some good parameters for a game. By now you should have an idea of what the genre is, what kind of characters are in the game, the lead characters, where the game/story takes place, the era, etc.

1. Write a one-sentence logline that defines the essence of your story. Use television and movie loglines for guidance.

---

[17] Role-playing games.

2. Define the who, what, when, where, why, and how of your story in succinct bullet points.

3. Expand these elements into a short document, no more than two pages, of what the story is all about. This is a brief story treatment.

Check your story.

- Make sure that the action that moves the story forward is based on cause and effect.
- If you can't fit this onto two pages, you're going into too much detail. This usually is a sign of getting hung up on the set-up, on a character, or on a particular scene.
- Make sure that your story has a short set-up, a meaty middle, and a nice short wrap-up.

Put your story away for at least three days. Come back to it with some distance and look at those checkpoints again. See how it works, and rewrite it to make it more clear, interesting, compelling, and fun, keeping it at two pages.

When you're satisfied with it, you'll be ready to expand it, but first, you need to do some character work, which happens in Chapter 5.

Story Checklist

❑ Story fundamentals include who, what, when, where, why, and how.

❑ In game design, this includes the characters and the player's interaction with them, the environment, levels, and puzzles, the mechanics, and the player's experience of gameplay.

❑ Story is defined around conflict and usually includes a protagonist and an antagonist.

❑ Story structure should be considered in three acts, with a beginning, middle, and end:
  - Act 1 is a short set-up for establishing the story.
  - Act 2 is the bulk of the character's journey.
  - Act 3 is the wrap-up of the adventure.

❑ Good storytelling is organic.

❑ Stories are generally a series of related events—*and because* instead of *and then*.

❑ Someone on your team should be responsible for all aspects of the story and keeping any story docs up-to-date as a script editor, writer, producer, or narrative designer.

Chapter 5
Characters Rule

"It all started with Lara—who she is and what we wanted to let people in on."

—Riley Cooper, Lead Designer, *Lara Croft Tomb Raider: Legend*

Whether you're doing a game that is rich in story, rich in mechanics, rich in graphics, or any combination of the three, one thing that is consistently becoming more and more important is how the player relates to the characters. Game developers are, across the board, spending a significant amount of time addressing the makeup of their characters' personalities as they relate to the story and the experience of gameplay.

Even companies that produce games that have traditionally had minimal story want their characters to look really cool and be fun to play. But there's more to making a great character than just telling the artist to whip something up. It all starts with something more. It starts with creating some personality.

Lara Croft in scene from *Lara Croft Tomb Raider: Legend*. Image © 2006 Eidos Interactive Ltd. *Lara Croft Tomb Raider: Legend,* Lara Croft, *Tomb Raider,* and the Tomb Raider logo are all trademarks of Eidos Interactive Ltd.

Concept art group shot of characters from *Death Jr. II*. Image © 2006 Backbone Entertainment. Death Jr., the Death Jr. characters and logo are trademarks of Backbone Entertainment. (See color plates.)

"There are a handful of different elements we start with, but you have to figure out your characters before you can focus on the game."

—Joe Morrissey, Lead Designer, *Death Jr. II: Root of Evil*

AUDIO/VISUAL PROCESSING
- There are a few voice mails:
  - Angry voice mail from Contractor.
  - Voice mail from stripper thanking him for gift.
  - Angry voice mail from mother about promised campaign contribution that never materialized.

BRASS 12.75
We'll need to strengthen this Search Warrant.
REQUIRES: Mom Denies an argument about money took place between her and the Vicitm.
REQUIRES: Angry voice mail from mother about promised campaign contribution that never materialized.
- Warrant for Search (HOUSE)

INTERROGATION ROOM13 (Suspect: Contactor)
- I didn't kill him!
- Okay, okay, I wrote the note. He owed me money, but it was no big deal, just a friendly game of poker and he wouldn't pay up. I wrote it in a moment of anger because he was dodging my calls. I left it for him in his mother's garage; she told me he was going to pick up some camping gear there and I knew he'd see it.
- I lied when you asked me about the sodium monofluoroacetate pesticide because I'm not licensed to carry it. A "friend" got me a large quantity at a discount rate.
  - Of course I read up on the stuff, it's dangerous, I gotta make sure no one gets hurt!
- Poisoned! Hey man I've very careful with this stuff. I wear gloves when I handle it and I always let people know what it is I'm spreading around.
- The jar that belongs to the lid? I'm not sure, really. I use the stuff on a lot of jobs. Works real good killing pests you find in homes when you're remodeling. I know I had some at the Victim's home. The Wife asked me all kinds of questions about it, told me she was worried their cat might get sick. Funny, don't remember seeing any cat around.
- Bootprint (GIFT from Contractor) ➔ Contractor's bootprint INTR13
- Alright, alright! Yes, we got into it before he went camping. He saw my note and drove to my shop in a rage. He went after me and I popped him in the head with the rake handle to protect myself. He stormed out,

CSI3_Case4_Treatment tv.doc   Page 18 of 24   1/10/2007

CSI case treatment. See Appendix A for full document. Courtesy of Ubisoft.

What's My Motivation?

The well-known cry of the method actor, *"What's my motivation?"* is really right on the mark when it comes to thinking about character development. What *is* this character's motivation? Why does he do what he does? Why does she think the way she thinks? Why would she respond one way versus another? Why does he feel the way he feels?

In Chapter 1, Noah Falstein mentioned that game designers are great for being curious about what makes people tick. Character development really starts with that concept. What makes this character tick? Because actually, when you come right down to it, what you're really doing is creating a person's psychology. The way to do that is to develop their backstory and document it in the character or story bible.

Anatomy of a Backstory

The typical character bible consists of some pretty extensive background on each of the main characters, about two to five pages each, not counting artwork, plus some broad strokes on the secondary characters, which usually translates to a couple of paragraphs more or less. This document is used in the game-design process by everyone on the team—artists to help create the look and animations of the characters, level designers to put them into play in appropriate ways, audio for casting talent, and the talent to understand who they're portraying and what they need to convey in their delivery. The character bible is *the* document that ensures everyone is on the same page when it comes to dealing with these characters. Its name, the "bible," gives you a clue about how important this document really is.

Using brainstorming techniques discussed earlier, you start by creating the broad strokes of the character's makeup and get a clear vision of some of the big picture issues. What do they look like? What role do they play? Obviously, you're going to have different dynamics if the player is meant to be sympathetic versus scary. This initial work pretty quickly leads to details popping into your brain as you start to think of cool things the character can do. So once you have their general physical appearance and temperament, soon you're into creating their psychology. This can be complex, but it doesn't have to be hard. Just remember: stay away from stereotypes.

Let's take a look at a couple of characters in *DOOM 3*, for example. The Lost Soul is one of my favorites. For starters, there's the name. It elicits an emotional response that touches a core theme in the human condition. Graphically, its underlying doll-like face is in stark contrast to the horrific overall appearance. There's no doubt that this character gives you the creeps. But there's something more to her than meets the eye at first glance. She is crying.

Lost Soul character from *DOOM 3*. Images courtesy of id Software, Inc. (See color plates.)

"The Lost Soul never became a 'full' demon in the *DOOM* universe—instead, only the head and partial soul survived. The Lost Soul is trapped between the world of the living demons and that of the spirit world of Hell. The Lost Soul is always seeking death to help it on its final journey even though that journey is a sentence of eternal damnation." —**Tim Willits**

Marine character from *DOOM 3*. Image courtesy of id Software, Inc.

"The *DOOM* Marine is no one in particular but rather everyone who plays the game. We wanted to create an average male image in the character. He has a unique look but doesn't have any unique features, which helps him look tough but also average, helping the player identify with him but also want to be him. We wanted him to be the Marlboro Man of demon fighting." —**Tim Willits**

> *"It's like a puzzle—if things work out well, you end up with four or five key characters whose backstories make something that can't be pulled apart."*
>
> —**Rob Huebner, Nihilistic**

This character has emotional depth written all over it. It's creepy, it's sweet, it's sad, it's haunting, it's horrifying, all at once. And it does a great job at getting the desired emotional response.

In contrast is the player character, Marine. In the book *The Making of DOOM 3*, Kenneth Scott explains that this player character had to be both strong and vulnerable. "With the kind of experience we wanted to impart, our boy couldn't look so heroic and powerful as to be beyond worry. He's fit, but not a weightlifter. He's plausibly good looking, not 'comic book' severe. Boy Scout; not badass. I wanted someone softer, more friendly and likeable versus the over-angular, steroidal, mean-looking antihero that's archetypical of most fps.[1] It's really dependent on how empowered you want the player to feel, and I think it's more interesting to make the player feel inadequate to the challenges ahead."

The requirements of each project you work on will be different, but the more thorough you can be in giving some depth to your characters, the easier you will make life for everyone on your team. And the more connection you can create with the characters, the more you can grab and keep the interest of your audience. Clearly, both of these are very important goals.

Obviously, not all games are after the same kind of response from the player. Although what they

---

[1] First-person shooters.

do have in common is their need to connect with the player on some level so they'll want to spend their free time playing with them. They have to be engaging.

One project that I worked on required the development of five original lead characters who would interact with the player extensively throughout the game, but the player would never actually see the characters. They would only hear the characters. Although they could, as play progressed, go to a simulated website located inside the game to see pictures and bios on them. This meant that we had to write backstory for our use in story development,

Concept art of Pandora character from *Death Jr. II.* Image © 2006 Backbone Entertainment. Death Jr., the Death Jr. characters and logo are trademarks of Backbone Entertainment.

audio, photo shoots, etc., and then also draw from that backstory for the public-facing character bios that were in the game's simulated website.

The story for this project was huge—it originally had 80 plot points in the game, which were revealed to the player as they progressed in their gameplay. The challenges were to motivate the players to actually want to play the game in the first place, to make and keep the game compelling, to make sure the characters seemed absolutely real, and to move the story forward through the player and character interactions. Oh, and it was an *algebra* game.[2] And as if that weren't enough, the target audience was 12- to 15-year-olds, sweet spot of 13–14.

The good news is that this game did everything we had hoped it would do, and more. And it was IMHO[3] in big part because of the characters and fun gameplay they provided. The biggest rewards of all came from the kids who emailed the company. Many requested the email addresses of the characters in the game. Thanks to the simulated website, they thought the characters we made up were real people. And many kids sent us email telling us how much they loved the game and couldn't wait to come home from school every day and *play algebra*. The game was named one of the *U.S. News and World Report's* "Top 12 Titles of the Year" and was cited for great, real characters who never talked down to this very difficult market of young teens.

Here's how we did it:

---

2 *Grade Builder: Algebra 1.*

3 In my humble opinion.

We needed five main characters in the story who would be tutors, mentors, and friends to the player. So the first thing we did was develop 20. In big
broad strokes. We knew the target age of our audience, so we used Hollywood
parameters when deciding the age of our characters. Hollywood, in its nearly
100 years of existence, has found that kids look up to other kids who are two
to three years older. If they're much older than that, they are seen as authority
figures and might as well be portrayed as adults. We wanted only one authority figure in our game, and only somewhat of an authority at that, so we made
him in his early 20s and gave him a great rock-band bio so the players would
have a fun, cool, and hip guy to relate to. But the rest of our characters had to
fall within our main target audience's age parameters.

First, we developed a pool of characters, identifying age, gender, and a
few key characteristics, about a paragraph on each character. Then we went
into focus testing. As is typical, in my experience, we didn't have a lot of surprises.[4] For example, one character was a 15-year-old girl who was somewhat
klutzy, and she was a big hit with the boys in our target market. Why? Well,
in real life, 13- and 14-year-old boys are somewhat klutzy, and so they felt
that they could really relate to her. "She seems nice," and "kind of cool," and
"funny," and "someone I would like to know." She was a keeper.

We validated on some characteristics we felt this market would relate to:
smart, but not acting better than others; into music; into cars; into sports
but not jocks; and so on. We had these characteristics spread across the 20
characters to start with, so it was easy to go to the next step, which was to
consolidate down to five key characters and add depth.

This was the start of our backstory development. Next, we went into
greater detail about their background. This involved finding out (making up)
a lot of specifics, things like their family life, their school life, their relationships with friends and the other characters in the game. Specifically, here are
some of the elements we developed for each character:

- Full name, and any significance to their name (for example, if they were
  named after a relative, family friend, celebrity, etc.)
- Age
- Birth date

---

4 Focus testing is a valuable tool to use in game design. My experience has been that any game
designer with any amount of experience has a pretty good intuitive sense of what their audience will
relate to, and in this case focus testing is very useful for validating what you already know. In addition, however, you always learn something new when you present to your target audience, so even if
you get main ideas validated (you're on the right track), you'll also end up with some interesting and
fresh ideas to potentially weave into what you already have.

- Place of birth
- Where they grew up (if multiple locations, explain)
- Physical attributes (eyes, hair, body type, ethnicity, etc.)
- Health issues, if any
- Childhood traumas, if any, from their POV[5]
- Religious beliefs
- Standing in the family (first born, middle child, etc.)
- Siblings' names and ages and brief characteristics
- Relationship with each of their siblings (both from the point of view of the character and from their sibling's perspective)
- Parents' marital status
- Parents' relationship with each other
- Parents' relationships with and feelings/attitudes about each child in the family
- Relationship of the main character with their parents—this is different from the relationship of the parent with the character because it's from the character's POV
- Relationship with extended family (for example, are their grandparents alive, do they live nearby or far away, do they see them frequently or never, is there a close bond, do they have older siblings out of the house with whom they do or do not have a relationship, etc.)
- Family pets—what kind, how many, the name(s), how did they acquire the pet, whose pet is it really, how do they feel about the pet; if they don't have a pet do they want one, if so why don't they have one and how do they feel about that
- Who their favorite person is (relative or friend or pet) and why
- What their home is like, both in terms of physical environment (decorator design, garage-sale design, etc.) and atmosphere (calm, quite, chaotic, hectic, etc.)
- What kind of neighborhood they live in
- Family's financial situation and what effect this has on family dynamics
- Their relationship with school, the teachers, and other kids, including grades and who they feel they really are in regards to school that can't be measured academically
- Extracurricular activities at school, for example, clubs, sports, etc.
- Activities outside of school

---

5 Point of view.

- Community involvement/volunteer work
- Hobbies
- Their relationship with the opposite sex
- Their opinions and feelings and hopes and fears about going to college
- Their hopes, dreams, and aspirations
- Their general life fears and phobias
- What makes them happiest
- How they feel about material things, and what their favorite material possession is (for example, are they into their car, clothes, musical instruments, shopping, not shopping, etc.)
- The circumstances that led to them being here (where they are in the game), and how they feel about being here
- How they feel about each of the other characters, and who their least and most favorite of the others are
- Favorite foods
- Pet peeves
- Quirks and habits
- Key personality traits
- And more

You can imagine how knowing this much about each character in the game made it easier for everyone to work with them. These characters became living, real people. This is why the kids who played the game wanted to communicate with them in real life. And it's why the game was cited for its portrayal of characters who knew how to talk to this very specific and hard-to-reach target audience.

When it came to our next task of writing the storyline, the plot points, the script, and the dialog, having this kind of detail made it apparent which of the characters would do certain things. Character choices to handle specific activities became obvious. While it took some real effort and time to create all of this backstory, overall it exponentially saved us time.

Another huge advantage was that it made the entire audio process a dream to manage. In this case, the audio lead read the bios and had a very good idea of what he was looking for in casting. Everyone on the production team also read the bios, so when we got down to the top candidates for each voice-over recording (the casting decision was a team decision), we all knew what we were expecting to hear. We were surprisingly in agreement on which talent to cast for each character.

The talent loved the bios, because they felt they really knew the characters they were playing. The director knew how to pull what he wanted from the talent because he was so familiar with who the characters were. And when we ran into a few stumbling blocks during recording, like fumbling over lines, we could easily rewrite the dialog on the fly and keep the cast completely in character.

There was real connection on this project, and while it was a lot of work over 18 months, it was fun. There is no greater pleasure on a project than when everyone is happy with their work.

Key Personality Traits—Tips and Tricks

Really, when you think about it, coming up with key personality traits for someone can sound a little daunting. It's like you're actually creating an entire person, which is a little bit of an odd thing to do. And it's not like you're creating a "perfect" person, which on the whole sounds a lot easier—someone who's always agreeable, does and says everything you want, looks beautiful and flawless, and never makes life difficult. We all might have fantasies about having a person like that in our lives, but that kind of character would be (a) non-believable and (b) really boring.

What you really need to do is create a character with flaws, foibles, and fears, hopes, dreams, and desires, sprinkled generously with quirky traits and maybe some annoyances. The good news is we all know annoying and quirky people, so we can use them as material.

But think about your character. Are they socially inept? Are they laid back and don't say much, but when they do it's a major cut? Are they completely irresponsible? Are they hard-core serious? Are they afraid of heights, or the dark, or nails on a chalkboard? You can have a major badass who is afraid of heights. You can have an arrogant jackass who, when things get tough, will be there for you. Be specific.

For years, I have kept a quote at hand by John Vorhaus, a seasoned comedy writer, that reminds, "You have the right and obligation to tell people what to do. That's what a writer does." It is your obligation to define your characters so you can confidently tell them what to do when situations arise that need their action. There's really no room for ambiguity in character design.

Brass character screenshots from *CSI: Hard Evidence.* Images courtesy of Ubisoft

Looking at this kind of detail is like taking the elements in your life that make you you, and defining those same kinds of elements in someone else's life that makes them them.

How do you do that?

Well, the best way I have found is to go directly to the experts.

The good news is that there are a gazillion books on the market that help real people, like you and me, be better individuals. These how-to books are filled with great insights on self-improvement, and that means they're loaded with things that explain how people tick. I use these as tools for character development. And I go straight to a few well-known experts for ideas:

- Deepak Chopra for some spiritual and karmic insight
- Anthony Robbins for modality work,[6] self-esteem traits, hopes, and dreams
- Stephen Covey for guiding principles

I like using all of these as resources, and it's hard to pick a "favorite," but I'd have to say the one I often springboard with is Covey. When you ask yourself "What drives this person?" the choices you make for that answer create some great starting points. What's the most important thing to them?

The Marine character in *DOOM 3*. Image courtesy of id Software, Inc. (See color plates.)

Freedom? Career? Family? Money? Religion? You get a fundamentally very different character based on the answer to this question.

There are two more resources that I use in character development that are extremely helpful. One is that I sometimes start a character by basing them on a real person, often someone I know. It doesn't have to be the whole person. It can just be a trait or a feature they have that you use as a launching point.

Kenneth Scott of id used Kevin Cloud's "monkey hairy arms" as a character feature in both *DOOM* and *DOOM 3*. That's not psychology, but it's fun, and there's nothing to say that you can't do the same.

One of the characters I developed in the aforementioned math game was inspired initially by one of the guys on our team. I knew nothing about this person's background, but I thought he had some really nice traits that would appeal to our audience. So I started with those and spent some time

---

[6] In this case, meaning are they visual, auditory, or kinesthetic—and understanding what that means in how they behave and relate to others.

thinking about how he might have come to be the way he is. I worked up an extensive backstory, that I utterly made up, using the guidance of the self-help gurus above. And *then*... I tweaked it with the *other* resource I use in backstory development that is really off the wall and fun to use.

It is... well, first let me tell you why I use it.

I have found this resource to be invaluable in developing both big personality traits that are core to everybody, and those finer details like shyness, moodiness, loyalty, flakiness, that sort of thing. You can pick this resource up at any bookstore for about $5 in paperback, and it is full of *really* great material.

It's an astrology guide. Yep, the "what's your sign" kind of astrology guide. This is not about believing in astrology. This is about using a resource that is full of human features that are already spelled out for you. And here's a cool bonus: if you know when your character was born, you can go straight to the section and get great specific information about their personality. Let me explain how that works.

In the above example of our team member on whom I based a character, I looked up the birth date in the astrology guide, found a few traits that didn't quite ring true, made a few minor adjustments, and discovered that the rest of them were luckily right on. When he read the bio, he was stunned. He said it was as if I had followed him around from birth to age 16 and knew everything about him. It was kind of spooky. And very cool.

For another one of the characters, the astrology guide didn't really match up at all with the personality traits I had given her. So I looked for a sign that more closely reflected what I wanted. Fortunately, I didn't have to look far. I moved her birth date to a few weeks later, which put her under a different sign, and those traits were almost an exact match to the kind of person I needed. And it gave me some things I hadn't thought of to work into her profile.

The whole point here is that you can use the resources that already exist to help you round out your characters and make them interesting, flawed, and completely believable.

Character Arc

And now, a note about character arc. This might be *really* going out on a limb given the opinionated diatribes in our community on character development. As Mary DeMarle of Ubisoft puts it, with a laugh, "Character development, well, that's another interesting debate going on in the game industry right now, and I'm not prepared to step into the middle of it." She's got a point.

But, in an effort to continue the growth of the art and craft of game design, I feel that I should speak up. So here goes.

Character arc is a key component of most character work in other entertainment media. So here's my suggestion: maybe it would be cool to learn about character arc and fold it into the game designer's psyche. Because if you don't, you will ultimately end up with the same characters being used over and over again, and that presents a high risk of losing the audience's interest. This was, in fact, a big problem that Crystal Dynamics faced when they undertook revitalizing *Tomb Raider*. Lara Croft had grown stale.

Lead characters in books and movies step into that first scene with baggage in tow. As the story unfolds, they're faced with new challenges, are urged to rise to the occasion usually through angst and upheaval that takes them well outside of their comfort zone, and by the end of the experience they're in a very different place emotionally and psychically than when they started.

Pushing a person to perform outside of their comfort zone, in life and books and movies, causes a change in the person that cannot be undone. And that is personal growth. The character expands, usually in a profound way, and in the end is more dynamic, bigger in spirit, and better for having had the experience.

This change in character that takes place from the beginning of their adventure to the end of the story is called the *character arc*.

Typically in game design, once the characters are developed, they show up the same way in the franchise, game after game. But as game companies are starting to see, this is tantamount to character suicide.

My challenge to you is to go beyond the parameters of the current norm in our industry and innovate characters who are deep with backstory *and who grow through having gone through their adventure in the game*. So that when you do your next title in their franchise, your players have something "more" to look forward to. Make it serial. Otherwise, like the old television show, it's just Batman fighting the Riddler this week and the Joker the next. How much more interesting Batman became when we started learning things about him and seeing things from the past show up in new adventures.

Character Lite

Character art of Tetsuo in *Antigrav*. Image provided by Harmonix Music Systems, Inc.

The *Character Lite* version of character development is used for lead characters when you need more depth than secondary characters and NPCs, without getting as robust as the main characters described earlier. You might use

Character Lite because of the type of game you're doing, the amount of time in the schedule, mandates from above to come up with something short and sweet but compelling, or any other factors of reality.

In Character Lite development, you just need to create an interesting enough backstory to have your characters show up as somewhat unique and appealing to your audience. Start with the clichés, remove some of the stereotypes and replace with some twists on the theme, and be sure there's originality.

The character bios on *Guitar Hero II* read like a logline to a story, which in essence they are—the backstory. Judy Nails is "A fan of distorted feedback and roller derby. Judy Nails has been a pioneer of alternative rock since her first tour at age 17. Known for her diverse collection of vinyl, Nails always brings a smile, and a lot of pedals." She's not psychologically deep, but she is interesting and fun.

Greg LoPiccolo, VP of Product Development for Harmonix, says "The characters in *Guitar Hero* were all archetypes of rock players. Half the people in the company are in bands or have been in bands, so when it came to character development we did rock-and-roll archetypes—the blue-collar metal head, the punk girl. It was all about making it hard core rock and roll, and at every step in the game design we asked, 'Is this rock and roll?'"

At Backbone Entertainment, the challenge for *Death Jr. II: Root of Evil* was to come up with an interesting and unpredictable villain to duke it out with their hero, Death. "We asked ourselves, 'What would be Death's ulti-mate villain?' says Joe Morrissey, lead designer. "And the answer we came up with was Life, because it's the opposite. But then Life is supposed to be this good thing, right? So how do you make Life the evil thing? How do you spin that? The answer was that she wants to be evil because all of her life everything has gone good for her—she's an angry teenage girl rebelling against her mom.[7]

Backbone's approach, like Harmonix's, was to create interesting charac-ters that had enough backstory to make them understandable, yet were also organic to the game. They fit in well with the requirements of the gameplay, are interesting for the players, and have some twists that make them fun. Even for the villain.

And speaking of villains…

Character art of Napalm in *Guitar Hero II*. Image provided by Harmonix Music Systems, Inc. (See color plates.)

---

7 Life's mom is, of course, Mother Nature.

The Lessons of Hannibal Lecter

In June of 2003, the American Film Institute announced its choice of the greatest villain in film history. It should come as no surprise to anyone that it was Sir Anthony Hopkins' portrayal of "the brilliant, cunning, and psychotic" Dr. Hannibal Lecter. If you want a good villain, there is no better role model around. And it's not his dietary preferences that make him so good at being so bad; it's his humanness—those very real and believable personality traits that allow us to relate to him as a human being even though he is one of the most heinous characters imaginable.

The biggest mistake usually made in the villain-creation process is making the character evil just for the sake of being evil. The real question is *why* he is bad. Some would answer "He's bad because he's the bad guy." Wrong answer. All that supplies you with in the end is a very flat and uninteresting character.

"We use Hannibal Lecter as a massive reference. For any character that you paint evil as simply a black character, it's so predictable, so boring. So how about creating an evil character everyone can relate to? That's Hannibal Lecter. A character who truly frightens people because he is so evil and yet so human."

—Denis Dyack, Silicon Knights

This is what makes Lecter such a great model. He is, in fact, a walking contradiction of bad and good qualities. Lecter is intelligent, engaging, present, cunning and well read. He has the ability to pull you into conversation and then say something with complete deference that scares the hell out of you. His personality was defined by some very horrible yet very human events that would probably turn anybody into a psychopath. So we have sympathy.

"Hannibal Lecter was born in Lithuania in 1938 to a wealthy aristocratic family. His father was a count and his mother a descendant of the famous Visconti family of Milan…he is said to be a cousin of the artist Balthus. He had a younger sister named Mischa. In 1944, when Lecter was six, a group of German deserters retreating from Russia shelled his family's estate, killing his parents and most of the servants. Lecter, his sister, and other local children were rounded up by the deserters to be killed and used as food during the cold Baltic winter. Mischa was killed and eaten, but young Lecter managed to escape."[8] The beginnings of the life of a really great villain.

In villain creation, it is of the utmost importance to always keep in mind that this character is a person, who is the way he is because of what has hap-

---

[8] Nice simple write up, quoted from Wikipedia (http://en.wikipedia.org/wiki/Hannibal_Lecter).

pened to him.[9] Maybe he's sorry or remorseful after his villainous deeds, maybe before them, or maybe not at all. Maybe he got slow-boiled into the role he's in.[10]

It's up to you to determine what kind of life the character had and why. Look at Lecter's background. Use other fictional characters for inspiration. Use people from real life. Use the techniques mentioned earlier. Take those twisted ideas from your imagination and combine them all to come up with really good villains. Your players will love you for it.

Secondary Characters and NPCs

When developing secondary and non-player characters, the backstory process doesn't need to be nearly as thorough as it does with lead characters. Secondary characters are meant to be supporting cast to the leads. This can be anywhere from "best supporting actor" caliber to someone resembling more of an "extra" who populates the scene but doesn't need to be heard from.

That doesn't mean, however, that you can't make your supporting characters or NPCs interesting. As mentioned in Chapter 3, you can take a seemingly nondescript character and give them just a little more attention to provide some oomph to their existence. Again, it's all about avoiding stereotypes and clichés. But don't spend more time on them than you really need. Like

Smith and Weston character from *Death Jr. II*. Top image: sketches. Middle left image: sketches tweak. Middle right image: additional sketches. Bottom image: renders. Images © 2006 Backbone Entertainment. Death Jr., the Death Jr. characters and logo are trademarks of Backbone Entertainment.

---

9 It doesn't matter whether the "person" is a human, by the way. We're talking about personality and characteristics, and we can use them across species.

10 I use the term slow-boiled frequently to explain how situations come about without being stopped. It relates to the lore that if you put a frog into a pot of boiling water it will jump right out, but if you put a frog into a pot of cold water and turn on the heat, you will slow-boil the frog to death. This is what happens to people a lot in their lives—in relationships, in jobs, even in political situations, and this concept is very useful for explaining why a character is the way he is. He was slow-boiled and never realized that there would be a resultant change in his life.

everything else in game design, it's a balancing act. That said, don't sell your secondary characters short. Give them *something* interesting that makes them unique.

Include your secondary character descriptions in the character bible, but keep these bios short. Typically, they should be a couple of paragraphs long and be just the essence of who they are. The granny described in Chapter 3 is a relatively good example of a secondary character or NPC.

Backstory is Not Front Story

One thing to keep in mind during all of this character development is that backstory is not meant to be front story—it's background information *only*. It should not directly come up in the story or script in any expository way. It should only *inform* the choices you make in narrative, dialog, and game design going forward.

Backstory will help you create situations in the plot in a very natural and organic way. Backstory will help you write the character dialog. It will help the artists give their personal touch to the characters. It will help the talent and directors. Again, it will not show up in the game as written in the bible. If it does, you're just being lazy.

Create your backstory. Love your backstory. And use it for what it is intended—background information.

Backstory and Marquee Characters

So far, we've been dealing pretty much with backstory design on original characters. Sort of the 'what do you do when you need to make up somebody from scratch' approach.

But what do you do when somebody hands you a character who's already established and you have to "enhance" them? The key rule here is *make it organic*.

Organic.

Organic.

Organic.

I can't stress enough the importance of this concept. Organic means that it has to be natural to the character, the environment they're in, the story you're trying to tell, the experience you want the audience to have. Make it real. If it is *not* organic, I guarantee that you will take the player out of the experience. You want to avoid that.

Crybaby Doll and Bitter Bear concept art from *Death Jr. II*. Images © 2006 Backbone Entertainment. Death Jr., the Death Jr. characters and logo are trademarks of Backbone Entertainment. (See color plates.)

Characters need to be revisited when they cross over from one medium to another, when they are placed into a new context and it has an effect on the story, and when their franchise is being revived.

Case in point: *101 Dalmatians* the adventure game came out of the book *The Hundred and One Dalmatians*, the animated movie *One Hundred and One Dalmatians*, and the live-action movie with Glenn Close. It had gameplay that took place in the DeVil mansion, and while this is conceptually a well-known location, all we knew of it physically were the few rooms they built on the set. Well, a few rooms does not an entire house make, so it was our task to build out the house to allow for lots of gameplay. What does this have to do with character backstory? Plenty. This was Cruella DeVil's childhood home. What do you know about Cruella DeVil as a little kid? Exactly. Nothing. So, as the game designer, you have to enhance her character and make up an organic backstory to support the gameplay you want in the house.

Organically: If she grew up here, her childhood bedroom would be upstairs. If she grew up in a mansion, she must have had a nanny. Suddenly, you're beginning to see some questions that need to be answered. Like, what did Cruella look like as a little girl? What was her relationship with the nanny? She's a twisted adult; was she a twisted kid?

There are some major responsibilities that come with working on an iconic character. You can't do anything that will take the audience aback. So how do you portray a little girl and make her Cruella DeVil? Was she a blond? A brunette? Long hair? Short hair? Princess? Tomboy? You can see the difficulties already. But not if you go organic. Cruella as an adult has the signature half-black half-white hair. The picture in the house of Cruella as a little girl shows her wearing ponytails on the sides of her head—one black, the other white.

Cruella as an adult is into skinning helpless little puppies. How did she get this way? The answer lies in the large, menacing taxidermy bear in the downstairs foyer, and upstairs in her childhood bedroom where you'll find, in the same pose, a taxidermied hamster.

Based on other backstory decisions, we were able to make several playable elements in the game. The dumbwaiter was added to the game, which would have been used when Cruella was a child to bring food up from the kitchen on the first floor. We used this device as a major feature for some of the puzzles we built into the game.

The thing to keep in mind with pre-existing characters is that they already have an audience, and they have expectations, and you can't stomp all over them. Stay true to the spirit of the character, be organic, have some fun with it, and your character enhancement will be fine.

Scene from *Lara Croft Tomb Raider: Legend*. Image © 2006 Eidos Interactive Ltd. *Lara Croft Tomb Raider: Legend,* Lara Croft, *Tomb Raider,* and the Tomb Raider logo are all trademarks of Eidos Interactive Ltd. (See color plates.)

Lara Croft and *Tomb Raider: Legend*

One of the most visible pre-existing characters to come through a successful character expansion is Lara Croft. In this case, the *Tomb Raider* franchise was one that had gone from the pinnacle of success to the verge of going down the tubes if something different wasn't done. Staleness can happen to even one of the most recognized characters in gaming history.

"We went through like two phases when we got this franchise," says Riley Cooper, lead designer on *Lara Croft Tomb Raider: Legend.* "One was excitement because it's such a well-known license and there's this great opportunity. Then a pressure set in because you've got to live up to *Tomb Raider.* We had a little skepticism and fear, too, because we were thinking, 'Is this license still interesting to people?' We found out the answer was "yes," but before you get there, you just don't know.

"We didn't want to alienate anyone who had gotten to know Lara in the previous six games. We didn't want to trample anything, so we had to familiarize ourselves with her and the other games. After that, there was plenty of room to expand the character. She was always a little aloof, so we tried to give it a little more of a personal angle with the storyline, a little more of why she goes after things, without removing any of the mystique.

"We wrote truckloads of things for this game before we did anything. We rebuilt large aspects of our system to develop things we hadn't done before.

Lara Croft in action in scene from *Lara Croft Tomb Raider: Legend.* Image © 2006 Eidos Interactive Ltd. *Lara Croft Tomb Raider: Legend,* Lara Croft, *Tomb Raider,* and the Tomb Raider logo are all trademarks of Eidos Interactive Ltd.

We had to speculate quite a bit. It's pretty unanimous in the industry that the ideal way to build a game is to just get something on the screen and see what's there. But we used reams of paper first. Many a tree sacrificed itself for us. We did bios on all of the characters in the game, and story treatments at a very high level, a few iterations of those, some script samples, all the way down to writing the exact script.

"There's a lot of discussion at first between people on your team who are officially responsible for creating the story or overseeing development of the story, and team members who are particularly passionate and have something to offer. It's almost like a writer's group—you get those people together and really start throwing darts at the board until you see something that's exciting to people.

"Step one was looking at her history. Given this, what's the biggest missing thing we can start to fill in? In the case of *Tomb Raider*, we can actually start to say more about Lara herself. From there we say who Lara is, what do we want people to know about her that we haven't said before. Then what sort of uber-situations can we use to bring that out. It all started with Lara—who she is and what we wanted to let people in on.

"Then you work with almost every aspect at once; that includes story development, art development, code development. You do the quickest, fastest thing that tells you what you're trying to accomplish, and you repeat that until you get it done.

Lara Croft in *Lara Croft Tomb Raider: Legend.* Image © 2006 Eidos Interactive Ltd. *Lara Croft Tomb Raider: Legend,* Lara Croft, *Tomb Raider,* and the Tomb Raider logo are all trademarks of Eidos Interactive Ltd.

"In art, the first thing you do is get a concept artist to give you a concept sketch, and all of a sudden you have a picture. Before that there are lots of conversations and some writing, then you go to model sheets, more detailed and specific design on how the character looks, then modeling and texturing. Then once you have the model everyone sits around and looks at it and says what works.

"Lara's ability to move is really important, and we tested that, but until you put her in a tomb you don't really know how it's going to feel. You start with a paper map—it doesn't have to be pretty. You get artists and everybody working on the project to look at it together and see what works, what they think they can build. Also they tell you if they think something's not fun, and that's critical."

Lara Croft in action in *Lara Croft Tomb Raider: Legend.* Images © 2006 Eidos Interactive Ltd. *Lara Croft Tomb Raider: Legend,* Lara Croft, *Tomb Raider,* and the Tomb Raider logo are all trademarks of Eidos Interactive Ltd.

Suspect under interrogation in *CSI: 3 Dimensions of Murder.* Image courtesy of Ubisoft.

CSI

"Ubisoft picked Telltale Games to do *CSI* [in 3D] based on our goals for story and our cinematics quality, and also because our engine is really all about characters talking to other characters," says Greg Land, lead designer and lead writer on both *CSI: 3 Dimensions of Murder*, and *CSI: Hard Evidence*. "It's not an action engine, it's a character engine.

"I think it's always great to start with a character that you really respond to in some way. For instance, we wanted to do something with an Anna Nicole Smith–like character. We found her really fascinating, so building a case around that character there was a lot to dive into and have fun with. She's just over-the-top luxury and also a certain campiness. She was an inspiration for a character design.

"With character development, for me, it's making really dramatic choices for characters, giving them a really rich history. A lot of times I'll sit down and just spend some time making up how old they are, what's their relationship to x-y-z people, what's their temperament. I try to give them really extreme choices and then play up those choices the characters make. We're more interested in dramatic choices than we are mundane choices. And we're interested in ordinary people doing extraordinary things, where there's a lot of emotion and conflict. We're really creating emotion and conflict for the characters."

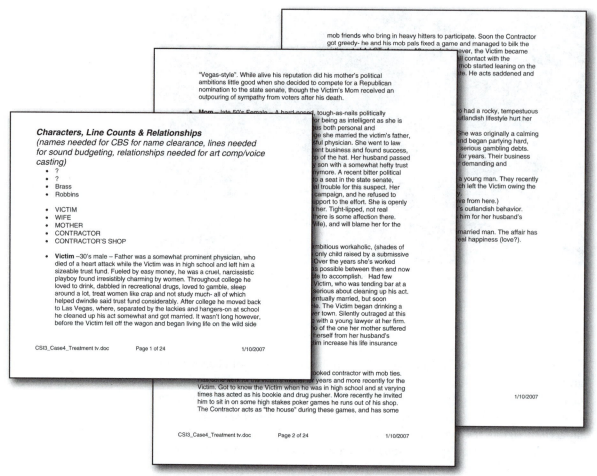

CSI case treatment. See Appendix A for full document. Courtesy of Ubisoft

Silicon Knights

Denis Dyack, co-founder of Silicon Knights, is completely dedicated to creating titles that are steeped in story and populated with rich and full characters. And he is the first to admit that his background would suggest otherwise.

"I have a master's in computer science, and I have an arts background from before that. It might surprise you, but in school I was horrible with literature—I did not do well and I hated Shakespeare. I took computer science only because I wanted to make video games.

"But while I was in school I was lucky enough to be exposed to people like Peter Drucker, and that shifted my thinking. Suddenly I didn't see technology as a god, I saw it as a means to an end. I also got a master's in neural networks, AI, and user interfaces. So, as a programmer, I could talk the talk.

"It's really easy to say 'no' to something in our industry when there's some new innovation being proposed. So when people say, 'No, that can't be done; the technology doesn't support it,' I'm thinking that I have the tools, and I run the company, and so I would say, 'Well, I can tell you this is how *I* would do this,' and then that idea of 'it can't be done' starts to fade away. Really all this is about is understanding technology and getting it there, and then getting the right collection of people together to understand that technology to use it as a means to an end.

"So, in order to create that kind of innovative interactive content, we want technology and art to come together to create something that is more than the sum of its parts. If we take advantage of what technology can do, and create content people have never experienced before, that's where you'll have a win.

"For example, when the PS1 came out, I suddenly could stream audio, and I knew if we were going to do what I knew we could do with that technology, we had to have good voice acting, equal in par to the movies. And that's what we did. Since then, games companies have gone more to audio because they've seen what that technology can do to enhance their games. It's just getting the right group of people together to think outside the box, and then use that box in ways people haven't thought of before.

"If you take content, gameplay, technology, artwork, and audio and combine all those things, the game becomes more than the sum of its parts. We call that *engagement theory*. We develop games around the content, and there's a strategic reason for that.

"We come up with content we think is interesting. So for *Legacy of Kain*, you play a vampire who hates himself because he has to kill people in order to survive, and everybody is trying to kill him, but he's the only one who can save the world. Then we build the graphics and mechanics around that.

"Character development was the first thing we did in *Legacy of Kain*. It was a big thing for us. But one of the first things we wanted to do was break the traditional band with 'this one is evil, this one is good.' The movie *Unforgiven* is one of my favorite movies, not because it's a Western, because I usually don't go for Westerns, but this was such a great story because of the characters. In *Unforgiven*, all of the characters you thought were good were bad, and all the characters you thought were the bad guys also had some good in them, and it turned them upside down. The good characters really were bad. It's a great example of characters.

"With *Legacy of Kain*, we wanted to develop characters with substance. The definition of a good script is these characters motivate you, you can relate to them, they have foibles, you can look up to them, this makes them real. Without that, you don't have real entertainment.

"We need to develop games on a content level instead of just on technology. For example, in *Eternal Darkness* you play 12 characters over a time period of 2,000 years to defeat this one character who is immortal and trying to destroy the world.

"We try to merge the world with the characters. And as independent developers, we really feel that's the way we have to go. When it comes to characters and story development, if the characters aren't very strong you're in big trouble.

"It's the same rules for Hollywood or for books, but as an industry we're still skewed by technology, where we can have bad story and characters but good technology, and that's what the games are based on. But those days are going away. Soon, everybody will be able to do great graphics, and everybody will have great technology, but where's the substance? It's like the latest *Star Wars*. Sure the technology was there and the graphics were great, but where's the story?

"Another example is the latest James Bond movie. On the Metacritic[11] site, *Casino Royale* is scoring high, and it's because of James Bond. The character development in that movie is probably enough to revitalize the whole Bond franchise.

"What it comes down to after a while is that you get that initial punch with the technology, but the character is the substance, and without that substance you're losing longevity."

Nihilistic

"Character development is definitely more story-driven than art-driven," says Rob Huebner, talking about Nihilistic's approach to designing interesting characters. "We start with the main character first and always make sure we come up with a character the player wants to be. How do they want to be powerful? How do they want to be empowered? We get that person identified first. The key is looking at the story and identifying key characters who compliment the story and who complete the main character.

"In our current game, we have a main central character with a female ally who is like a mirror image of him, and we developed her character as she relates to him. Then we developed the main bad guy, his nemesis, and figured out how he can fit with the two protagonists.

---

[11] http://www.metacritic.com/

"The artists also make suggestions. In this game, we started with a stereo-typical young tough protagonist, and one artist thought it would be interesting to make him older. He's still handsome and virile, but he's older and more mature. Visuals can definitely feed back into the story. The artists provide this, and when they make contributions like this, it's really good.

"It's like a puzzle—if things work out well, you end up with four or five key characters whose backstories make something that can't be pulled apart. We find ways to use the characters to tie the story together. So what you end up with is that the story is bound up with the characters and the characters are bound up with each other, and you find the loose ends just wrap themselves up. If you tie this thing to that, it's a self-completing puzzle to some degree."

Splinter Cell 5

Mary DeMarle has seen the benefits of taking this very thorough approach to character design on the many titles she's worked on, including her latest project, *Splinter Cell 5*. DeMarle is the narrative designer on *SC5*, in charge of making certain that the desired player experience is delivered in every aspect of the game, including story and character. According to DeMarle, "I'll create a very detailed bio on this character, defining two or four main characteristics of this person, of how they get expressed, and I will almost tell you the story of this person from birth on up. And everybody who is going to deal with this character needs to read this bio.

"The artists will create the visual look of this character, and when they read the bio there are certain details that strike cords with different people who work on this. So, for example, the character artist will create a visual of them, and there are always elements they've captured and created that they get directly from the bio. Then from there, the animators will take it, and they need to read the bios because they need to know what this guy is like. Maybe he's a little bit timid, a little bit shy, and they'll catch that and start to animate it, and it will affect how they make the character walk. I don't tell them "this character walks a certain way," but they internalize the characteristics and create the walk that fits the character. And then, when the actor knows the background of this person, they'll start adapting that in, and that characterization will come across. It's this mutli-layered process.

"I don't expect that half of what I write about his character will come in at all—it's trivial detail. It's also funny because projects I've worked on where I've created characters, everybody always seems to have a real clear image of who these characters are.

"On this project, I've created them, it goes to the scriptwriter, then we did casting. We pre-selected the director, and we pre-selected the ones we felt were the best picks, the top choices for each character we would play to the producers. We had four different characters and we played the recordings, and it was funny to listen to everyone in the room talk about them. Everyone had a very different vision of what this character was. They were starting from my vision of this character, and they were very opinionated on these characters—they all think they know them.

"And sometimes I learn.

"For one character, there was a situation where he was blocked at some point, and I wrote a piece of dialog that was something like, 'S***, the door is blocked,' and the creative director came back to me later and said, 'I don't really think he would say s***. I don't think he would ever admit he made a mistake, and saying s*** is admitting he screwed up and he would never do that.' Or I've have a head animator come to me and say about another character, 'He would never say a line like that, and he would never even admit he had a thought about that, and saying that line would be admitting he had that thought and he would never do that,' and I'd have to say, 'You know what? You're probably right,' so I would change the line. And I don't think that would happen if you didn't have that kind of a character bible.

"My bios are about a page and a half at most, but that's single-spaced. The main characters are two pages, with main character traits attached and expressed as how this would show up in their character, and that's an extra two to three pages. The character traits are more visual, more like a diagram, where you have a main character trait in a circle in the center, and it has lines coming off of it showing other traits. Lets say, for example, that the character trait is 'nervous,' so off of that we have 'chews gum all the time,' 'taps fingers,' more stuff like that.

"I can create very strong, realistic characters with full-fledged depth to them. But how that gets expressed in the game, well, that is crucial."

Character Exercises

Exercise 1: With your story from Chapter 4 in mind, we're going to work on character development.

You now have a logline and two-page story treatment for your game. If you already have some characters in your treatment, use them as a starting point to complete this exercise.

1. Write a one- to two-sentence description of ten characters that could populate your game, including your antagonist and protagonist.

2. After you have a clear definition of each of these characters, that anyone could pick up and read and "get" who they are in a couple of sentences, expand their descriptions into a paragraph or two, giving each one some unique characteristics. Use characteristics from people you know or celebrities to kick-start this process if you'd like.

3. Select your antagonist and protagonist, and write a backstory on them of at least two pages each.[12] Include in your backstory the following:

   - When and where they were born, their age

   - Where they grew up

   - A description of their family of origin and their relationship with them

   - Their three biggest weaknesses

   - Their three best traits

   - What drives them

   - Who they are and what they do at this stage in their life, including their attitude about themselves and about the world at large

   - The relationship of the lead characters in the story with one another, why are they in conflict, if applicable, and how they got to this point in their lives

   This is the beginning of your character bible.

4. Look at your remaining characters and see how you can now add some elements to them to make them a little more interesting. Then determine how they relate to your leads.

5. Add some visual sketches or drawings of your characters to your bible if you would like/are able.

6. Now, go back to your story, and knowing what you know about your characters, expand your story treatment to ten pages. If your story starts to change, it's because you've done some good character definition. Go with it, and see where it takes you.

---

12 Double-spaced.

7. How many characters do you really need in your game? Start to think about them based on your new story treatment, and define who they are, either in Character Lite or in full-blown backstories, as appropriate.

8. Adjust your character bible as needed.

Exercise 2: Choose a well-known character from a movie and expand their backstory.

As your second exercise, work on fleshing out a character that you are already familiar with, and imagine that you are going to put them into a new game. Keep them in their known environment if this is easier for you (for example, if they live in Chicago, you don't have to move them to Juno).

Using what you already know about them as your starting point, write a synopsis of who they are now.

1. Start with a one- to two-sentence description.

2. When you're satisfied that you've captured them in this brief description, expand it into a paragraph, still using what you know about who they are now.

3. From here, organically build out their backstory into a two-page document. Avoid clichés. You can be as wild as you'd like, but make sure that even if their backstory is fantastic, it's believable. Look at the elements in Exercise 1 as a starting point for expansion, or select some described in this chapter.

Character Checklist

❏ The lead characters in your story are the protagonist (hero) and the antagonist (villain).

❏ Avoid clichéd and stereotyped characters.

❏ To develop an extensive backstory, you need to determine a range of personality traits, including flaws and fears, dreams and desires.

❏ Use resources that already exist to help you develop traits for your characters.

❏ To develop a Character Lite backstory, work with and past clichés and add some twists to create a brief summary of a unique character.

❑ Make certain that your villain has a reason for being the way he is, rather than "He's a bad guy because he's evil."

❑ Spend a little time on your secondary characters and NPCs, giving them some unique features that make them interesting and fun to encounter.

❑ All character development should be organic. This is especially important when dealing with pre-existing characters.

❑ Use your characters to help you evolve story development and gameplay.

Chapter 6

The Hat Trick of Game Design—
Environments, **Puzzles**, and **Levels**

"Game design is not one person's vision; one person pushes the group and the direction, but game design is the vision of everyone involved."

—**Tim Willits, id Software**

Everyone from kids to hard-core gamers love the payoff of winning a level and advancing to the next. The thrill of victory, the challenge of the unknown, the belief that with enough skill they can get better and better, conquer the mysteries that lie ahead, and become masters of the universe. Levels keep the game interesting and the players engaged long after they should have quit and gone to sleep. And as a game designer, there's just about no better reward. Putting the story and characters into the environment and making them work, fleshing out the levels in their many iterations, adding interesting puzzles to the mix, that's where you get to the meat of things—going from paper to pixels.

Up to this point, we've seen many ways in which companies start new game development. Tim Willits and the crew at id Software first decide if they want to expand an existing franchise or create a new IP and then figure out when and where they want their game to take place. Saber Interactive builds a cool game mechanic then wraps a story around it with all of the specifics of who, what, where, when, why, and how for a high-concept game. Crystal Dynamics has

Venue concept sketch of Record Store in *Karaoke Revolution*. Image provided by Harmonix Music Systems, Inc.

Screenshot from *Karaoke Revolution*. Image provided by Harmonix Music Systems, Inc. (See color plates.)

Lara Croft in *Lara Croft Tomb Raider Legend*. Images © 2006 Eidos Interactive Ltd. *Lara Croft Tomb Raider: Legend*, Lara Croft, *Tomb Raider*, and the Tomb Raider logo are all trademarks of Eidos Interactive Ltd.

Lost Souls in-game shot from *DOOM 3*. Image courtesy of id Software, Inc.

a great character to work with in Lara Croft, and they place her in a cool environment with a story that would be fun and compelling. Telltale Games has an existing property in *CSI* and comes up with new stories that are consistent with the franchise and in new locations in which the player explores and interacts with characters to solve mysteries. And then there's Harmonix with music-centric levels. And we haven't even talked about MMOs yet.

Even with all of their unique requirements, every game takes place *somewhere*, and whatever and wherever that environment is, it is inextricably tied to the characters, the story, and the mechanics. Levels are based on what happens in the environment, sometimes with puzzles, and usually relating to story, or characters, or both in varying degrees—from "deeply involved with story" to "not a lot of story, but it's fun." When puzzles are present, they are almost always environment- and/or story-driven.

The big-picture question of "Where does this game take place?" is usually asked within the first 30–90 seconds of the new game development discussion. An answer to which everyone *agrees* can take a little longer to come up with, but suffice it to say it's one of the first decisions made. Once that's settled, it's time for specifics, and that means writing up what everyone said they wanted and making sure you're all on the same page.

"Creating story-world docs for a game is my preference for beginning a project," explains Matt Costello. "I will talk about the world, the environment look and feel, what makes the environment tick, wherever it is, whether it's places with pirates or places on Mars. If they're well done in words, the person producing it will get the image and the feeling that works with the story. This is not just arbitrary. You can carry it to the art director and the people making it and building the levels so they can get a sense of it and of the overall integrity."

This first document can be short, a relief I'm sure for those who would rather be dropped into a pit of snakes than have to read a document. Short, but not lacking. As Costello notes, it is supposed to go beyond just stating the facts of "game played here," and reach the realm of giving a real sense of the place—pulling you into the environment, making you want to play there, and getting a real visual and emotional sense of what a cool place it is. This is very much akin to the story treatment, but it's all about location, location, location. The ambiance, the atmosphere, the prose of it all.

Between the initial steps of creating a world overview and getting it to a place where you can turn it over to artists and level designers to start to build, a lot of other things usually have to take place. The characters need to be figured out, the story bible gets written, and flowcharts are created somewhere along the way. If you're doing this before you've signed with a publisher, which is common, such details as timelines and budgets need to spec'd out.

It saves considerable amounts of time and ibuprofen if this is all done before things go to level design. Puzzles might be created as part of the story doc, or this task could be something the level designers do. It depends in large part on the type of game. Some companies, with varying degrees of success and failure, just skip the whole planning thing and jump right into the deep end and start prototyping. That's one of the industry's hot topics. To paraphrase Shakespeare, "To write and read documents, or to prototype: that is the question." We'll get to various answers to this in Chapter 10.

World of Waffles screenshot in *Death Jr. II*. Image © 2006 Backbone Entertainment. Death Jr., the Death Jr. characters and logo are trademarks of Backbone Entertainment.

Screenshot from *Antigrav*. Image provided by Harmonix Music Systems, Inc.

"Part of the kick-off process is a detailed summary of how many levels, characters, and hours of play time are in the game. And they want that in the contract, along with all of the players' mechanics, the actions they can take like shooting, the types of guns, jumps, sneaking around corners, all the different core abilities. It usually ends up being exhibits or appendices to the contract, so this has to be succinct. It's approximately 30 pages worth of stuff, with 20 pages of contract on top of that."

—Rob Huebner

Enemy Name	Abriviation	Forest Path 01	Forest Path 02	Toy Cemetery 01	Toy Cemetery 02	Toy Arena	Saw Mill 01	Saw Mill INT 01	Llama Farm 01	Llama Farm 02	Base 01	Base 02	Wafflehouse 01	Wafflehouse 02	Saw Mill 02	Saw Mill INT 02	Mall 01	Mall 02	Styx 01	Styx 02	Tree 01	Tree 02	Tree Arena
Action Hero - Regular army guy	Ah_01			X	X																		
Action Hero - Ranged Character	Ah_02			X	X																		
Animatronic Llama - Regular Llama Robot	Al_01												X	X									

Death Jr. II enemy location list. Image © 2006 Backbone Entertainment. Death Jr., the Death Jr. characters and logo are trademarks of Backbone Entertainment.

Once the environment is nailed down, thoughts lead to level design. And while level design is important for figuring out the fun in the gameplay, it's also part of the more mundane requirement of figuring out the number of hours of gameplay. Some companies, like Nihilistic, have the levels and timing synced to each other with graphic flowcharts and timelines that line the wall of the conference room in which daily meetings are held. Others might keep this all in a wiki.

Costello has seen the number of hours of gameplay come down over recent years. From the early days of game design when, as Rob Swigart recalls, nobody even asked that question, to just a few years ago when, Costello says, "They were thinking 20 to 40 hours of gameplay" was the target everyone was shooting for.

"We knew in *The 7th Guest* how many rooms there would be," explains Costello, "and each room when you unlock the puzzle would trigger the next ghostly video and open up other areas in the house. There were between about 15 and 20 rooms, and each one would have a puzzle, and the puzzle would take as long as it took you to figure it out. For example, you'd get a puzzle and a telescope where you're looking at Mars, and you'd have to figure it out. Some puzzles could stop you cold and others you could breeze through. I would guess it took on the average 20–30 hours.

"But we know now that the average age of a gamer is 28 or 29, and we're thinking eight,

"There's a huge difference between designing a single-player game and designing an MMO. And to this day I'm still searching for the right analogy. Like a lot of designers, I live by analogies. It's like designing a bicycle versus designing a rhinoceros. I can't even think of a way to tell you how different they are."

—Mike Sellers

nine, maybe ten hours of great gameplay. And that sounds just right to me, because if the game is great, you'll play it again. I sense that shifting all over. Before, you had endless levels doing the same endless things, so that's a pretty good change."

Puzzle development in level design must always stick to the rule of "organic." And as Joe Morrissey reminded us in Chapter 4, your goal should be to love the player, not kill the player. You want to make it challenging, but don't get them in a cycle of "eternally stuck." Accomplishing that balancing act, however, is a little tougher to do.

The key really is to think about the situation, the environment you're in, and the player's overall goal and make the puzzle a natural narrative-related obstacle, which is conflict, which is good storytelling. In *101 Dalmatians: Escape from DeVil Manor*, the whole game was a puzzle. How do you get the puppies out of the DeVil mansion? Before Cruella arrives? Without getting caught by Horace and Jasper?

Concept art for Waffle House in *Death Jr. II*. Image © 2006 Backbone Entertainment. Death Jr., the Death Jr. characters and logo are trademarks of Backbone Entertainment.

How do you get them safely through the countryside? And find the way to London? It was an adventure game full of exciting gameplay that was puzzle-rich through and through.

One of the things we wanted to do was use the dumbwaiter as a device to move the main character puppies throughout the house to discover a way out. This would give them access to the basement, the kitchen on the first floor, the hallway on the second floor, and the attic, opening up four levels of rooms for mischief and play. But puppies are little, and the dumbwaiter was too high for them to reach. What do you do?

Everyone I know who's ever worked in puzzle design will tell you to work backwards. When you have a puzzle, think of the end result you're trying to achieve and backtrack how you can get from there to here and make it happen.

So, how could little puppies get up to a dumbwaiter that was as high as the kitchen counter? My thinking went somewhere along these lines, backwards in order:

- Dumbwaiter
- Kitchen counter

- Open cabinet drawers
- Floor

There was no way the puppies could jump up as high as the counter, but they could absolutely make smaller jumps. So we devised a series of open cabinet drawers on which the puppies could jump, and we made it a memory game as well, making some drawers with missing bottoms so that if a puppy jumped on one of these it would fall right through and have to start over. So, to get them to the dumbwaiter it went:

- Start on the floor
- Jump onto open cabinet drawers
- Make it up to the kitchen counter
- Head into the dumbwaiter

Fun gameplay—and once the puzzle was figured out, which drawers had solid bottoms and which did not, the puppies could quickly jump up the right combination of drawers to scramble into the dumbwaiter and take a ride.

The answers to dilemmas in a game are obviously up to the player to figure out, but it's also up to us to help them accomplish their goal without making it maddening for them, or too easy. You also don't want to throw the player a curve by sticking something bizarre in the game that feels like it was inserted as a placeholder and then forgotten. This might seem obvious to you, but it is not always obvious to others.

Fortunately, game developers and publishers are thinking that they want to keep the player playing rather than fuming, and that means moving them along through the gameplay experience. This is especially significant as we bring in some of those markets we looked at in Chapter 1—like adults who are new to video games. We have the casual-games market to thank for this expansion, because as newbie game players get comfortable playing games that don't require too much attention, or thinking, and are fun and satisfying to play at the same time, they are able to move into games that offer them some more diversity in their gaming experience.

"Whenever I have to think in a game, I usually stop playing and start reading email," says Dan Conners, founder of Telltale Games. "Most people don't like to be stuck, not even for 20 minutes. It's key to keep them moving, and it's hard to keep them engrossed in a game if they're stuck."

Conners and his team went to a tough crowd for focus testing on the Ubisoft franchise *CSI*. Gaming virgins.

"One of the most common responses we heard was, 'I've never played a game before.' We want it to be rewarding and enjoyable to them, as well as

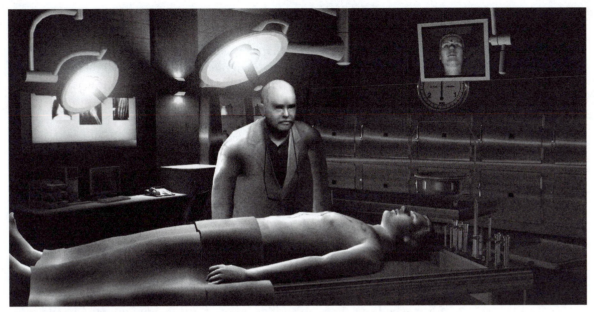

CSI: 3 Dimensions of Murder body in the morgue. Image courtesy of Ubisoft.

people who do play games." *CSI* ended up being "twelve and half hours long for play through. And when you finish it, you feel like you got your money's worth because it's not expensive."

Dave Grossman on Puzzle Design

Dave Grossman is a senior designer at Telltale Games who has been in the business since 1989, starting at LucasArts on *Monkey Island* and currently steering the helm on *Sam & Max* games. He shares some thoughts on puzzle design.

"Stuff I work on, we insist that the player be clever in order to succeed, and actually most of the challenge is to make each puzzle be exactly a question of difficulty level and what is the conceptual leap you have to make in order to solve the puzzle.

"I can imagine, for example, that you come to a stream and the path is on both sides of the stream but you can't get across, and you ask the player to build a bridge. If the stream is too small, there's no challenge. If it's too big, they can't get across.

"There has to be some 'Ah-ha!' moment for the player to figure out the puzzle. You can't just give them, 'Here's what you have to do, go do it,' and no fun. People don't like to be lost, and they don't like to be told what to do. And in the middle of that is the ultimate puzzle.

"Once you figure out what they need to do in response to a particular situation, you can help them figure it out so that their response is, 'Oh boy, I figured that out by myself.' Then if they still can't do it and they have to get help, I want their response to be, 'Oh, I should have thought of that,' rather than, 'How did they expect me to figure that out?'

"There's a lot of voodoo involved in puzzle design. I tend to approach them the same way I would if I were playing the game. I start with the problem and come up with a solution. The princess is up in the castle; how do we get her down? And then I try to think of all the ways I could do that in this world. Is there a ladder? Do I have a rope or grappling hook? If there are too many solutions and I can't think of reasons they all wouldn't work, then I change the problem because it's too easy.

"I like it if there are a few things you might think to try, if it's not a problem that only has one solution. I might put a ladder and grappling hook around the tower to solve it and invent some reasons why that wouldn't work. Or maybe I put shoes on springs. A lot of it is imagining how I would solve the puzzle and think, 'How am I going to think of something that is going to be fun for me and that I'll be able to help them think of?' And then there's insuring that the problem is stated correctly.

"You want to do something maybe a little more than just, 'Oops, she's up there,' but not so much as, 'I need a ladder.' I tend to graduate the presentation of the information, so it's essentially a series of hints. The more you try to solve the puzzle, the more you're talking to the person involved. You want to push the player gradually along, but I don't like to ever out-and-out tell them what to do. I just want to state the problem with increasing narrowness.

"The *Sam & Max* stories are all original. We're doing them as an episodic game. Each episode stands on its own, and they also have a story arc. So you're doing a case, and then it comes to a close, but they're all related to each other. They solve one little mystery each time, but there's something bigger going on and sometimes they're connected to that. We're working toward an actual conclusion at the end of the season. I don't want to leave a giant cliffhanger at the end. Each one you can enjoy on its own, and hopefully you will enjoy them enough that now you want to pick up the next one.

"Our games are so story-intensive that character is everything. It's not just about figuring out how people look and how they talk, but it's best if you make the nature of the puzzles and gameplay support the nature of the characters and license as a whole. *Day of the Tentacle* is an example of that done really successfully. You're entering a cartoon world, and you have to think about being a cartoon character. You have to place the white stripe down the back of the cat to make it the skunk.

"Whenever I'm starting on a game, if there's any existing IP, I steep myself in it as much as possible. I'm a big believer in research. A lot of people don't do that, and I don't know why. With *Sam & Max*, we have them as central characters, and we're inventing everybody else; it's all new people every time. So part of the challenge is, 'Who are these people, and how do they fit in with the world?' They have to feel right. They have to feel quirky and oddball in a particular way that will fit with Steve Percel's[1] particular sense of humor. And with this one, we're lucky to have a little access to Steve. So we make up some stuff and run it by him. We look at character sketches, and sometimes he improves them drastically.

"I find that for story and puzzle design both, it's helpful to have a small group involved in it. About four people is the right amount for brainstorming on stuff. When it's [a co-designer] and me, just the two of us, it gets a little slow. When you get more than four of five, it gets slow again for other reasons.

"I have perfect numbers for anything. If you're trying to complicate a puzzle, you divide it into three. It's enough that it seems complicated, and it's few enough that you can remember all the pieces without working too hard at it. As soon as you get to four, it's hard to remember—'The fourth thing, hmm, let's see, I had to go get some pepper, and a screwdriver, and a steering wheel, and what's that fourth thing? Damn! I just can't remember.' It's the maximum number of things I can remember.

"I usually come out of a brainstorming session with some idea of what the story is basically about, are the characters going to have to learn anything, challenges they're going to face for simple games. I like to use some variant of a simple three-act play structure—a little at the beginning getting used to characters and environments, getting used to the gameplay, a little about how to use the interface, and as they play they're going to be picking up on stuff. Then some big story point happens and you go off in a different direction from the story and puzzle point, then another twist on that and you have an exciting bit at the end.

"And then there's an exhaustive filling-in-the-details period, which because we have to come up with interesting puzzles to do at each step, that makes it a lot more work than it is if you're just writing a story. You're more limited in what you can do, because of the fact that all of these little bits and pieces have to be 'figureoutaboutable' by someone with an ordinary brain. It's

---

1 Steve Percel works at Pixar and is the creator of *Sam & Max*.

fun to do fun, but you have to figure out how to allow them to be solved in different orders. Not 'first you do this, then this.' You don't realize when you lay out a movie what a luxury it is that you get to decide the order until you work in a form where that's not true."

Matt Costello on Puzzle Design

"First of all, puzzles are really just problems. For example, in your kitchen you could have a drawer that gets stuck. What's the secret strategy you can use to get the drawer open? That technique is used on a large scale in all the great novels, to do things that essentially are real-life puzzles—a configuration and a problem you have to solve. For classic puzzles, there's a whole formula. My book on puzzles covers pretty much the gamut of classic puzzles, and they all fall into different categories, 25 or 30 of them, and rarely do you have new ones come along like Sudoku, which is kind of like magic squares but it's different. That happens maybe once every ten years. It's rare.

"Look at puzzles, whether they're magic squares, or a pictogram with words, or a sliding block thing, all of them are just brain challenges but transformed into a physical universe with something at stake, something that matters that can become compelling, and real experiences to drive the fiction. Think of *Alien*, *The Da Vinci Code*, a show like *24*. The key thing is to make it so the puzzle belongs in that world. When you come to an alien space lock and it has a big symbol grid on it, that may be a pattern and you have 60 seconds to figure out the attributes of the alien system. The puzzle is set into an environment that fits. It perfectly makes sense. And it's no longer a puzzle, it's the alien door lock.

"In *The 7th Guest*, we intentionally decided that puzzles should just be puzzles. But what I did, for example, was for the toymaker I'd have the puzzle be in the toymaker's realm. Having them embedded in the world, they became logical. The *Indiana Jones* series of films is action adventure with puzzles embedded. It's a perfect example. To a lesser extent, so are the James Bond books and films, Robert Ludlum, all of his work.

"Now, when people say they 'don't have puzzles, what can you do?' these strategies apply. Look at the environment. What situation would be challenging that works in the context? Then, work backwards to find the mechanics to make that fly. You wouldn't do it the other way around. Let's say you have a medieval knights game. What does the castle look like? Does it have catapults? Spiral staircases? Rows of armor? Shields? Think about shields. They have a pattern. Look at the story context. Story and environment go together, and that will suggest the type of things you have in it."

Hal Barwood on Puzzle Design

"How do I approach puzzle design? Backwards. You look for a goal and then figure out what you would need to have that goal realized. Let's say you want to steal a document. First you have to have access to that location. How are you going to get the key? If you can't get the key, how are you going to get in? You back it in. Usually that suggests puzzlely elements that you have to consciously be looking for—the interactive ideas.

"It's a funny abstract skill you cultivate. It's like hunting for elves. They're hard to spot, and you have to sincerely believe they exist, and when you see one out of the corner of your eye you have to turn suddenly and grab it, and then it turns into concrete and it's a substantial idea you can do something with.

"That technique is also useful in brainstorming. A lot of things go by that drift though your consciousness that you don't observe, and you have to learn to observe those things that drift through in a way that feels self-conscious at first. One of my favorite lines comes from Sherlock Holmes, when Sherlock says to Watson, 'You see, Watson, but you do not observe.' You have to be aware and put the grab on them.

"And if that fails you can always make lists. It's never a bad idea.

"'Okay, I need to get into this building. What are all the ways I can think of to do it?' Make a list of things that are the widest possible array of things that can happen. This isn't such a bad idea because one of the things you're always trying to do creatively is to find the maximum number of ways to express everything that can be expressed. You try to exploit the material as much as you can, and find all of the different ways you can do it. Whether you're throwing a pot, designing a game, or building a bridge, I think that's true."

CSI

"Second to characters, their environment is the next most important thing," according to Greg Land, *CSI*'s lead designer at Telltale Games. "When the characters are not on the screen, the only other thing you have to look at is that environment. So creating an evocative place to be for ten minutes or so is very critical for us, because it's all about searching for evidence. We

CSI: Hard Evidence Warrick in the studio. Image courtesy of Ubisoft.

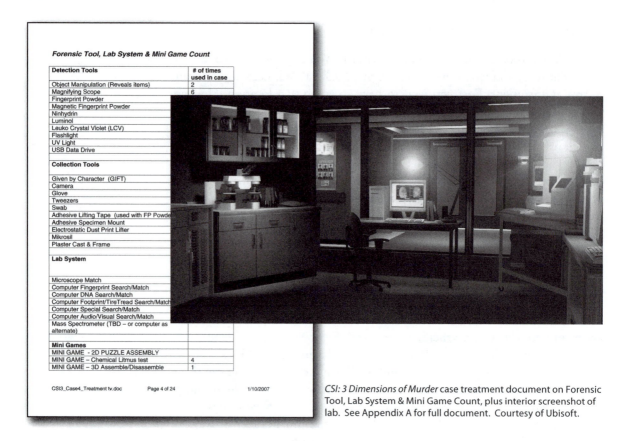

Forensic Tool, Lab System & Mini Game Count

Detection Tools	# of times used in case
Object Manipulation (Reveals items)	2
Magnifying Scope	6
Fingerprint Powder	
Magnetic Fingerprint Powder	
Ninhydrin	
Luminol	
Leuko Crystal Violet (LCV)	
Flashlight	
UV Light	
USB Data Drive	
Collection Tools	
Given by Character (GIFT)	
Camera	
Glove	
Tweezers	
Swab	
Adhesive Lifting Tape (used with FP Powder	
Adhesive Specimen Mount	
Electrostatic Dust Print Lifter	
Mikrosil	
Plaster Cast & Frame	
Lab System	
Microscope Match	
Computer Fingerprint Search/Match	
Computer DNA Search/Match	
Computer Footprint/TireTread Search/Match	
Computer Special Search/Match	
Computer Audio/Visual Search/Match	
Mass Spectrometer (TBD – or computer as alternate)	
Mini Games	
MINI GAME - 2D PUZZLE ASSEMBLY	
MINI GAME – Chemical Litmus test	4
MINI GAME – 3D Assemble/Disassemble	1

CSI3_Case4_Treatment tv.doc   Page 4 of 24   1/10/2007

CSI: 3 Dimensions of Murder case treatment document on Forensic Tool, Lab System & Mini Game Count, plus interior screenshot of lab. See Appendix A for full document. Courtesy of Ubisoft.

do a lot of work to make sure that the evidence is compelling—that we're drawn into the environment so it's multilayered, not just one room. It's a room with another room attached, and in that room is a closet, and in the closet is a cutaway safe. It allows you to go deeper into the room and probe into this character's environment.

"With environments, we also really take a cue from the show to see how it's lit, and we try to match the show's lighting and types of light sources. For example, the show has windows that are glossed over with extremely bright light coming in, but the inside of the room is kind of shadowy, and we want that same kind of look and feel. We try to recreate the look of the show as much as we can.

"Environment also provides a real opportunity to speak to a person's character. In *CSI 3*, one of our suspects is an artist, and his studio is a reflection of his personality, where it's very cluttered and sort of dark. There are pictures of the victim in there that really show that this is the life he's been living. He has been drawing pictures of her and living with her image for years, and he's very eccentric and sort of an angry grumpy artist—a recluse basically. So it's a real opportunity with the environment to help show more sides of this character, and a lot of those details are figured out by our environment artists. Fortunately, the discussion with the artist and the designer creates a good understanding of what we're after. We're working together to help the game artist make those kinds of choices."

Halo 3

Justin Hayward, who previously worked on the single-player version of *Halo 2* at Bungie, explains his role as an artist and level designer on the multiplayer version of *Halo 3*.

"On the multiplayer team for *Halo 3*, I have a lot more input into design than on the single-player team. The design team is much smaller because the artists take a larger role in the design process. Also, they tend to be smaller spaces because of how vigorously they're played, so the environment very much dictates how they play in these spaces. So part of the design is deciding the paths people can run on, where they can jump to hiding spots, things like that. And because environment artists are coming up with the themes for these crazy spaces, we're also figuring out if there are special gameplay elements, like force fields you can't shoot through, or jump pads that can get you places very quickly, and how those relate to the overall theme of the environment.

"We have a design team and the art team and the programming team and then the management group, and those are somewhat broken up between single-player and multiplayer. The multiplayer group is smaller because the single-player group has to deal with integrating story and game cinematics into the spaces they're creating, and syncing up the audio cues, and there's a lot in the story; there's a lot of ground to cover. These environments tend to be much, much bigger, so it needs a bigger crew. In the multiplayer group because of the size of the group and the size of the environment, it allows us to have more input and more of a fast turn around.

"We start out with giving general guidelines as to what we want the individual environment to be and how many players we want it to accommodate. Then we come up with a basic mass out [initial 3D iteration after a paper design] of these spaces, and it's sort of putting some real rough sketches on paper, and building that in very rough form in three dimensions. And that allows us to get a really good feel for what this space could turn into.

"From there we do quite a bit of molding, and that could change the environment quite a bit from the original idea—molding meaning manipulating, tweaking around where things sit, and how the tunnels, or whatever they are, are laid out. And from there we go to architecting. At that stage, we start locking down what these game spaces are and how they're laid out, and at this point we're playing the game and the designers as part of their job set up regular gameplay testing—every day they bring folks into the office and have them run around in the spaces in this very unfinished state to find where the problem spots are, where it's working, where it isn't. And this allows us to lock down some of these elements.

"Then we bring it to a state where we complete all the major alterations and the locking down of all the geometry. And then at that point we go into polish, and polish is taking all of those surfaces and further refining the shape of doorframes and rocks, things like that. It's what we call *resing up* the geometry, which means adding a lot more vertices to create more defined shapes, more detail in geometry. And part of the process as well is to apply texturing and shader work, and start laying out where effects will go, and special objects that are activated or are moving, that sort of thing where those exist in the environment. And we haven't really reached the next stage on any of our maps yet. We're saving that until last, and we're calling that *finishing*. Finishing can be thought of as polishing because it's going over all the surfaces and tweaking them to our liking but not adding anything new.

"Designers tend to have the last say on what the layout of the space should be. They can extrapolate quite a bit from what they see people doing or not doing. They stand in these rooms and take notes and see where folks are getting hung up and come back to the artists and say, 'I really see people getting hung up in these spaces, and we need to come up with a solution.' A lot of times they have a solution, and other times we have a conversation and come up with a solution together. And that's where multiplayer artists tend to have more say in the design process. It tends to be back and forth between the artist and designer as part of the solution for design problems.

"The dev cycle tends to be about two and a half to three years total, and three is maxing out. Multiplayer maps with these processes I told you about where we're massing out and finishing, we tend to mass out one map and mass out another and come back and architect the one we did first so we sort of jump around. It might take maybe three months or so on an individual multiplayer space.

"We really want the art and design for multiplayer and single-player to feel like they're part of the same universe, so you just feel like you're stepping from one realm to the other. So there are people constantly looking back and forth from single-player to multiplayer to make sure the environments and themes we're creating fit in the *Halo* universe."

id

"When we create levels here at id, it's always a balancing act, because you have fun things you want to do and you have to figure out how it fits in with the story," explains id's lead designer, Tim Willits. "So we come up with overall level missions—a generic mission where you come up with fun gameplay, ideas, challenges and puzzles. I write up the ideas, and once we agree on that direction we go to graph paper with the pencil. Before anybody touches a computer, it's paper and pencil.

"We start sketching out the general flow of the level, and I go over it with them, the overall flow, the gameplay with traps, puzzles, what they have to jump over, and then the flow of the map—and once we're happy with those three elements we go into the map editor and do a rough block out. This is with really crude geometry, just to show where the action is going to take place. And once we walk through it, we go back and make sure the overall mission is still fine, the gameplay is fine, and it all flows well.

"In this first part, we will get a concept artist to come in and talk about what it would look like, for example, 'This is an abandoned site, and it's this year,' and he'll do a room or two. Once that's done, we give it to the texture artists and they'll work on one hallway and one room, and once we're happy with that the level designer will take that and proliferate that and work it out. So, we take concept art, then give it to the texture artist to make textures for a small section of the map, then once that looks correct the level designer can take it and do the whole map.

"The early maps can take two months, meaning the first maps you make in the game-design process take longer because you're figuring it out. First maps you make may take two to three months, but then you know what you're going for, and in the end you can get the whole process done in a month.

"Activities and stories can get pretty huge, like with *DOOM 3* it was hundreds of pages. Coming up with a way to keep track of all of it is hard. I'm using this mind-manager program, and it is easier for taking that game design and putting it into digestible chunks for the developer to understand. Getting that across to the level designer who has to make that one map that fits into the game, they have to know about that whole map but they don't want to read about the whole game. So each section has to be self-contained. But the overall document has to be quite huge. But I'm the only person who understands that whole document.

"Each level has to have a story, and why it fits the background setting, what you do, the risks and rewards through the level, and it all has to be repeated though every level. Most of this I keep in my head.

Pinky and Sawyer from *DOOM 3*. Images courtesy of id Software, Inc. (See color plates.)

"With our brand new game, John [Carmack] isn't done with outdoor rendering technology, so until we get that, because it's a major point of the game, it's not something we'd want to demo to publishers yet. But we're still working on levels and missions. One thing that's different with this game and *DOOM 3*, for this game I'm actually working with the designers individually and having them write a lot of it. It's one of those things: 'If you want to learn something, you teach it,' and if you want someone to read something you have them write it.

"Our team is writing missions that revolve around sections of the game. We still have levels, but they revolve around a bigger world. In the new game it's a larger world, and you go in and out of a bunch of levels. It's still chapters, but the level designers have in the story, 'This is what's happening,' and they come up with what goes in the chapter, 'This is what you need, what you do, and the overall arc.' It gets more people involved. Game design is not one person's vision; one person pushes the group and the direction, but game design is the vision of everyone involved."

Backbone

"We flowchart out the gameplay, for example, an easy hover jump goes six meters, a hard jump goes eight meters, a deadly jump is eight meters over lava, and the first five levels are easy, then a little harder, and then a little harder," says lead designer Joe Morrissey on *Death Jr. II: Root of Evil*, "and what we're shooting for is eight to ten hours of play. In *DJ II*, we had 17 levels roughly, and each level was a part of a bigger world. For example, the toy cemetery is a world, so from that we come up with how many levels fit into that, and you

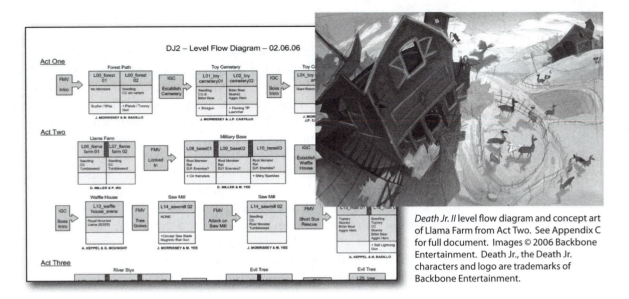

Death Jr. II level flow diagram and concept art of Llama Farm from Act Two. See Appendix C for full document. Images © 2006 Backbone Entertainment. Death Jr., the Death Jr. characters and logo are trademarks of Backbone Entertainment.

determine the level by how long you want a person to play between breaks. We're on a handheld, so people who play our game aren't on a couch in front of a big TV; they're on the train, or at school, so they need shorter levels that can't go on for hours.

"So let's say we'll have the levels be 15–20 minutes each. From that we say, 'This is how big we're going to make the levels.' I can't really have any complex platform mechanics, so I figure out that I can only have jumps and maybe a ledge grab, then you lay out what elements you want, like story elements. There's a lot that goes into it. It's crazy."

Golden Llama sketch, Llama boss sketch, and Robo Llama concept art from *Death Jr. II*. Images © 2006 Backbone Entertainment. Death Jr., the Death Jr. characters and logo are trademarks of Backbone Entertainment.

Silicon Knights

"How we approach level design is we take the storyline, the content and plot of the initial core of the game, and interweave story with the experience, with what we're tying to achieve with the story," says Denis Dyack. "We have secondary scripts that move the player along through the levels that have multiple goals—we want them to have fun, we want the content and the story that we want to tell to support beautiful visuals and the technology, and all of those things we interweave into the levels.

"We create cross-discipline committees of strike forces—music, content and story, gameplay, and the technology group. Game design has to sync up from top to bottom, so with *Too Human* [for example], we always relate back to 'What does it mean being human and being a cybernetic god?' We flesh those elements out, and we relate them back to our themes. It's very much like the process they go through in a movie—we create a movie experience *and* we're adding interactivity."

Saber Interactive

"At Saber, we have a level-design and level-scripting department," explains Saber's Matthew Karch. "We create a list of events of things we'd like to see happen in a game level, and then we come up with a theme for a particular level, whether it's a story-driven theme or a game-driven theme. Then we do a low-res blocked-out version of the basic geometry, and this is by scripters/ level designers and artists. The way we flow is by low-resing them. Well, first we start by putting things on paper, but I can't tell you how many ideas that we've come up with that sound good and look good on paper that stink in the game.

"We come up with a progression chart in Word and then test it out in a prototype. We can prototype extremely quickly, which makes it a lot easier to do these types of things effectively. So many people are having problems with off-the-shelf engine solutions; having our own technology, well, not only does it make us more valuable to publishers, it's also more valuable to us.

"Then, once we script out the gameplay so you can play these levels in low-res form—we want to make sure it works in a low-res setting, and sometimes it's *really* low-res, like just a moving block on the screen and we don't even animate it—then we do multiple testing. Then we go to high res, where we're starting to do motion capture and creating detailed lists of scenes. It starts out in iterations, low-res scripting to low-res artwork to high-res scripting."

Greg Land

Prior to joining Telltale Games, Greg Land was a level designer at LucasArts for eight and a half years. Land gives us his take on how level design fits into the process.

"Lead level design works closely with the designer and producer to basically come up with scenarios the player gets to experience. You're involved at the ground level to take the high concept and break it down into smaller chunks that players will play through. So let's say you might have different planets you play on, then you start breaking it down to smaller chunks and seeing it through to make each chunk as fun as humanly possibly, and fit that into production and technical constraints of course.

"By and large, you start with paper designs and get those approved first. And then level design is tricky because it's not always obvious. It's difficult to describe on paper the experience the person is going to have who plays the game, so a lot of level designers don't always conceive of things from that paper framework. They want to mess with things in the engines, to see what works and what's fun. So what you try to do is make it so that you allow for organic work while covering your basis with paper design. If you don't have a solid up-front plan, you're probably in trouble, or at least your producers will be very skeptical.

"Paper design usually is a top-down map, and a lot of times you will have a question list, like we created an info sheet that goes into details like: Who is in this mission? What happened just before this mission? What story elements does the mission communicate? What types of enemies will you be fighting? What type of set objects are in the level? Will it be in a Wild West saloon or out in the street—where is it going to be? So you can combine the map with a very detailed list that gives the scope and intent of the design. And it's also good to include what's the biggest payoff you're trying to achieve with the level, in other words something like, 'This level is all about blowing up these guys with the sniper rifle, and that's what I'm going to deliver.'

"And if time permits, its always good to have any other visual aids that will help communicate the design vision of the level to a broader audience—that can be photographs, materials like movie stills, or clippings, or even drawings of how you might want a layout to appear. This is largely related to action games. In level design, you're working hand-in-hand with the lead level artist as a team.

"As a lead level designer, I would work with the team to come up with these ideas and present them to the rest of the team—the artists, producers, and programmers in our team meeting, where I say this is our plan for the levels, on a high level, and the goal is to get buy-in from the team that, 'Yes, this is the type of game we want to be making.'"

Hal Barwood

"Levels in the kinds of games that I work on have to fit into the story structure, so they have to be effective and be an interactive form of chapters or of territories. If there's a serial sequence that you expect people to go through in a level, something happens and sends them to another level, it's very much like chapters. But if you want to do it in an open sandbox sort of way, you have to find ways to vary the game and ungate access to the larger world especially if it's going to have a lot of player volition involved in where you go. For example, in *Vice City* there's a hurricane warning, so you can't cross the bridge to get to a larger territory.

"The fundamental thing is to understand what the level is doing. It's a section of a game. It's a small game within itself. In today's world of real-time 3D, this often appears as chunks of architecture. But it's a mistake to think of them in the same way an architect would think about a building. You're trying to create a game experience that will unfold, and the architectural trappings are really parts of an interactive set. They're not really a building. You're trying to get through an experience, and you have to understand the visual cues, the place, and the design challenges that will pull the player through. You have to learn how to give the player as much freedom as it's useful to have without confusing the player. You have to learn when it's very important to tighten the constraints, so the player is forced through a pipe. Even RPGs and shooters have puzzles. They're usually very primitive, so you don't spend a lot of time with them.

"The secret really is interactivity. If you just cruise along through some visual world, you're not really exploring that world. Exploration isn't just the discovery of territory; it's the character discovering the territory, whether it's you or an avatar. In order to have the character come to grips with the world, you must have puzzles or if not puzzles then dismal hard work."

Tracy Fullerton

"One thing we see a lot of is that levels are about the game getting harder, but that really locks out a lot of casual players. They might be able to play some simple levels, but they can get lost in deeper levels of play. I see levels not about being more difficult, but a richer level of experience, more interesting, give it a twist and reinvigorate it without alienating people that aren't hardcore players.

"Level design in general is a very interesting thing. Something I do with students is give them a simple puzzle game and have them tweak five levels of the game. They quickly discover that by adding one or two more elements, suddenly it is wildly out of control. They didn't understand how difficult it is to create that ramp, and how different a response each player will have to the game.

"At USC, we do extensive usability testing on all student games, and this is the place where you see the biggest eye opening. They'll design the game and make it too difficult from level one, so the player's eyes will go back in their head. When I see that, I'll say, 'That's probably a level five, so let's back out and teach the player how to get there.' You haven't brought the player to that level yet—you have to lead them to it. Some of the best campaigns will subtly lead to an introduction of concepts and rampings of the story, and they're all integrated well, and when that happens that's really nice."

Corey Bridges

"Most of the MMOs out there now have one style of gameplay, that the goal is to make your character more powerful, to level up. You start off at level one, and your goal is to go to level sixty. Most MMOs have a system by which your character levels up and becomes more powerful, or parallel to that, you get better at certain skills, like sword fighting or mining or blacksmithing. So when we develop a code that lets our customers implement a skill system or leveling system in their games, first you ask, 'What's the architecture that lets them do all of these things that have been done before?' And then we think, 'Okay, what are some *other* ways that people could become more powerful in games? What other types of skill systems or leveling systems people might want to do?'

"Some games you get better at a combat skill by fighting, and you can improve that skill by practicing it—it's related to the real world. But what about a game that's based on social interaction and the way you level up is the number of friends you have, or the depth of

Screenshot from *Force of Arms*, a game by Wardog Studios on the Multiverse Network

Screenshot from a Multiverse demonstration world under construction in the Multiverse World Editor tool

friendship you have with a few people, or the breadth of friendships you have? And I don't know any games like that.

"To do that you build in layers of abstraction where you don't hard-code in something and say, 'Skills are built in this way and this way only.' What you do is put in instead this layer of abstraction, and it's an arbitrary skill, maybe it's combat and maybe it's cooking, and then you put in another level of abstraction so skills don't improve just on practice but there are other ways, and somebody decides how they get better.

"For example, let's say my game has dancing skills and you get better by eating the special pomegranate of love, or whatever the hell the trigger is. You put in the levels of abstraction so the mechanics are there to develop the gameplay structure the developer would want, without forcing them to do it one certain way.

"You could take this to ridiculous extremes, so you have to make some hard choices at some point. For example, version one of the Multiverse platform is best for games that move on terrain. But we did not include any code that will make it especially easy for somebody to do a 3D space-simulator game where every character has its own subjective up and down. Our platform doesn't keep you from doing that, but you would have to build it yourself or wait for version two. And that's one way to define the value an experienced platform-creation team brings to something like this. We have a good sense of what can be abstracted and what should be hard-coded, but we leave ways for people to build around it."

Greg LoPiccolo

"The biggest issue that we have had to get our heads around with respect to level design is that, for us, the *songs* are the levels," explains Greg LoPiccolo of Harmonix. "The design task becomes not so much to design a level in the conventional manner that pulls the player through at a prescribed pace with a prescribed amount of challenge, but more to design gameplay that flexibly interprets the song information into gameplay information and that translates differences in song tempo, arrangement, and overall style into meaningful gameplay differentiation.

"If you are making a platform game (or shooter, racing game, etc.), then you have the burden of designing the terrain to provide an environment for the player that supports your design goals. In a music game, the song *is* the terrain, and the design process is twofold: (1) design a system to allow for the interpretation of song data into gameplay data, and (2) author lots of songs using the system. Most of the action is in Step 1. Step 2 is labor-intensive and time-consuming but proceeds according to a fairly rigid rule set.

"We use comparatively junior staffers to do a lot of our song authoring, since they don't need to make big calls; they just need a decent ear for music and then need to follow the authoring rules prescribed by Step 1. Ideally, you want a metal song to seem metal when you play it, and a pop song to seem pop, but the actual process of authoring rhythm action gameplay is pretty fixed; the audio team drops gems onto the relevant spots in the musical track to outline the actual music. By the way, this will all make a lot more sense if you play *Guitar Hero*, or any Harmonix rhythm action game, for an hour or so.

"The cool and exciting thing about this approach is that you get all this cool design variety out of the source material for free, sort of. You need to craft the interpretation, and actually author the material, but the levels kind of design themselves, since the songs are already written. Every song presents its own complex and unique playscape, just derived from the composition and performance of the song itself. It's almost like you are hijacking the song for your own purposes. No one (yet!) writes music to serve as gameplay levels, but they have enough relevant attributes to make them a great source for gameplay experiences."

Mike Sellers

"Once you put your game in the box, you're done. That's the entire mindset ultimately that goes into the production process with boxed games. But that is the furthest thing from the truth with an MMOG. When it's out there for people to get their hands on it, that's when things really begin. You have to do something I think some people do better than others, and that we as humans aren't built very well to do—you have to think along emergent lines. In

Top image: sketch of StoneHenge venue in *Guitar Hero II*. Bottom two images: screenshots from *Guitar Hero II*. Images provided by Harmonix Music Systems, Inc.

designing an MMOG, you have to consider what are all of the ramifications of all the rules you give people to work with.

"For example, in *Ultima Online*, when someone near you uses a skill, you learn that skill. Let's say you want to learn to cook. But you can only have a total of 700 skills overall, and when you reach your limit and learn a new skill, the top one goes away. So people started griefing one another and playing in a way that harms someone else's game. I could go and sit down in a group and start cooking, and because I start cooking, everyone around me loses their top sword ability. So I could affect your character in a negative way without your approval, and that's a form of emergent griefing.

"If you give a player a way to create boxes, they absolutely will create swastikas, swear words, spell out their girlfriend's name, and do all kinds of things you never intended them to do with those boxes, just because they can. In one game, I got a call one day and was asked, 'Can anyone get on top of the buildings?' We had made sure when we built the game that no one could get on top of the buildings, so I said, 'No,' and they said, 'Well, someone's on top of a building.' Now, we had thought we had taken care of that, but we had shovels in the game, and these shovels were stackable. Because they were stackable, you could climb on top of them. So someone built a ramp out of shovels, walked up it, and went on top of the building. These kinds of consequences are pervasive in MMOGs, and you don't see them at all in single-player games.

"I often hear designers say, 'Well, in this game, the player does this and then the player does that.' In MMOGs you really don't know what the player is going to do. There are thousands of viewpoints, and each one is valid.

"When you're designing an MMOG, you try to think out all of the consequences ahead of time. And this is where having trusted friends with good design heads is invaluable. It happens a lot where you're in a design meeting and you come up with something and someone says, 'Okay, the first thing I'm gonna do with that is take it and misuse it.' So you try to guard against misuse, but you'll never catch it all. Something always comes up that was unexpected. 'I didn't realize that if you put that sword and these boots together something incredible happens.'"

Environments, Puzzles, and Levels Exercises

You've expanded your story treatment into a ten-page document (Chapter 4), and you have a very good start to a character bible (Chapter 5). You already have a good idea of where the story takes place and what the action is. This is your foundation for environments and levels.

1. Knowing what you know about your story and characters at this point, think about how to make the story work in ten hours of gameplay. You're going to need to expand it and chunk it out into many levels, which means more locations and potentially some mini-games or puzzles, depending on your genre.

2. Write a two-page synopsis describing the main story world in which your game takes place. Image that this document will be turned over to the lead artist on your game so they can start on sketches. It needs to be a rich and yet succinct visual description.

3. Be prepared to use this document to work on your flowchart (Chapter 9).

Environments, Puzzles, and Levels Checklist

❏ The synopsis of the world should be a rich visual description of where the action is.

❏ Consider how many hours of gameplay you'll have to create with levels, puzzles, and action.

❏ Keep puzzle development organic within the environment.

❏ Keep the action organic to the characters, story, and level design.

❏ When trying to figure out puzzles, start at the end and work your way backwards.

❏ Love your player—don't try to make the puzzle too easy, too difficult, or impossible to solve.

❏ Always keep your gameplay in mind when working on the environment.

Chapter 7
There's a Whole Lot of **Testing** Going On

"One of our most successful cases is when we worked with the Bungie team on *Halo 1*. There was a belief at that time that you couldn't create a good shooter on a console because to date they had all been on PCs, and the mouse allows for very precise control of aiming … So the Bungie team asked us to help them with aiming mechanics on the console."

—**Dennis Wixon**

From concept to completion, there's a whole of lot of testing going on in a game's development cycle. This of course depends on the company, but testing can be part of the process with everyone from marketing in the early stages to QA at the end. But we're not talking about bug testing here.[1] We're talking about putting the product in front of its potential users and getting feedback from people who don't make games for a living.

There's a lot to be said for talking with others who don't have the same skewed sense of reality that you do. But sometimes, people in our industry think "Why bother?" On the one hand, you're an expert at what you do, and you should know what works, what doesn't, and why. Some people think this is good enough. Sometimes it is. Sometimes it isn't. Because on the other hand, after a while you're not looking at the game with fresh eyes. And things can come up for inexperienced or new users that you would never even have in your peripheral vision. So it's good to have your market, game players, tell you what they think is cool and what isn't, and find out what doesn't work for them, because remember, you're the kind of game designer who loves your players. And besides, if you work with one of those big publishers on a AAA title, you have no choice—testing is part of the package.

From her beginning in the industry, Tracy Fullerton has been a true believer in the power of focus testing. "Somehow I lucked out very early in

---

1 Also known as *recon* (at Microsoft, for instance) or *game balancing*.

my career, doing that first casual game with Microsoft. They have a strict policy on user testing, and they took the game and focus-tested it and came back with improvements; they were so great. I became a believer right away. Sony did it. Intel did it. It always surprises me when I work with big companies and they don't do testing. Or they do it at the end. What are you going to do with it then? That's one of the reasons that when we started the program at USC, one of the first things we did was build the usability-testing lab. And I am hoping to ingrain in them this process so when they go out and work on a project they'll say, 'When are we gonna test it?'"

One of the first focus tests an IP encounters is usually in its embryonic stage, when a developer pitches to a publisher and gets them interested enough to consider doing the title. As Rob Huebner pointed out earlier, a publisher won't even commit to a project until marketing has done focus testing on it. Huebner's current project is *Lost King*, but he adds, "*Lost King* is the working title; it will not be the final title. It's all a marketing decision. It's very marketing driven. They focus test everything."

Focus testing can happen in a lot of different ways, from casual conversations with a couple of friends and acquaintances at a party, to detailed computerized analysis of a highly targeted group's gameplay. In the algebra game I mentioned in Chapter 5, we did several rounds of focus testing to validate and inform. These tests took place in very impressive professional focus-testing facilities and involved the highly coveted one-way–mirror approach. On one side of the mirror sat our facilitator and the guinea pigs in a rather large conference room, and on the other side in a smaller, tastefully decorated and comfortable room with a few rows of chairs set up theatre style was our team—the producer-designer, director, writer-designer, and at various times the lead SME,[2] lead artist, and lead programmer, depending on the particular focus-test topic.

For this project, the focus test was conducted by a highly trained, and I might add very effective, marketing person who really knew how to get the audience to open up and glean valuable information from them. We listened in, took notes, ate donuts, and went back to work enlightened. We got to eat donuts on several occasions. The many focus tests we did informed the game concept, the aforementioned character development, story development, and the overall game, including tone, fun factor, and playability.

Focus testing occurred again at the end of development, when it was time to name the product. Marketing met with the team, we gave our suggestions,

---

2 Subject-matter expert.

they added their own ideas, and focus tested for a title. This was not done by our regular fabulous focus tester, whom we all loved and adored, nor were we invited to sit in. Consequently, they ended up with an awful title as far as the team was concerned. We protested. Marketing won. And so it goes. Except for the "title issue," this rated as one of the better focus-testing experiences. Many are not run so well, or by someone so capable. We were lucky.

Sometimes focus testing is a very casual affair that happens a little more spontaneously throughout the development cycle—friends and family focus testing. This isn't necessarily a bad thing; it's just very different from the serious corporate testing scenario above. Maybe it involves getting the neighbor's kid to bring a few of his friends over to talk to you about what they like and don't like about certain kinds of games, which they all play all of the time. Or maybe they're giving you feedback about your game in particular during a specific phase of development. You give them pizza, they get to tell you what they'd do if they were in your position, and a fun time is had by all. The people might change depending on the type of game. The activity you bring them in for might change, depending on where you are in the development cycle. The food is usually pizza, though. All in all, it's the same sort of process. Sometimes this works great. Sometimes, not so much.

In the case of *CSI*, they did a little from column A and a little from column B. They discovered in market research that their audience consisted primarily of "fans of the show, 70% of whom were females, and 57% of whom were over the age of 35." Telltale and Ubisoft knew their market was the same demographic as the casual-games market.

Telltale was taking the franchise, which already had three 2D titles, and expanding the gameplay and hopefully the market by creating a new 3D game. They discovered in their *CSI* study that over 90% of the people who had played the game had rated it excellent, 72% had played two or more of the titles, and there was an 80% completion rate. They did focus testing and targeted people who had *not* played games to get some fresh perspective on opening up the market.

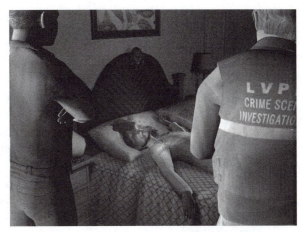

CSI: Hard Evidence victim in bedroom. Image courtesy of Ubisoft.

The audience was looking for "authenticity to the show and an uncomplicated user experience," says Dan Conners, Telltale's CEO. According to Conners and Greg Land, the lead designer on *CSI 3* and *CSI 4*, they also used the friends-and-family method of focus testing. "Around the office, it was, 'Hey, did you call your mom yet? Is your sister around?'"

One of the things that the *CSI* focus testing informed was the game's system specs. Since their primary market is about as far away from hard-core gamers as you can get, the users were not likely to have the latest and greatest technology with which to play the game. They were also very interested in getting those repeat 2D players to play the new 3D version. And while they wanted to wow their audience with the way the game looked, they did not want to lead them down a path of frustration with multiple disks and high specs that created problems with their computers. "We didn't want to alienate the 2D players, so we aligned with the *Sims 2* minimum specs and leveraged the strengths of our engine," explains Conners. "Everything is really low poly[3], but we made strategic use of shaders. We had a strategic approach to not being poly hungry."

Focus testing can help you align your product throughout its development cycle. And there are many approaches to getting that critical feedback. Sometimes the developer initiates the testing, and sometimes the publisher requires it at certain stages.

If you happen to be working with Microsoft as your publisher, it's a seriously complete process. They pull out all stops. They have focus testing down to a science. And if you want to call in the big guns, Dennis Wixon is your man.

Dennis Wixon on *Halo, Forza,* and *Age of Empires*

When it comes to uber focus testing, the crème de la crème is Microsoft Game Studios in Redmond, Washington, where Dennis Wixon is the user research manager who oversees the many levels of testing on products. Wixon and his team have focus testing down to a science, and their findings have informed some of the industry's most well-known games. Wixon explains how things work in his department and uses specific examples from *Halo, Forza,* and *Age of Empires* to illustrate how the testing process they put the games through improved the gameplay and the user's experience.

"How this differs from other kinds of testing," explains Wixon, "is that we don't do the kind of quality assurance often known as bug testing that other teams sometimes do. There's a testing team that tests for bugs at Microsoft. We don't do any of that. It's also called different things in different companies. Here it's called recon. At other places it's called game balance, where they hire

---

[3] Low polygon—using a small number of polygons to approximate a three-dimensional model.

people on an hourly basis with a fair amount of expertise in a particular kind of game to play through it and give feedback. That's not what we do. The differentiation is we are testing our target audience for the game. If it's a casual game, we test casual users. If it's shooters, we bring in people experienced in those and test the game for the audience for which it was intended. That is where our work really lies.

"One way to look at our job is that it's to take questions that designers and program managers have about user experience and turn them into usable researchable questions. How do you take questions and morph them into meaningful questions you can collect data on and turn that back around to program managers, executive producers, people on the business side, and help them make trade-offs and decisions? That is the essence of the work we do.

"Another way to characterize our work is that all games begin with design intent—designers intend users to have a certain experience. This experience can be created by visuals, storyline, characterization, but the differentiation is that games have a set of mechanics, behaviors that users have to use to move through the game. In all other forms of entertainment, the users don't have to do anything. They're meaningful emotional experiences, but they don't have the same level of intensity because that behavioral element has the potential to make games an intense experience that most other mediums can't really match. And that's where most of our research and testing lie. The intended experience should be created in part by mechanics of the game, and we can bring people in to see, 'Did the mechanics deliver, or was there a blocker that gets in the way of that?' A large part of our job is to uncover those blockers and make it more straightforward for people to get to the fun of the game, to the emotional intensity of it, and that ranges from the installation and set-up of the game to the details of how that game is played, the mechanics of the game.

"One of our most successful cases is when we worked with the Bungie team on *Halo 1*. There was a belief at that time that you couldn't create a good shooter on a console because to date they had all been on PCs, and the mouse allows for very precise control of aiming. And with a console, you just have small thumb sticks, and you can't do a good shooter because you can't aim well. And aiming is a fundamental mechanic of a shooter—you have to be able to aim well to be a success on a shooter. So the Bungie team asked us to help them with aiming mechanics on the console.

"There were a few shooters before *Halo* on consoles, and we brought them into our lab and had people come in and play them. This was a typical usability lab where we talk to people as they play and videotape them playing.

And what we found was that people typically tended to overcorrect as they played. They would be to the left of the target and they'd push the joystick and then they'd be too far to the right, so they'd push it back to the left and then they'd be too far to the left, so they'd push it back to the right and they'd be too far to the right again, and then the left, and the right, and back and forth and *finally* they could end up being on target. That's not a very rewarding kind of experience, and it was a fundamental problem with aiming.

"So we took that information and worked with the *Halo* team on the mechanics of aiming. Targets in *Halo 1* have a certain amount of gravity. What that means is that as you get close to the target, the targeting reticle tends to zero in on the target—it's just like the target has gravity. What's really happening is the gain on the joystick is slowing down, which minimizes the overcorrection we were seeing on the joystick. A key breakthrough was getting that tuning right. And at the same time we found a few other things, like targeting vertical was more difficult than targeting horizontal. So in the early parts of the game there was more horizontal targeting play to get people used to the tasks.

"The second thing we found was in a game you're always trying to get the right level of challenge. You can't be too simple or it's not fun. [Nolan] Bushnell's famous quote is something along the lines of, 'A game should be easy to pick up and impossible to master.' We want that sweet spot where there's always another threshold to cross. In *Halo 1*, as we improved targeting, we found it was too intelligent and too simple. It was pretty straightforward for the Bungie team to fix that—they could make the targets move more, or seem to move more. For example, the grunts talk, and talking makes them seem more intelligent and more active, even though the mechanics are the same as if they don't talk. So we can change the details of perception.

"In addition, we found that when we'd run tests there are little things you can tweak that will make a big difference in the game. In our original test in *Halo 1*, half the people wanted the joystick to work like a mouse, and the other half wanted it to work like an aircraft control. And each of these groups felt very strong about this. The difference is, if you push the thumb stick forward, should the reticle go down or up, and if you pull it back should it go up or down? There were strong differences between people. They were very opinionated about this, with lines drawn in the sand. So, in *Halo 1*, as the master chief is being brought out of cryo, he's getting used to being thawed out and they have him go through this exercise looking up or down, and they ask him if that's working for him or if he'd like it reversed. The user is stetting it up—it's built right into the game, and they don't even remember actually setting the preference.

"Another problem arose because of the spaceship design. Bungie had designed a very complex spaceship, and when the master chief was first brought out, the player would get lost wandering around the spaceship. Now, it's not that fun to get lost, in life or in a game. So as soon as the master chief is lost, a marine comes out and says, 'We need to get to the bridge, sir; follow me,' and we put markers on the floor to the bridge.

"There are a couple of things working with Bungie that we did in *Halo 1*, and it is one of our best success cases. One is tuning of aiming, tuning of a very specific design mechanic that has to be right in the game because it's fundamental to the game. The other thing is noticing things users do and exposing those and coming up with really creative solutions. It's a very close relationship between user research and design that goes a long way to making the games successful.

"Relative success of both *Halo 1* and *2* is kind of legendary from a business perspective. We saw about a 60% attach rate between *Halo 1* and the Xbox. If you take the number of consoles out there, and how many games sold with the console, 60% of the Xboxes being sold were sold with *Halo 1*. You could make a case that *Halo* contributed substantially to the Xbox as a viable platform for people to play games on. Truth in advertising—this is our greatest sort of success story. But there are other ones that are not quite as compelling from a business and design perspective, but still very telling stories.

"For example, if you play *Forza* on the Xbox, you'd notice this thing called a drive line. As you're driving on the track, you'll see a green line of arrows that will turn yellow if you're going too fast and red if you're going *really* too fast. For a person who doesn't normally play a driving sim game, the hardest thing to learn is steering and speed. The drive line helps them get more in the groove.

"The reason I like the drive line so much is that we uncovered a lot of problems users were having staying on track. The drive line was not part of the game originally, but it *was* something the *Forza* team was using in testing internally. Once we found out they were already using it, we said, 'We could expose that to the users,' and that was a great idea. And it's one of our more successful elements of *Forza*—if you've never played a drive game you could pick it up and start to learn how to drive with it.

"Those are the kind of examples we love to see, and they're happening at various levels all the time in game design and development. In *Halo 2* there were hundreds of spec changes made to the game as a result of our working closely with Bungie designers and testing the game as much as we possibly could throughout development."

Classic Usability Test

"We have three different kinds of categories that testing fits in. One is the classic usability test—you bring in a small number of people, test in a room with a one-way mirror with the design team often watching, and this can occur in the development cycle whenever there's something to test. In *Halo 1*, we were testing aiming before *Halo* had aiming because we brought in competitors. That is useful because it can focus on a specific part of a game, because you're giving the user something specific to do and talking to the user as they test. If graphics are not complete or some other element is not complete it doesn't really matter. We can focus on elements the design team is interested in and uncover really interesting elements. This can occur any time during the development cycle."

Play Test

"The second kind of testing is play test. We bring in groups of people and tell them, 'Play this game the way you would at home if you just took it out of the box.' We test in groups, and we do collect video but we don't interact with them while they're testing, and we give them fairly extensive questionnaires when they're done—'What are you feeling and thinking about your experience in the game? How do you feel about the graphics? How do feel about the controls?' The challenge of the game at various levels. It's designed to get more at the quantitative elements. We do this on our competitors within a few weeks of when a competitor releases a game, and we do it on our games when they're in final forms just before they're released to manufacturing so we get a comparison of our own games and the competitors in the same genre.

"We also do this in the early parts of game development, but we're more focused. We will give them a specific task to do, and then have them fill in a questionnaire so we get their reaction. Because we're testing groups and getting value responses, we need the game to be more developed—a little more complete and a little more polished. In the play-test lab, the game has to be pretty much robust so that 15 to 50 people can play it for an hour or two without crashing."

Instrumented Testing

"Third is instrumented testing, where we actually tap into the activities that people are doing as they play the game. One way to describe this is that most games collect information about what the users are doing—did they die, kill a boss, which weapons are they using, how much ammunition do they have, etc.—the game needs to know that to work. We work with the tools and technology team (TNT), and they put hooks into the game to collect that data to see what kind of progress users are making.

"So we can collect that data and produce graphs on how many people are dying at what point and what is killing people at that point in time. And then this information goes back to the design team to see, 'Is it performing the way we expected it to?' If they get through the mission in ten minutes, is that happening because it's supposed to be taking them ten minutes, or is it supposed to be taking them an hour and they're getting it done in ten minutes anyway? Maybe 30% of the people are expected to die, but everybody is dying. We're collecting that data, and we have the tools to analyze that data within a few minutes of when it's collected. We can provide feedback on how well users are actually doing, and is that what the designers had hoped or intended them to do?

"We used to have to make a trade-off between quantitative work collecting surveys and qualitative work with video feedback. Now we can collect in qualitative ways and find that too many people are dying. Why? From plasma grenades. Where are they coming from? Oh, the grunts are throwing them. Now let's look at a particular user and see how that's happening. We know why people are dying, and we can retune the game, get the data very quickly, and give designers a point to get into that is in line with the intent the designers had originally. It's been a great breakthrough in the last couple of years, these new tools that allow us to get that specific.

"This is what we do 'routinely.' Collecting that kind of data is an extremely complex undertaking. Remember, were collecting on a game as it's being developed, not after it's done. We can test 15 to 50 people over an entire weekend, each playing six hours at a time, and have data including video on all those people in reports by Tuesday. That's a pretty amazing accomplishment, and you could not do that in a usability lab—it's detailed data on a few people versus detailed data on a lot of people.

"Instrumented tests can be on people playing for just an hour or two, but they can also run on weekends and be on people who play for six hours. One of the great things about games is people will come in and play on weekends. We can 'type' them in terms of their experience with various genres, so when Bungie would ask for one lab full of people experienced in shooters and then another lab filled with people that are only moderately experienced in shooter games, we can get down to that level of detail. Each lab will handle 17 people at a time and we have three labs so we can test 52 people simultaneously, in different genres, with different experiences, and on different games. We will run between 7,000 to 15,000 test sessions per year. That's more than any other game publisher anywhere."

RITE Testing and *Age of Empires II*

"In both serious and more casual games we do an approach called *RITE testing*.[4] The way this was developed was that *Age of Empires II* came to us and said, 'We would like to expand the market for RTS games, but RTS games are pretty complicated. So we want to design an excellent tutorial for it, but we only have six weeks to do it, but we can send our best tutorial designer to work with you for six weeks.'

"In a typical usability test, you run 8 to 15 people through, and it takes a period of about two weeks, and then you get a report that tells you about issues and problems you uncovered, and people will discuss them in meetings, and they'll make changes, or maybe they'll argue about it—'Did you test the right people?' for example. People don't like to be handed, 'Here's 100 things wrong with your product,' and they don't always welcome your findings with open arms.

"So in RITE testing, we decided to flip things around. Since the designer was here, he sat in the lab with us and watched the tests. At the end of the day we asked (1) what are all the problems we saw—do we have agreement on these, (2) given that we saw this problem, do we think we understand what caused that problem, and do we have agreement on that, and (3) now that we're in agreement on (1) and (2), do we think we have a fix for it and are we in agreement of what that fix is? And the designers would have a fix for it, maybe make a conceptual sketch, and it would be something they'd all agree to. The next day, the designer would make the changes in the tutorial, and then the next day we would run another test. And at the end of the day we'd ask (1) did the problem show up again, and if it didn't then we knew we fixed the problem, and (2) if it did show up we knew we were wrong about the cause and we had to fix the fix.

"When working very close with the design team, and at the end of two weeks, what you have instead of a report, you have actually a game that has been improved in one way or another, and not only improved, but you now have documented evidence that this fix we put in worked. If you put the fix in and it never showed up again, problem solved. You get a more improved game.

"Also, you discover more problems this way. Because in the old ways of testing, you would see the same problems come up over and over instead of seeing new stuff. Now once you fix the problem, you have the opportunity to see new stuff you probably wouldn't have gotten to see before because the bigger problems were always in the way. The final thing is that this changes the relationship between user research and design—you're now working together

---

[4] Rapid iterative testing and evaluation.

to make a better game as quickly as you can—you're working toward that goal in a high level but this makes it very specific and concrete, and at the end of two weeks you have a demonstrably better game instead of a big report that's all about what's screwed up.

"With our teams, once they do it, they don't want to work any other way. Folks from big huge companies working on RTS games tell us, 'We get more work done in two weeks with you than we would get done in three months.' We've done this on games like *Rise of Nations*, and it's very effective and very rewarding. It was highly successful in *Age II*—we uncovered all kinds of stuff and did all kinds of tweaks, and *Age II* was highly successful commercially, and the people involved think they expanded the market because of the tutorial success."

Testing Exercise

You now have a clear idea of what the key components are in your game. It's time to run them by your audience

1. Identify a few key titles in your genre that could be considered competition for your game (if you say there is no competition, you're not thinking creatively enough, and you're certainly not thinking the way a publisher would want you to be thinking—there's always something that could be considered your competition).

2. Do a small friends and family focus testing. Based on your answer to the question above, find some friends and family (no more than five people) who have some experience with these games (this would suggest that they are in your target market), invite them over, order some pizzas (optional, but a good move), and discuss with them what they like and don't like about the competition. Take notes. Eat pizza. Thank your participants.

3. Assemble your notes, decide which information is valuable and useful, and compare to your game. Notice similarities with their feedback and your game, and *adjust your treatment* as necessary/desired to attend to the problem areas and enhance where possible.

4. Once you're happy with your treatment, pull together another session, this time specifically to get feedback on *your* game. Don't ask anyone who loves you to participate in this session. Points to keep in mind:

    (a) Be organized in your approach. Have questions ready before you bring people together.

(b) Keep the amount of questions to a reasonable number—this should be more like 20 questions, not 200 questions.

(c) Assemble questions about the gameplay, characters, location, experience, etc. This can be text-based questions, questions about visuals like character or game sketches, or some sort of mock-up or prototype of your game.

(d) Do not judge responses—stay neutral. You're just gathering information.

(e) Do not justify any elements of your game, whether someone says they do or do not like something—stay neutral. You're just gathering information.

(f) Have fun.

(g) Thank your participants.

5. Assemble your notes. Decide which information is valid and useful. Adjust your games as necessary. Repeat if desired.

Testing Checklist

❏ Know your genre.

❏ Know your market.

❏ Know what experience you want users to have when they play your game.

❏ Decide the results you want from your testing before you begin. For example, are you looking for character feedback, gameplay feedback, etc.

❏ Be prepared with questions before you bring in a focus group.

❏ Test your game with the audience for which it is intended—choose an appropriate focus group.

❏ Keep the testing to a reasonable amount of time.

❏ Do not judge your users' comments during testing.

❏ Do not justify your game during testing.

❏ If you're asked questions, be sure to avoid giving leading answers.

Chapter 8
The Many Faces of **GDDs**

"As soon as people don't understand what's going on, then they start to bitch about things."

—Tim Willits

And now for the juicy stuff! There is no subject more controversial in this industry than the topic of game-design documents, a.k.a. GDDs. Generally speaking, those who have a history of working with companies that use design docs are walking testimonials for them. Those who have worked with companies that go straight to prototyping and iterate through a design swear that this is the only way to go. The perception, on both sides, is that the *other* process is a waste of time and money.

The truth of the matter, of course, lies somewhere in between, and this is based purely on reality: (1) if you want a publisher to give you $10+ million, you're going to have to cough up something for them to invest in, which means a solid design explained in some sort of convincing documentation, and (2) every design requires changes midstream, so you must be both willing and able to work around problems, come up with creative fixes, and understand that you're going to have elements in your game that were not in your original plans.

Honestly, nobody in any professional capacity in this business suggests going directly from the idea stage into coding without some degree of pencil-to-paper design work up front. Where the controversy arises is in determining how much design is enough before jumping into production.

The culprit of all of this divisiveness seems to lie in the differences between two programming methodologies: classic vs. extreme.

"Extreme programming is a programming philosophy that is very germane to this industry," says Greg LoPiccolo of Harmonix. "Approximately 10 years ago, they came up with this revolutionary software-development set of theories.[1] In the classic theory of design, you make sure you have a really solid design and plan it out in detail before you do any coding. Extreme programming has revolutionary tenants, like everybody always programs in pairs, and you code to throw away. In classic, the coding is redundant, it's robust, and it has well-defined interfaces to other pieces of code.

"In extreme, you work as quickly as possible and don't worry about the quality of the code. You expect to throw code away, so you build and review and revise, and you have that process—of build, review, revise—as tight as possible. A lot of the more progressive houses have familiarity with extreme processes. It is totally relevant to the way we work."

Extreme programming, or XP, is an agile software development methodology. Where agile means the ability to rapidly change direction, repeatedly throughout the development process. The thought is that this reduces costs in the long run, avoiding design specs that are cast in concrete on the front end, which require costly change orders to fix in the middle, and reducing the crunch factor at the end.

Opponents of XP believe this approach is actually more costly with wasted coding throughout the entire process, and that it encourages the dreaded feature creep. The philosophy in XP is that this methodology better lends itself to meeting the changing needs of the customer, and therefore the project, and henceforth improves quality and time to market. For a philosophy that espouses flexibility, it originally had some very disciplined prescribed practices, and it still does. And yet, true to its mandate, it has been flexible enough to evolve as people work with it as a methodology.

There is a lot of waste in XP by its very nature, and this is acknowledged by proponents and opponents alike. Coding is considered king, as you might expect. But in XP, there is absolutely no problem with coding a bunch of different options to see which one best solves a particular problem, keeping the best/simplest solution, and tossing the rest. Whereas in a more traditional approach you program for excellence, in XP you program for expedience. And as LoPiccolo explained, you're *expected* to throw code away.

Major problems can and do occur on projects when there is a lack of communication about the approach being used in development. When part of the team spends time creating specs and design documents that are turned over to another part of the team that doesn't read design docs and is looking for a more informal approach to communicating needs, a lot can be lost

---

[1] Created in 1996 for the Chrysler Comprehensive Compensation System by Kent Beck, Ward Cunningham, and Ron Jeffries and released in a book entitled *Extreme Programming Explained* in 1999 by Kent Beck.

in translation. Mostly because nobody even considered that they needed a translator.

Classic programming relies on a strict method of communicating changes. XP often relies on a loose and free style and can be as informal as walking into an office or picking up the phone and saying something along the lines of, "Hey, listen, you know that thing we talked about? Yeah, let's do that." There's often no documentation of the request or the change, or the direction the project is headed. When things go wrong with this process, it's usually because of miscommunication. The team of designers and developers are literally and figuratively not on the same page. It's chaos. And it's maddening. And people become unhappy very fast. The toll it takes is sometimes fatal to the project.

Anybody who has worked for any amount of time in this industry will tell you they've worked on more projects that have been cancelled than on titles that have been published. Poor planning and lousy communication are big contributing factors to this unfortunate phenomenon.

> "There's a saying that anybody who builds anything is familiar with—it's 'measure twice, cut once.' And there's a reason for that. You want to be sure of what you're going to do. And when you don't follow that, it gets you… As a publisher, I would be hesitant to invest several million dollars into a moving target."
>
> **—Chris Ferriter, Ubisoft**

"I cringe when I hear people say, 'We just want to start building,'" says Chris Ferriter, producer at Ubisoft. "My thought is great, we feel better because we've started producing something, but at the end of the day we're going to have to take stock of what we're making and say okay we're on target, great, we got lucky, or we're off target, and in very bad situations we need to invest more money, get more staff, or kill this project because it's not what we thought it was in the beginning.

"There are various reasons why things get killed, but when somebody pitches a game or you get a developer to do work for hire to build a product, and you don't spend enough time in the beginning to clarify what the publisher's goals are for that project and what the developer can commit to on the project, it can be a recipe for disaster. Down the road, the publisher says, 'This isn't at all what I thought we were getting,' or the developer says, 'We underestimated what it would take to deliver what you wanted,' and nobody's happy."

And it's no fun at all working on a project that has this kind of fatal flaw. "The worst situation is where you don't know who's running the show, who you're supposed to be talking to," says Matt Costello, "and you don't have the clear vision that there's someone steering the ship. That's not good at all."

Where's the Beef?

Nobody minds reading a movie script. Many people complain about reading a design document.

Historically speaking, design docs have always been huge. I have accumulated many three-inch binders stuffed with documentation, and that's *per game*. Contrast that to a movie script, which is typically somewhere around 110-120 pages. A complete, final interactive script, not including flowcharts, early design work, asset lists, character and story bibles, and separate dialog script can easily come in at 500 pages. As a screenwriter, it might take a year, or two, or three, to complete a screenplay. As a designer-writer on a game, the most insane timeline I've had has been as little as 6 weeks to design a project and write those 500 pages. A movie lasts for about two hours. A game usually plays for anywhere between 10 and 40 hours. So, really, if you're just looking at the ratio of paper for the script, versus entertainment time, it's not so bad.

> "The biggest challenge in leading a game-design team is making sure everyone knows what they're doing, because developers are notoriously bad about not reading design docs and emails. It's important to make sure everybody is on the same page. As soon as people don't understand what's going on, then they start to bitch about things. You solve this with constant human contact. Small meetings, discussions, explaining over and over again what you want, what you're trying to accomplish. If you hand an artist a 300-page document, you might as well just throw it out the window. You need to put it in small chunks."
>
> —Tim Willits

But the problem with developers when it comes to design docs is the volume of paper and the need to know what's in those docs in minutia. For starters, nobody wants to read 500 pages. And as you get into development and you need to find just one little piece of information about a feature in the game, again, you don't want to have to look through 500 pages, or worse, a half dozen three-inch binders, to find what you're looking for. And while more and more companies are using a wiki to keep track of design specs, again, there's the searching. So, rather than looking for the proverbial needle in the haystack, it's easier for people to just ask somebody for the information they need. This is where Costello and Willits point out that there needs to be someone who is the keeper of all of this information.

Another solution is to create smaller design docs. This happens organically in the beginning of a project. "I like to lay out how I see my work developing," says Costello when he starts a project with a developer, "that we're going to start very small and build out from there. Basically this includes who the characters are, the world, a little background and then the next steps, and then signing off each step of the document. This naturally leads to a larger document, but everybody has signed off so there are no surprises along the way—they saw it when it was three paragraphs long." There's an added bonus with developing docs this way, says Costello. "It's a good way to maintain enthusiasm because people always have comments and you can easily incorporate them—it's a very back-and-forth process."

When Costello worked on *Just Cause*, he had this kind of relationship with the producer, who acted as the key point person, expanding the concepts with his team and Costello. "He takes it and broadens it out with key members from the development team. That's probably the best way, when the producer and the writer can sort of develop and nurture the idea a bit and then bring other people in.

"In the case of, say, *DOOM 3*, I went out there and met with them and got some feeling of what they wanted to do and what they needed. The original *DOOM* didn't have a lot of story or world behind it, so that had to be built. Tim showed me what they were thinking. Then I worked on the backstory doc of what was going on on Mars before all hell broke loose, then on what's happening on Earth, then they got the documentation and gave me feedback."

Nowhere is it more apparent that every project is different than with design documents. Here are some a project might include:

- Executive summary or pitch document—a global look at the game, the mechanics, story and characters, plus the team, the competition, the market, and a production schedule.

- Concept outline—a brief outline of a few paragraphs to a couple of pages on the concept of the game. This is the evolution of what comes out of brainstorming; an overview.

- Context outline—this is similar to a step outline in movies, in which each scene is stepped out, literally outlining the entire movie on a scene-by-scene basis; it's an outline of all of the components of the game within context of one another. In this case, the game is stepped out with what happens with the main characters, the storyline, and the gameplay from beginning to end.

> *"Every project is unique, so when it's done I put it on the shelf and move on to the next new project."*
>
> **—Matt Costello**

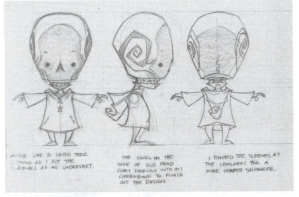

Sketches and concept art of DJ turning for *Death Jr. II*. Images © 2006 Backbone Entertainment. Death Jr., the Death Jr. characters and logo are trademarks of Backbone Entertainment. (See color plates.)

From top: concept art of DJ in action, render of DJ, game mechanics for the PSP, in-game dialogue, and voice-over list documents for *Death Jr. II*.

Images © 2006 Backbone Entertainment. Death Jr., the Death Jr. characters and logo are trademarks of Backbone Entertainment.

See Appendix C for full game mechanics document. Courtesy of Backbone Entertainment.

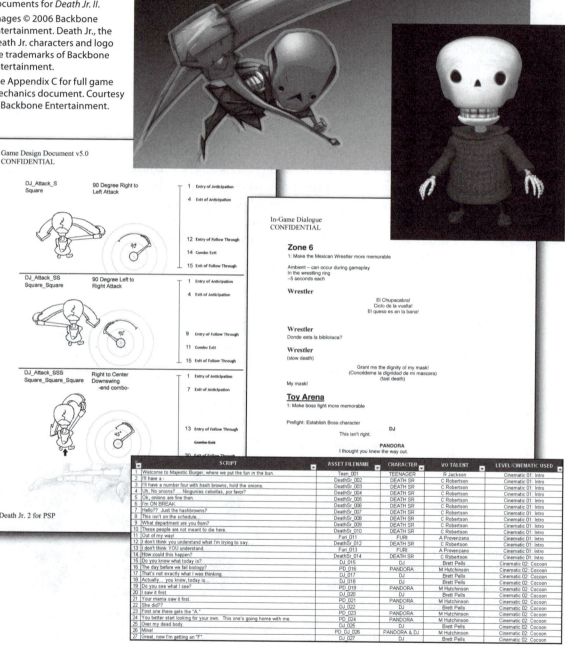

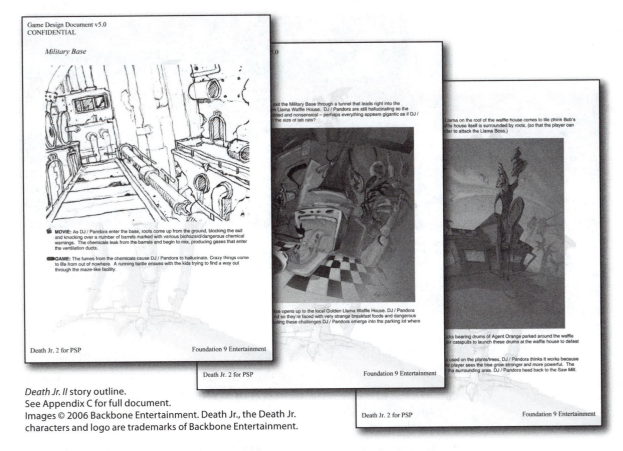

Death Jr. II story outline.
See Appendix C for full document.
Images © 2006 Backbone Entertainment. Death Jr., the Death Jr.
characters and logo are trademarks of Backbone Entertainment.

Usually this is agreed upon in a big-picture sense, before going into further detail. This can also be given to level designers to build out levels.

- Bibles—characters and story are thoroughly explained to help inform art, the flowcharts, and the script.

- Flowcharts—worthy of a chapter of their own, flowcharts are used for a variety of purposes, such as working out the flow of the environments, the story, and/or the characters' moves.

- Script—because this is a linear representation—page after page—of a nonlinear medium, the script becomes gigantic. It is used in conjunction with the context outline and the flowcharts to make sure everything is captured. It can include narrative, action, camera direction, cinematic scenes, and dialog.

- Asset lists—charts containing all of the art assets, props, environments, and characters that need to be developed for the game.

Sketch and screenshot of Majestic Burger venue for *Death Jr. II.*
Images © 2006 Backbone Entertainment. Death Jr., the Death Jr.
characters and logo are trademarks of Backbone Entertainment.

- Dialog script—this is all of the dialog pulled out of the overall script, so that the talent can easily go through their recording process. The dialog script is presented in the same format as a movie script, usually without any narrative, and includes things like 35 ways to say "hello," or "stop," or whatever.

- Cinematics script—this is the same format as a movie script and covers the cut scenes and cinematics of the game only; smaller than the entire game script, it does include narrative and so is more in context than a dialog script.

Now, back to the "every project is different" concept. This is the kind of documentation that a designer, or a lead designer, or a level designer, or an artist, or a writer, or a writer-designer, or a designer-producer, or a producer, might be asked to create for the project. In some cases these documents are created as a team effort at various stages and then *somebody* (listed above) will be asked to go off and pull the document together, expand it, and get it back to the group. In other instances, it is only a team effort in the very early stages of game design, and then *somebody* is in charge of making sure all iterations that occur are documented and kept in a centrally located place. Some companies might do all of these documents, and some might do none of them.

The other tricky thing about documentation is that it gets used not only in various degrees but at various times throughout the process. Some companies might be diligent in their documentation from the beginning. Usually, people are good about producing documentation when money is on the line, meaning they'll do it to hook a publisher and then often they let it slide after they get a green light. Other times people stick to keeping documentation up-to-date throughout the process. Here are some scenarios:

- Come up with a new game, write some minimal documentation to get a demo built to pitch to a publisher.
- Publisher says "maybe," but needs more specifics, so the requested documentation is written to get a contract.
- Publisher says "yes," so the project is greenlit but requires pre-production milestones to be met.
  - In some cases this includes a requirement for more documentation, which now has to be passed by the publisher for approval at every step of the way, and this is built into the contract.
  - In some cases the publisher just wants to make sure the milestones are met but they don't need to see any more docs, so companies drop their documentation efforts. If they're well managed, this can work. If they're not, the project risks being killed.

For companies that do not work with a majority of these design documents, they have other methods of making sure things stay on track. It's scheduling, scheduling, scheduling. That's the case with Harmonix.

"The basic challenge we have," explains LoPiccolo, "and the fundamental problem we're trying to solve, is to have a high degree of scheduling rigor and focus, but at the same time have the ability to be really flexible and to adjust our plan very quickly in response to changing circumstances. And those two things are very difficult to reconcile on an ongoing basis. So our planning is built on the ability to do that, and the reason that's important is because the kind of games we make are innovative games, so we don't have the luxury of assuming the design is going to work."

Image provided by Harmonix Music Systems, Inc.

The way Harmonix approaches this dilemma is with tight and flexible scheduling. Every six weeks they figure out the big picture, detail what needs to happen during the next six weeks, and then break that down into one-week increments, then daily tasks. This kind of structure helps them get products out in very short development cycles and minimizes crunch. The team feels secure with the structure this kind of scheduling provides, because there's no ambiguity.

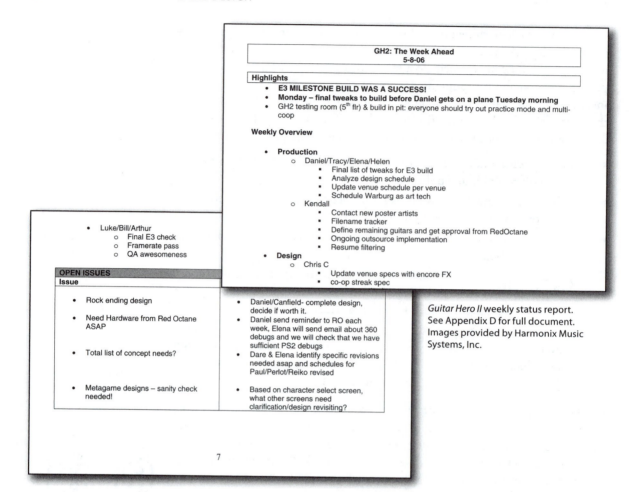

GH2: The Week Ahead
5-8-06

Highlights
- **E3 MILESTONE BUILD WAS A SUCCESS!**
- **Monday – final tweaks to build before Daniel gets on a plane Tuesday morning**
- GH2 testing room (5th flr) & build in pit: everyone should try out practice mode and multi-coop

Weekly Overview

- **Production**
  - Daniel/Tracy/Elena/Helen
    - Final list of tweaks for E3 build
    - Analyze design schedule
    - Update venue schedule per venue
    - Schedule Warburg as art tech
  - Kendall
    - Contact new poster artists
    - Filename tracker
    - Define remaining guitars and get approval from RedOctane
    - Ongoing outsource implementation
    - Resume filtering
- **Design**
  - Chris C
    - Update venue specs with encore FX
    - co-op streak spec

- Luke/Bill/Arthur
  - Final E3 check
  - Framerate pass
  - QA awesomeness

OPEN ISSUES

Issue	
• Rock ending design	• Daniel/Canfield- complete design, decide if worth it.
• Need Hardware from Red Octane ASAP	• Daniel send reminder to RO each week, Elena will send email about 360 debugs and we will check that we have sufficient PS2 debugs
• Total list of concept needs?	• Dare & Elena identify specific revisions needed asap and schedules for Paul/Perlot/Reiko revised
• Metagame designs – sanity check needed!	• Based on character select screen, what other screens need clarification/design revisiting?

7

Guitar Hero II weekly status report. See Appendix D for full document. Images provided by Harmonix Music Systems, Inc.

"We have to assume our plans will change on a week-to-week basis, as we discover the gameplay, but at the same time we can't afford to experiment in an open-ended way because we have schedule and budget constraints that we need to take heed of. Every team member is scheduled on a daily basis. This is developed on Friday, and laid out in our leads meeting on Monday morning, where we go over what slipped, why it slipped, and what to do to fix it. We have to be on a very tight schedule with the ability to be flexible, because the reality is it will change day to day—we'll change our minds about a feature or lop off parts of the gameplay. The producers keep everybody on track all week, and at the end of the day on Friday we start our schedule for next week, and we go over that Monday morning. We do this in six-week intervals. When we ship something and meet a milestone, we start on the next milestone.

Scene from *Lara Croft Tomb Raider: Legend*. Image © 2006 Eidos Interactive Ltd. *Lara Croft Tomb Raider: Legend,* Lara Croft, *Tomb Raider,* and the Tomb Raider logo are all trademarks of Eidos Interactive Ltd.

Scene from *Lara Croft Tomb Raider: Legend*. Image © 2006 Eidos Interactive Ltd. *Lara Croft Tomb Raider: Legend,* Lara Croft, *Tomb Raider,* and the Tomb Raider logo are all trademarks of Eidos Interactive Ltd.

Screenshot from *Karaoke Revolution*. Image provided by Harmonix Music Systems, Inc.

Character art of Napalm in *Guitar Hero II*. Image provided by Harmonix Music Systems, Inc.

Concept art of DJ turning for *Death Jr. II*. Image © 2006 Backbone Entertainment. Death Jr., the Death Jr. characters and logo are trademarks of Backbone Entertainment.

Concept art group shot of characters from *Death Jr. II*. Image © 2006 Backbone Entertainment. Death Jr., the Death Jr. characters and logo are trademarks of Backbone Entertainment.

Sketch of lead character for Backbone Entertainment's original intellectual property (IP) *Death Jr.* Image © 2006 Backbone Entertainment. Death Jr., the Death Jr. characters and logo are trademarks of Backbone Entertainment.

Hairless Lab Rat concept art. Image © 2006 Backbone Entertainment. Death Jr., the Death Jr. characters and logo are trademarks of Backbone Entertainment.

Bitter Bear concept art from *Death Jr. II.* Image © 2006 Backbone Entertainment. Death Jr., the Death Jr. characters and logo are trademarks of Backbone Entertainment.

CSI: Hard Evidence screenshot with Brass. Image courtesy of Ubisoft.

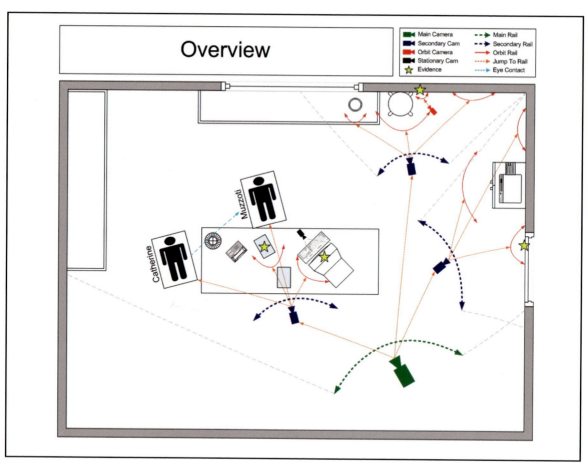

"I created this Visio file to communicate how the camera system should work within the environments in *CSI 3*. It was based on the first prototype delivery we received from Telltale, and the original file contained hyperlinks on all the objects and rails so you could click on any object or area and it would take you to the page that related to that object, so you could essentially navigate through the environment at a rudimentary level just as the player would navigate through the game." —**Chris Ferriter**

See Appendix E for full document. Image courtesy of Ubisoft.

Characters from *DOOM 3*: The Marine (left), Pinky (top right), and the Lost Soul (bottom right). Images courtesy of id Software, Inc.

Biodome shot from *Enemy Territory: Quake Wars*. Image courtesy of id Software, Inc.

Plaza color study for new original IP. Image courtesy of Ron Kee for Nihilistic Software.

Sample concept art from original IP—*Zombie* pitch. Image courtesy of Bren Adams for Nihilistic Software.

"So basically, we're trying to balance a lot of focus and clarity. At the same time we're closely tracking what people are working on so that people have a sense of feeling that their work is efficient, and they know what they need to get done, with the ability to revise along the way and respond to problems that occur, which always happens. Things slip and change and yet we have to continually focus on that core."

To develop a rigorous schedule that allows for change, Harmonix starts their development process with design docs. "We usually do at the onset of development a short high-level design doc that lays out the overall scope and focus of the title, what we're trying to accomplish. That's usually about two to three pages, and it may grow to ten pages. It includes the overall philosophy of the title, what experience we're trying to get the player to have, major play modes, assets, number of characters, number of venues, things like that, with some concept art sprinkled into it, too.

"Subsequently, we have tons of documentation organized in a wiki format live online with major topics like design, code, art, and so forth, and documents are hung off of those branches. It's a whole series of not more than a page or two associated with each little bit that needs to be understood.

"And we try to get the gameplay nailed as early as possible to start working on the prototype, which borrows from the code from our last project. And we have a prototype spec, a spec on what we want to build, then we build it, analyze it, and then spec the revisions. Everybody does this to some degree—you have a design doc and it becomes irrelevant at some point in building, and that's probably earlier for us than others because we don't have a design approach to building our games.

"That's because with an RPG, for example, the mechanic is pretty much nailed, and the storyline and content are most of the process. Whereas in our case, most of our content is the music. We have characters, shell screens, venues, and so forth, but most of our content is songs and the design emerges from what we build. We spec a little tiny piece of it and play

Screenshots from *Amplitude*. Images provided by Harmonix Music Systems, Inc.

Screenshot from *Antigrav.* Image provided by Harmonix Music Systems, Inc.

it, and then we revise that and we do it like a zillion times. We don't have a design process where somebody writes a design doc and other people implement it. Instead we have a small interdisciplinary group where they design collaboratively.

"The thing that seems worth emphasizing is if you're trying to develop games that innovate, that you really have to strive to keep the cycle between design and building and evaluating as tightly as possible. You have to always be playing the game you're making, and anything that gets between you and the game you're making has to be ruthlessly stomped down. Even if it's ugly or incomplete, you have some good subset of the game to work with and you have something that you can try out. We borrow liberally from the extreme-programming agile-development mindset. We're not a classic extreme shop, we're not religious about it, but we see a lot of relevancy to what we do."

Riley Cooper

"Our approach to gameplay, when you're starting from nothing and you don't know what you're doing at all, is to make a document and say everything we feel very confident of at the beginning. But the truth about games is that paper does not compare to building something and playing it. It gives you your superstructure to start with, but it becomes almost obsolete from the moment you finish writing it. It's kind of like booster rockets on the space shuttle. Once they're spent, they're garbage.

"So, for example, we might do a design doc on a boss and say this is how he moves, these are his attacks, this is what you have to do to kill him, these are his special abilities, and then you get it into development and find that at least 20 percent doesn't work like you thought it would. This is a common problem in design, and anybody who tells you different is lying through their teeth.

"Sometimes, a concept or a license or a sequel is pre-approved, and starting from the executive level down they figure out who is going to do it. Occasionally it happens the other way—in all honesty, that's a rare path—where you start with a smaller group who comes up with an idea and that gets pushed outward. Sometimes it's qualified—you're greenlit but only to go to the next level, which is usually documents. You start with a one-to-two-pager like an initial concept doc to give people a rough idea of what you're talking about. Then that gets more fleshed out, like 15 pages or so.

"The pitch doc includes more than the concept. It includes enough ideas about how the gameplay would look, and it includes story and art, and a competitive outlook of who the competitors would be. Usually that gets tailored to different groups, executives or brand, for example, then from there the real production docs start to get made."

Chris Ferriter, Ubisoft

"I'm a very visual person. I really believe that a picture is worth a thousand words. And it has been my experience that people on the publishing side respond very well to documents that are visually stimulating. When you just put a whole bunch of words on a page, it makes it difficult for people to focus on the writing and to understand what's in your head.

"When I was designing, I would try to make docs as visual as possible. When describing the interface, I would put mock-ups of that interface and I would include flowcharts of how the user interacts with that interface, and right there you've saved yourself a thousand words on describing how it works. It makes it easier for people to use the documents.

"It's very common for design docs to be created and shelved and never used again because they're big and unwieldy and not always kept up-to-date. So six months into a production when programming has a question about how a game mechanic is supposed to work, they're unlikely to go back to that doc and find the one paragraph to describe that. Instead, what they're going to do is go to the designer and have a meeting about it, and the designer will have to convey how this works. But this is lost efficiency.

"So what I would try to do is make a document that people will be likely to go back to. Make a document that's easy to read and easy to pull out pertinent information from. The other thing I've always been a big proponent of is going from concept doc to feature spec on a specific feature. So instead of writing one giant document, I'd write a document specific to one thing. User interface, sound, AI, specific game mechanics, would each have one document. Then it's easy not only for that doc to be updated as things would change throughout development, but it's easier for teams to find what they need, which results in more efficient workflow.

"There's a saying that anybody who builds anything is familiar with—it's 'measure twice, cut once.' And there's a reason for that. You want to be sure of what you're going to do. And when you don't follow that, it gets you.

"As a publisher, I would be hesitant to invest several million dollars into a moving target. If I am gong to purchase something, I want to know what I'm going to purchase. I don't want to know 'kind of' what I'm going to get at the end of the day. It's dangerous from a development standpoint, and it is bad business practice. Certainly if different practices work for you, I wouldn't want you to limit yourself to what is in this design document as, 'This is law,' because things need to be able to change and you need to be able to course-correct. But it is foolish to say you don't want to try to be as accurate as possible in the process.

"It boggles my mind. What other industry would do something like this? I mean it really is akin to saying, 'I'm going to build my dream home,' and I pick up a piece of paper or go to a whiteboard and draw a little house with a chimney and some smoke coming out of it, with a stick figure in front, and say, 'All right, build it.' It doesn't make sense. There is so much more that goes into it. Land surveys, architects, meetings with the planning commission. You wouldn't do it anywhere else, but we seem to accept it a lot in the game industry. It's, 'Throw away the design doc, we understand there are going to be mistakes along the way, and we'll fix them as we go.' But it compromises quality, time, or money, and often more than one of those."

Denis Dyack, Silicon Knights

"Usually we start with a three-pager executive summary. Ironically, this is most useful for non-executives. Our scripts are over 100 pages, and the game design doc goes to 200 pages when we start getting into a certain level of detail. And mostly no one reads these. So we start with three pages with lots of pictures—for us that is the way to go. Pictures have to be pretty to get everyone's attention. If it's the right documentation without pictures, no one's going to be interested in it.

"We have the storyline and graphs, and we post stuff all along the walls so we can suck it in through osmosis. You would recognize our scripts as Hollywood standard scripts, and we interweave them with other things like storyboards. We base our work on a good foundation. Documents are about communicating. And that's about getting people to believe and get passionate and getting them to contribute."

Greg Land, Telltale Games

"A lot of times design is a very hard thing for people to evaluate. A lot of people like to come up to an artist's screen and go, 'That's really cool,' and you can respond to it because you can see it. Designs are often hidden in documents—they're intangible—and people don't come up to you and say, 'Wow, this is a really cool-designed game,' especially during the process. It's something that's just not as easy to respond to from the outside. And it's also because a good designer takes ideas from the entire team. They're not always the one who has the best idea, but they're responsible for getting the best idea from wherever it comes. It's almost an invisible art, because the results aren't really seen except by a combination of every other element.

"One thing that has been on my mind lately, one real difference is that in film when a screenplay's done, everybody on the production gets the screenplay and they read it. Well, this very rarely happens, it almost never happens in games, so we've recently started addressing that. We're building in time to sit down with the team and explain the case to them so they don't have to just go away and read a document. We need to really communicate well, because these people are going to be working on details of the game much longer than I work on the design, so it's important they're working on the same roots."

Dave Grossman

"I'm very messy in my personal process, and here I'm actually lucky because I have another designer working with me and I get them to do the hard-line documentation. Because everybody who's working on the production needs to know what they're going to be doing without asking me several times a day. We have lists of animations, models, sounds, pieces of music—all this has to get written down because production schedules are insanely short.

"I have bunches of notepad paper with notes scribbled all over them in different directions, and at some point I start to make diagrams with three or four lobes of what are the major pieces, like, 'In this part where do we go, to the TV station, or on a car chase?' Then I make a puzzle-dependency diagram where I match out each puzzle and what has to happen for it to work. I make a flowchart, left to right, of how long vs. how wide the game is, and I'm looking for a shape like the head of a Powerpuff Girl. A small blob, with a bigger blob, and then a smaller blob again. Essentially, it's a map of the dramatic structure. So I can tell from that if things are too linear or not linear enough. Actually, sometimes they can be too open. If I have too much choice at this point in the game, that's actually audience dependent. It depends how broad you want things to be. In traditional adventure games, the audience likes things to be pretty broad and complicated before they're happy.

"By the time that flowchart is done, we've now basically laid out the entire puzzle structure of the game, so it's like we have the entire script outline now. Then we do a paragraph about each of those pieces, describing it so we can go through it. We might have a puzzle about a coffee cup in the office, and so-and-so character is doing this with the coffee cup, so the artist can say, 'I have to draw this and do this in the room,' and we get a vague picture of the document. From there we make lots and lots of exhaustive lists. Environments of the game that have to get modeled, we specify everything that has to be in there, all of the objects we need, do we have to pick anything up, a list of all animations that have to happen in the game, sound lists. Meanwhile, while making those lists, we're also writing the script. Typically the designers do that, but it is dependent on having designers who can write. We already have an understanding of what the nuances are for that particular piece of the puzzle, but there are plenty of designers who can't write at all, and they shouldn't.

"The script is mainly to send off to voice recording. We do some specification of action in the script to provide context so when people start doing art and choreographing things, they can see the script and see the lines and spec out some of the action. The script looks a little bit like a screenplay, but it's more like if you wrote a screenplay and you took every draft of it and you cut them all into little pieces and spread them out and drew little lines between them. It would look like that. Lots of chunks of scenes that have to be able to play well together, which is where it gets both difficult and interesting.

"We keep it in a database, and we have a Telltale dialog tool with a hierarchical thing that spells out where all of the jumps are.

"I just think that my job requires a certain combination of left-brain and right-brain kinds of skills. You can be good at design if you're a creative person who thinks like a programmer part of the time. You do have to think of the script as part art and part programming, because you have to visualize the structures you're making. Maybe that's one of the reasons it's tough to find good designers."

Mary DeMarle and *Splinter Cell 5*

"We're taking a different direction in the design process on this project. We've spent almost a year in the concept phase with a very small team, and we did not produce tons and tons of documentation because we had such a small team that everybody could just get together and talk about issues we had with it. And we could do very small PowerPoints where you can summarize or do one-page graphics to get your point across.

"But now that we're moving into the production phase, where so many new people are coming onto the team and they haven't been here from the beginning, we have to get these docs created, because while we know what we're talking about, they have no clue. We're experimenting on how to do docs, so we've created a design database, and it basically contains in it the key points we want for every episode of the game. We describe what is the experience, what is the feeling we want the player to have, how is this expressed through visuals, how is it experienced through story, what's happening here, what are game design elements that will support this, what are the elements that the level designer can use to create their episode or level that will support all of that. We start with that, and then the level designers will take that stuff that solely relates to their part of it and then they produce their level-design docs. And that gets approved through the various departments; for example, does it fit with our story, can the programmers do it, can AI accept it, can art deliver it? Once we have that document approved, we'll go into production on it."

Mike Sellers and MMOG Design

"Depending on how technical your group is, some people go straight to programming, but that's a mistake. When you program something, you're casting it in stone. Yes, you can change it, one of the great things about code is that it's changeable, but the more you put into programming the more difficult it is to change it, for financial reasons and morale reasons.

"When we have a good idea on this game we say, 'So let's coalesce it more, let's create some mock-ups.' The act of writing down the design takes a lot of assumptions and ambiguity out of it that you might not see otherwise. Then we ask, 'What's the simplest thing we can program that starts getting us in the direction we want to go,' rather than a whole bunch of programming with no design at all, or with a 300-page doc in front of it. We do a more iterative method of design, writing it down, doing mock-ups, programming it out, trying it out, going back and doing it again, because the fact is nobody really knows if this is going to be good design until it's there in front of you.

"Documents are really variable. I have never found one format that works for all people in all situations. For me, I like to create a bunch of one- to five-page documents. There was a book in the early '80s, *The Society of Mind* by Marvin Minsky,[2] in which each essay is one or two pages long. The whole point in the book is that in the mind there is no single driver sitting at the dashboard. It's made up of independent pieces. There was no thought line to the book. It was all one-page essays, but when you see it as a whole you get the point; it comes across.

"Because the games I do are the furthest thing possible from being linear, it makes it difficult to have a design document with a beginning, a middle, and an end. I start with a concept doc, where I understand what I'm talking about, but there may be some very obvious aspect I missed that if others read the document they can point that out. So in this case it becomes an overview of describing systems, pieces, players' goals.

"I also like to include user scenarios, which I approach as ABC—Ann, Bill, and Carl, where Ann is a new player who doesn't play this kind of game, Bill might be inexperienced but he does like this kind of game, and Carl is experienced in this type of game. Then I look at what their gameplay is like, in a typical five minutes, and it makes it clear why we have to have what we have in the game. Each lives in its own document rather than one huge document that becomes out of date immediately.

"If you're just one person working on a game, and you don't know what it really is, then yeah you can fool around with it and eventually get a game. But if you have any kind of egos or opinions involved, which we're not lacking in this industry, then there's a 99% guarantee that you'll get in front of someone and you'll say, 'This is a game about x,' and they'll say, 'No, it's about y,' and someone else will say, 'No, it's about z.' I did a rock-climbing game, and when I was saying 'rock climbing' maybe one person was thinking Mount Everest, someone else was thinking the Appalachians, and I was thinking hiking boots. You see this happen all the time, and then a year into it they go, 'What

---

2 Published in 1986, based on Minsky's conceptual theories of how the mind works.

I thought we were doing was this.' That's why it is most important to write this down, and at a strategic level.

"The idea of abandoning the design doc seems suboptimal. There's so much difficulty in the process already. Making games is difficult and expensive, and you're always on the line—there's almost always a flashing green light—you could go back to yellow or red at any moment. Why would you want to do it in a way that would make it more risky rather than less? I'm not a believer in a design bible that's 200 or 300 pages of design work before you start programming anything. You do not know if design works until you can see it. What's important is having a good design head, and some people have that and some don't. There are execs at large game companies who can't tell a good design in embryo to save their lives. You don't what to show something you've just written to somebody who doesn't get writing.

"At a fairly high level, we do a lot of early design work without trying to iterate too long without implementing something. Because you can talk about something forever, and that's not good. And at the same time we don't want to rush into something. Our first playable or first vertical slice of a game shows this is what it feels like, these are the mechanics, here are the dynamics of how you play, and here's a complete list of art aspects we need, levels we have, boss monsters.

"I tend much more toward a lot of small design docs that each describe pieces of the game that are linked together. A wiki is a great way to go to manage this. It gives you a spot to put the visionary comments you have, and maybe you can't do them now, but that's what you're shooting for and you don't lose that along the way. You can keep everything here from text design, to pictures, to Excel spreadsheets on different aspects of the game. Then you can start programming it. When it's just written on paper, when you get to the interactiveness of it, sometimes it doesn't work at all. That's why it remains a highly iterative process.

"Ideally, in production you have no design going on at all, but that never happens. You're always learning things as you build, so we're moving toward blurring that line between pre-production and production. It's dangerous to be longer in production than you should be, or conversely to think that you know more about the game than you really do. I can spend time in concept work and pre-production, but if I feel like the combat system is in good shape we go into an Excel table and map it out; this weapon is +2, this is +5, and why. Whereas the magic system is still nebulous, and so we're still working it all out. And at the same time, it turns out bows are more fun than swords, so then we tone down swords, bring up bows, or change to bows in the game. This can lead to dreaded feature creep, but it could also lead to this being a much better product. I don't draw a line in the sand and say everything is production or not; that doesn't make sense. Flexible discipline is important."

GDDs Exercise

Write a one- to two-page high-level executive summary of the game.

Next, create a pitch doc of approximately 10 to 15 pages. Much of this information can be gathered from previous exercises. Organize this document so that each key component is easy to identify.

These two docs should include:

- Title of your game
- Genre
- Story
- Gameplay/mechanics/interface/AI
- Market
- Competition
- How you differentiate your game from others
- Overall scope and focus of your game—the overall philosophy
- Experience you want the player to have
- Major play modes
- Characters—who they are and how many there are
- Main assets
- Venues/locales/levels
- Sketches and concept art

GDDs Checklist

- ❏ GDDs keep everyone literally on the same page.
- ❏ Chunk your GDDs into small useful segments:
  - Character bible
  - Story bible
  - Main story world/environment
- ❏ Add visuals where possible to explain concepts (this is especially important in pitch documents).

❑ Make sure key team members sign off on docs as they progressively get bigger, i.e., everyone is in agreement at the three-paragraph stage, the two-page stage, the ten-page stage, etc. to avoid surprises.

❑ As information changes, keep the documents up-to-date, whether in files or on a wiki.

❑ Keep the team informed of changes—use "constant human contact" in small informal discussions and schedule meetings.

❑ A variety of design docs are used throughout the project, depending on the company, and on the publisher's requirements, which might include:

- Executive summary
- Pitch document
- Concept outline
- User scenarios
- Sketches (preliminary)
- Concept art
- Context outline/story outline
- Bibles
  - Character bible
  - Story bible
- Puzzle diagrams/lists
- Environments list
- Level design
- Maps
- Asset lists
- Prop lists
- Weapons lists
- Character lists/boss lists
- Flowcharts
- Storyboards
- Screenshots
- Script
- Dialog script

- Dialog list
- Cinematics script
- Character actions
- Animation lists
- User interface
- AI
- Mechanics
- Controls map/flowchart and logic
- Sound/audio/music
- Gameplay timelines
- Production timelines
- Schedules

Chapter 9

And Now for Something Completely Different—**Flowcharts** and **Storyboards**

"In *Revelation*… We had a huge board the size of one wall, where…You could look at that and it was the entire experience of the game through gameplay, what the puzzles are doing, what the story is at this point, what's the wow factor."

—**Mary DeMarle**

To a left-brainer, flowcharts are pretty much a no-brainer. You start at the beginning, chart out all of the possible paths in a logical and methodical way, and end up at the end. No big deal. To any self-respecting creative type, the mere mention of the word "flowchart" could be enough to make them consider switching professions. But, since we've already established, with the assistance of Dave Grossman, that a good designer needs a healthy dose of both right-brain and left-brain features, flowcharting is something you should expect to be a big part of your game-design career.

In Chapter 1, Chris Charla of Backbone Entertainment said, "You have to know how to do flowcharting…" It's key to be able to take "the behaviors of a character broken down into states, and flowchart that, instead of, 'Oh, he shoots a lot.'"

While it's true that flowcharts can seem a bit didactic, they are also a lot of fun because this is where you get to really step out the gameplay in visual chunks, where you're going to *have* to come up with very creative ways of doing this, and where you ultimately make sure that every possible gameplay element is considered so you don't end up with gigantic structural holes and opprobrious dead ends in your game. It is *much* cheaper to fix a problem in a flowchart than it is in programming. So your attention to this process is critical to the success of the game's development.

The great thing about flowcharts is that they happen very organically in the game-design process, because nonlinear thinking, which is an essential feature of a game designer's brain, begets nonlinear storylines and nonlinear

Zipline flowchart. Image © 2006
Eidos Interactive Ltd. *Lara Croft
Tomb Raider: Legend,* Lara Croft,
Tomb Raider, and the Tomb Raider
logo are all trademarks of Eidos
Interactive Ltd.

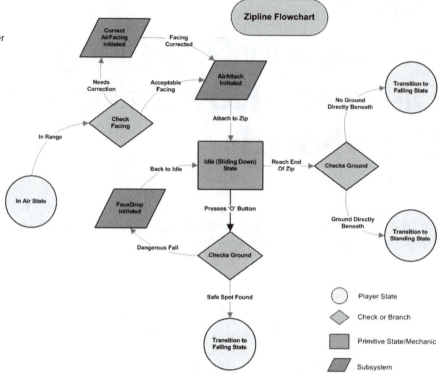

gameplay. It all has to be tracked somehow, and accurately, and the best way to track is with flowcharts.

We have been presented, throughout this book, with various ways different projects use flowcharting to help them track different components in their game. Flowcharts are used to:

- Track navigation
- Work through an environment
- Manage a storyline
- Work through gameplay
- Follow a character's actions
- Track game mechanics
- Structure a timeline
- Track gameplay as it relates to the timeline

We developed *Curious George Comes Home* as a prop-driven game in which the branching order of the gameplay, and therefore the story, was determined by certain props the player picked up. For example, if the player picked

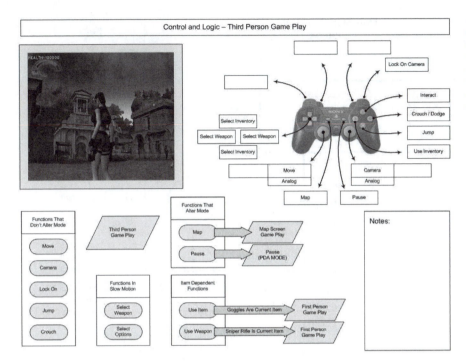

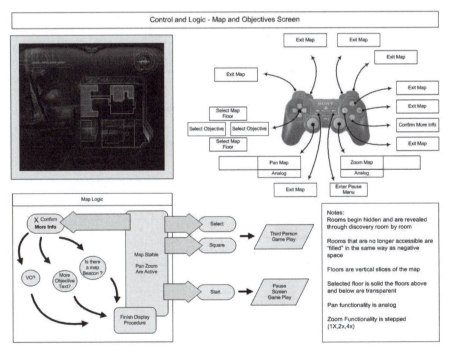

Control and logic documents. Images © 2006 Eidos Interactive Ltd. *Lara Croft Tomb Raider: Legend*, Lara Croft, *Tomb Raider*, and the Tomb Raider logo are all trademarks of Eidos Interactive Ltd.

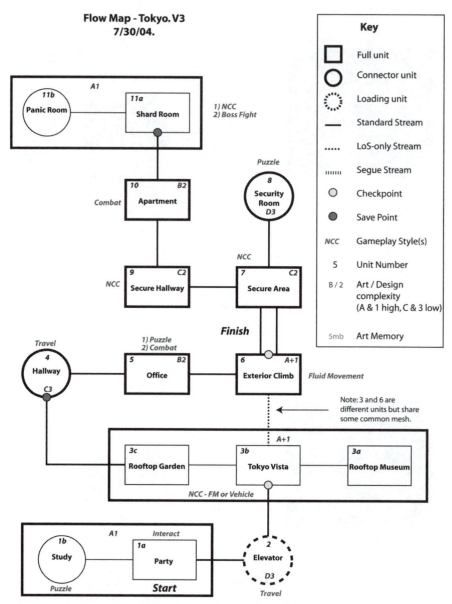

Tokyo flow map. Image © 2006 Eidos Interactive Ltd. *Lara Croft Tomb Raider: Legend,* Lara Croft, *Tomb Raider,* and the Tomb Raider logo are all trademarks of Eidos Interactive Ltd.

up the binoculars, they went with George through the "rhino story." And whichever direction the player went, they could at the end print out a *Curious George* storybook/coloring book of their adventure with the mischievous little monkey. That storybook structure was scrutinized and analyzed before we did any gameplay mechanics, and all of the stories and gameplay had to be captured and followed first in a flowchart.

Greg Land uses flowcharts extensively to track the clues in *CSI* as they relate to story and gameplay. "We do a flowchart for the story, and it shows that you can't collect a certain piece of evidence before x, y, and z happen. It helps you think through the story in a visual way. You keep track of all the details because you're trying to lead the player in a very clear way through the case, and it's important that certain things aren't done out of line."

At Crystal Dynamics, Riley Cooper explains, "One place you always use flowcharts is with menu screens. How does the player go from the start screen to the options—the start shell is what we call it—how does the player enter in and back out? What's the menu navigation? That lends itself to a flowchart.

"Lara's movement abilities were done in flowcharts to make it clear what the different animation states could be, and what buttons lead to those transitions. If I press x, I'll jump off the ladder. And pressing r or l, I'll laterally jump off the ladder. We make bubbles for those."

Flowcharts are a huge aid in working through story structure and gameplay. Like an outline, they help make sure there are no holes to the structure, no unwanted dead ends. If you have your game flowcharted, you can visually see very quickly where problems pop up. They are a great visual tool. They are also a key in helping to avoid the kinds of big communication problems that have been discussed throughout this book.

So let's take a look at some simple flowcharting. Sort of a "jump right in and face your worst nightmare" approach.

Take, for Instance, My House

You walk into my house, and you have options: you can go to the left, you can go to the right, and you can go straight ahead. Let's look at that using simple rectangular shapes:

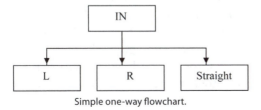

Simple one-way flowchart.

And there we have it—our first flowchart. What this flowchart conveys is that from IN, you can go left, or you can go right, or you can go straight. Easy. Not very exciting, though. But there is some additional information this flowchart gives us. It also says that while you can go forward in these directions, you can't go back. That's indicated by the one-way arrows. So let's add some flexibility to this. And let's name the rooms, just for grins.

Let's say we need to flowchart the house inside a murder-mystery game. We'll start out in the living room. If you go through the living room to the left, you reach the kitchen. Through the right, you reach the hallway. Off of the hallway is a bathroom, a bedroom, a closet, a door to the garage, and a set of stairs that takes you up to another level. Let's flowchart that. Oh, and by the way, you want to be able to go freely in both directions, so we'll add two-way arrows:

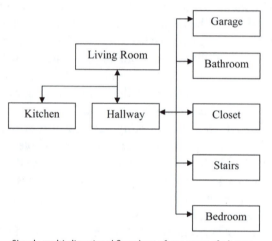

Simple multi-directional flowchart of one story of a house.

This is still pretty straightforward. You can guess that the main point of entry is the living room and follow the paths into a variety of other rooms in the house. And since the flow now goes in both directions, you can navigate around from one room to another.

But there's more to this house than you might think. Some of the rooms have doors that lead elsewhere, like outside. And some of the rooms have windows that any good murderer would be able to use to their benefit if they wanted and/or needed to make a fast escape. And what about the heating vent? If it's big enough to crawl through (we'll say it is), where does it go and how does it connect the rooms and how can we use it as a shortcut to get from one place in the house to another? Things start to get interesting. Let's make this flow.

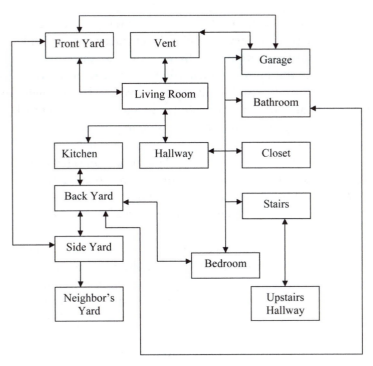

Expanded flow of a multidirectional flowchart.

Here we can see that the living room will actually take us many places—to the kitchen, the hallway, the front yard, and the vent. The vent leads us to the garage, which in turn gives us an easy escape route to the front yard or takes us back to the hallway off the living room. How do we get to the back yard? Easy—from the kitchen, the bedroom, and the bathroom. The back yard leads us to the side yard, which takes us either to the neighbor's yard or the front yard. The closet is an utter dead end. And, according to this flowchart, if we go to the neighbor's yard we're toast, because we can't get back into the side yard (there's no two-way arrow).

Is the gameplay different if you enter the house from another location? Yes and no. You still have the same flow through the house, but if you throw puzzles in the path of the player, that can make it a little more complicated to maneuver. Perhaps the doors are all locked and the player enters the premises through the garage. Now the only way into the house itself is through the vent, which may or may not be obvious. Once in the house, maybe they can unlock the doors from the inside, which will give them access back into the house from a different entry point if they leave and need to come back inside later. And so on.

And how do the characters play into this flowchart? Is the gameplay still the same? That depends on the nature of the characters and the rules you set up for them and their environment. Maybe you're an insect, yes literally the "fly on the wall" in this murder mystery, and you have to buzz around picking up clues and help your human counterpart, a two-bit detective who couldn't solve a case if it came with a user's manual, by bugging him so much that he comes after you singularly obsessed with swatting you to death, and that's how you lead him to the clues and win the game. Maybe you're a cartoon Sam Spade in a B-grade film-noir set, and like any cartoon character worth his weight in guffaws you can flatten out thin as a French crêpe and slide under doors, so that a locked door now has no meaning and new venues open up to you; for example, a crack in the floor that leads to a hidden crawl space where you find a major clue.

By now you can see that the simple little process of flowcharting one level of a house can quickly turn into a pretty complicated production. All of the connections need to be *thoroughly* thought through because they all need to be communicated to everyone on the team so that anyone who picks up the flowchart can tell where they are, how they got there, and where they can go from here.

The flowchart is *the* essential roadmap to the game.

One of the problems you'll notice immediately is that if every part of the flowchart is represented with the same rectangular shape, it can become pretty much impossible to figure out where things begin. And that is why those little plastic flowchart templates, and their digital cousins, flowchart programs (Inspiration and Visio, for example), come complete with a variety of pre-determined shapes. These shapes, as it turns out, actually mean something.

Do you have to follow/use them all? I'm going to go out on a limb here and say unequivocally "probably not." In fact, in every project I've worked we've always had our own bastardized version of flowcharting nomenclature. And every flowchart I've seen is a little different. But they can still all be read with ease. Generally speaking, though, usually the flowchart begins at an intro sequence or a point where the user makes a decision, and this has, sometimes, historically been represented with a diamond:

From here, you start connecting with lines and arrows, using one-way arrows if the player can only go forward from the starting point:

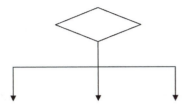

And double arrows if they can go back:

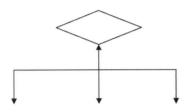

Typically, the main shape you'll use after this is a rectangle, which in my experience has been used to let everyone know that a change in location or action occurs. It is also the most common shape used in general, and sometimes it's the only shape used in a flowchart. It just depends on the company.

Alternately, you can use the rounded corner rectangle, but as I said, it all depends on how pragmatic you want to be and what the team is used to doing:

Once you start flowcharting, there will come a point, about 90 seconds into the process, when you've run out of room on a single page of paper, and *then* what do you do? Leave it to the flowcharting template gurus to come to the rescue with a connectivity symbol, usually:

These are commonly used to indicate that you've come from another page on the flowchart, or that you need to go to another page in the flowchart.

Put it all together, and we have a quick, simple flowchart using graphic templates:

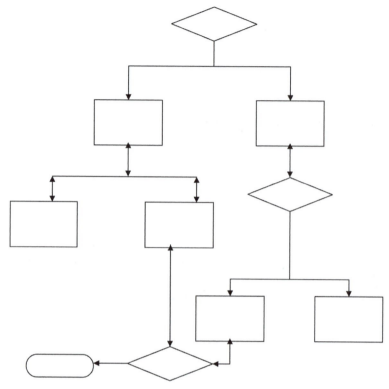

Multidirectional multishape flowchart.

Often, location flowcharting and action flowcharting work hand in hand as you figure out how you walk the player through the gameplay, and the two merge into one. Sometimes they're separate flowcharts, based on where you are in the design process. And sometimes you might want to do a little side flowchart to help you figure out some element in which you're having trouble, whether with some location in which you need to define its physical structure, or with how you effectively move through a place.

Doggone Gameplay

In *101 Dalmatians: Escape from DeVil Manor*, we started with a simple mandate: design an adventure game that combined elements from the original book, the 1959 animated feature, and the live-action movie. In the movie, the doggy parents save the puppies. In the game, the player gets to save the day through their fun adventures and clever gameplay. We had lots to figure out. And with treasured characters to work with, this required great care. The locations in the movie gave us the big-picture starting point for locations in the game—London, the countryside, and the mansion. And we had to build out from there.

Our foundation for designing the mansion's gameplay worked beautifully with the house's blueprints from the movie set. Obviously, the set builders didn't build the whole house for the movie—the action took place in only a handful of rooms and the rest of the house was implied—so we started with the few rooms we had on the blueprints and built the house out to accommodate the interactive gameplay. This process organically helped us figure out the puzzles we wanted to build into the game, like the kitchen-drawer puzzle mentioned in Chapter 6.

To end up with the kind of interactivity and puzzle play we wanted, we created four levels in the house—the basement, the main floor, upstairs, and the attic. The attic and basement were connected to the kitchen via the dumbwaiter, while the kitchen puzzle was built in to allow access to the dumbwaiter. The upstairs was also connected directly to the basement via the laundry chute. The player could run up the stairs from the main floor to the second, or with a fun puzzle could figure out how to bounce on a springy cushion and be propelled through a hole in the ceiling. And it goes on and on, puzzles and gameplay borne of flowcharting.

With all of the action going on in the house, it was fun to stay in there and play all day. But the title of the game was *Escape from DeVil Manor*, not *Hang Out in DeVil Manor*, and besides that, we had a whole world of gameplay to get to outside of the house. And worse yet, there was always the threat that Cruella would show up at any minute and turn us into haute couture. So we had to figure out a way out of the house, and it of course couldn't be an obvious "go out the front door or pry open a window" solution.

At this point, we, on the game-design team, were still stuck inside the manor. But since we had so thoroughly figured out the layout of the house in the flowchart, we were able to devise some wacky yet organic solutions consistent with the game's characters, its rules, and the environment. We were then able to create a major puzzle with a big payoff and move the player on their way to more hours of fun with the puppies.

Very little of this detailed action is ever decided *before* the flowcharting process is started. It happens as you work out the gameplay via the flowchart.

The Gestalt of a Flowchart

There are basically two steps to flowcharting, which can easily be summed up as "the big picture" and "the details," and this is, once again, really a lot like the process you learned for outlining those eighth-grade book reports. Big-picture flowcharts are the global concepts of how the game connects. They might take a few pages, maybe a dozen pages at most, to explain the overarching concept. These, in fact, will be representative of your conceptual outline. And, assuming you actually did a conceptual outline, the two should work together.

The detailed flowchart (sometimes called a level-two flowchart) is what comes after everyone agrees on the basic underlying structure you've put forth in your preliminary flow (sometimes called a level-one flowchart). Be aware, though, that just because everyone agrees on the big picture and you're moving forward to fill in the details, it doesn't mean that people won't (a) change their mind about the big picture or (b) give you stupid ideas that they insist you integrate into the gameplay. It can happen. Honestly, it *will* happen. In either of these instances, the flowchart can become your favorite ally.

The flowchart can help you figure out how to make changes work. It can also back you up in showing how the inevitable ridiculous requests, or ideas, or recommendations, or requirements won't work. "I'd love to have a milkmaid show up on the asteroid, Fred, and if it were up to me I'd do it in a heartbeat. But lookit here, I've been working on your great idea for three days and this stupid flowchart just won't let it happen." I'm not kidding. You would not believe the crazy ideas people come up with, even *way* into the design process. If you "can't" make it work, use the flowchart to back you up.

I've seen flowcharts done in a variety of methods, from those that resemble craft projects made by kindergarteners, to those that look like masterpieces. They all start the same way: with a large flat workspace—a floor, a table, a wall—and they all end up on the wall. Usually it goes something like this:

- Index cards: Each index card is used to represent one box in a flowchart, so that each location or decision point or action piece has its own card. Doing a flowchart with the index-card method is useful because it's easy to fix a mistake (just throw the card away [please, recycle]), and they're easy to move around to other locations if you change your mind on where something needs to be. Eventually the collection of index cards gets too big and unruly to keep on a table, and they get pinned or taped to the wall with some ubiquitous yarn connecting them all to show how the flow goes.

- Sticky notes: Alternately, a variety of colored sticky notes are sometimes used for the first phase of flowcharting, with some color-coded scheme to identify different scenes. It doesn't take long before this becomes impossible to track—usually you run out of colors. Besides, it doesn't really work all that well. I've seen these first two methods combined, however, in which the flow is done with index cards and occasional colored sticky notes are used to indicate change in flow or new decision points. This usually works okay.

- 8½×11 paper: Full sheets of paper are good for plotting out the flow of more than one element per sheet and are easier to handle than a bunch of little cards, but it's not so easy to fix individual mistakes or things that just don't work and can start looking pretty messy pretty quickly. Again, these end up on the wall and, if the flow is done right, can be taped together.

- Rolls of art paper or butcher paper: This method is good for plastering walls with paper from the get-go and drawing out the flow from a standing position, rather than bending over a table and futzing with little cards and crossed-out sheets of paper. It's also a lot more fun, somehow, drawing out flowcharts on big sheets of paper on the wall (at least for those of us who were discouraged from drawing on walls as children; there's some sense of "I'm being naughty and getting paid for it" pleasure here). If you have limited wall space, this method is nice because you can put one layer over another and still have access to the whole thing. Sort of like a humongous flip chart.

- Whiteboard walls: I have worked on projects in which our development room was floor-to-ceiling whiteboards. The advantage is that it's really easy to change something, and you can add illustrations and even color-code with different color whiteboard markets. BUT—make sure you have signs *everywhere* that say "DO NOT ERASE," and/or keep the room locked at all times and have only one person be the sacred holder of the key.

- Drawings: If you have the talent available, this is a great way to get an instant visual of the decision points and the paths that can be taken in gameplay. Sort of a flowchart-meets-storyboard approach. I've worked on a few games in which we've flowcharted with illustrations on 8½×11 paper, and it really made a difference in helping us make some crucial decisions. I've also only done this with very experienced teams; in other words, we all knew what we were doing so this was a feasible way to check out how the flow would look. Otherwise, this could be a costly and time-consuming way to go. A good compromise is to have quick illustrations done at a few key points in the flow that can help you in your decision-making process, rather than illustrating out the whole flow, in essence like a storyboard.

- Digital alternatives: There are, of course, the previously mentioned flow-charting programs, PowerPoint, and mind-mapping programs that can be used to create flowcharts, sometimes with better success than other times, depending on your needs. Remember, every project is different, so whichever method you use to get the job done, it ultimately depends on the company you're working with and their current preferred strategy.

Often, flowcharts start out using index cards and end up as a combination of 8½×11 or 11×14 sheets with illustrations scattered throughout. Know this before you start: flowcharts get huge! *Always*. I have seen them, many, many times, completely wrap around all four walls of large conference rooms, ceiling to floor.

The Hollywood Connection—Storyboards

In the world of Hollywood—film and television, to be precise—for the most part there's not really much need for a flowchart (exceptions, of course, are everywhere, and as films start to offer multiple complex storylines this changes, but "for the most part" scripts are linear). With a linear storyline, you simply follow a linear progression.

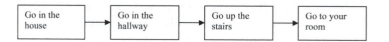

Really, there's no need to flowchart this; it's all written out in the script. But you *do* need to see how this is going to look in terms of angles, placement, etc., for shooting the script, and the Hollywood model for dealing with what all of this looks like before getting into the expensive production process is the storyboard.

In the game-design world, storyboards can be used to flesh out the details of the flow just as they do with Hollywood scripts. Here's how they work: Storyboards step through the script *one scene* at a time. Dialog, narrative, camera angle, cast positioning, prop placement, and action are all indicated in individual drawings, one per scene. The storyboard accomplishes a variety of tasks, from making sure that the scene can be played out as written, to getting everybody on the same page for production.

Interactivity by its very nature is nonlinear, but the storyboarding processes can still be valuable to the designer and the production team. Storyboarding can provide depth that would be impossible with the flowchart.

The job of the *flowchart* is to map out the game, work out the gameplay, and help make sure that none of your pathways fall into a black hole. The *illustrated* flowchart can give you a more focused picture of the decision points and help you make design choices. The *storyboard* gives you the ability of following a particular path from the point of view of the player, again, providing you with a clear detailed look at the environment, the camera angles, cut scenes, transitions, video sequences, and interaction with other characters.

The storyboard is a useful tool for the game designer especially when there's conflict on the team about how something plays out. It's not necessarily used to prove a point but rather to bring the team together to get on the same page. This is a visual medium, and different team members will have different visions of how things work. Communication can be made clearer with the storyboard. And executives who have been absent throughout most of the game-design process can easily be brought up to speed with a sequence of storyboards.

Storyboarding gets to the visual details.

In most instances, storyboards are used in conjunction with flowcharts on an as-needed basis. They do not have to be idyllic works of art. They *do* have to convey the important elements of the scene and can be more or less detailed depending on the need for doing the storyboard in the first place. Do you want to see where to strategically place a critical prop in a scene and follow how it plays out in a sequence? Or maybe you need to check movement through the environment, either the player's or another character, or their interaction together.

From the game designer's perspective, use the storyboard as an additional tool and leave the detailed artwork to your art team.

Rob Swigart and *Portal*

When Swigart developed *Portal* in the late 1980s, Timothy Leary called the book "spooky, audacious, breakthrough science fiction [that] pulls the reader through the page into the bleak terrain of an AI universe, a chaotic silicon landscape of ROM ghosts, short-circuited entities, and crystalline madness." The story, designed for interactive "gameplay," was one of the first ever to explore the use of interactive narrative in digital storytelling. It would have been impossible to create this new narrative structure without a flowchart.

Good stories and good concepts have long lives, a fact Swigart can attest to with this project. Now, 20 years later, Swigart's classic sci-fi novel, published both in hard copy and in game form, is taking its latest shape as a graphic novel.

Cinematics storyboard and corresponding rendered shots from *Death Jr. II*. Images © 2006 Backbone Entertainment. Death Jr., the Death Jr. characters and logo are trademarks of Backbone Entertainment.

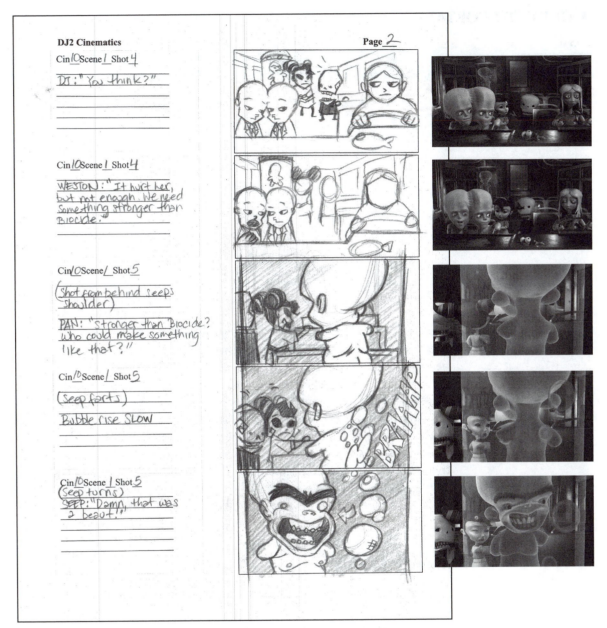

Cinematics storyboard and corresponding rendered shots from *Death Jr. II*. Images © 2006 Backbone Entertainment. Death Jr., the Death Jr. characters and logo are trademarks of Backbone Entertainment.

A GUIDE TO PORTAL

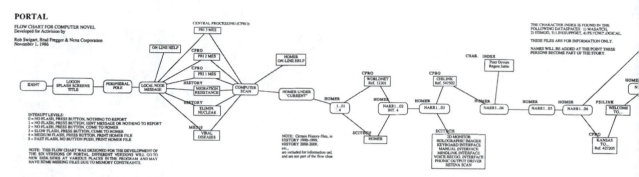

Portal flowchart. Courtesy of Rob Swigart.

Swigart sent me a copy of a short summary he found of *Portal*: "Originally published as an interactive novel on computer disk in 1986, *Portal* is the story of an astronaut who returns to earth from a mysteriously aborted mission, prematurely awakened from suspended animation. One hundred years have passed; animals and plants thrive, cities stand intact. Every human being, however, has disappeared. With the help of a slowly reviving computer network, the astronaut begins to piece together the events of the last century. He learns of the child prodigy Peter Devore, of a world orchestrated by stunning new technologies, and of Peter's race against time to unlock the secrets of the Portal." The longer summary goes into a good bit of detail, and the flowchart shows how important this tool is at holding together the interactivity, the player's experience, and the fundamental narrative of a nonlinear storyline.

A quick look at the flowchart for *Portal* and you can see why it has been described as looking like a giant python that swallowed a series of rabbits.

Mary DeMarle

"One thing I do find is that this is a very visual medium, and most people working in it are very visually oriented. I do create a very visual map of the game. On *Revelation*[1] we had this huge chart where we basically charted out

---

[1] *Myst IV: Revelation.*

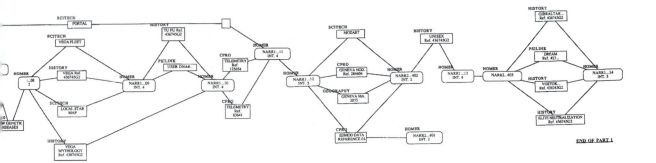

all of the player's experience. We create the experience we want and the various ways we're going to get that across in this area. In *Revelation* it starts in the home of the main character—what is the feeling we want to convey here, how do we convey that in a visual sense, the feel, the wow factors? We had a huge board the size of one wall, where we followed that. You could look at that, and it was the entire experience of the game through gameplay, what the puzzles are doing, what the story is at this point, what's the wow factor.

"On the project now,[2] we don't have the same thing. We do have an overall picture of the game, but it's expressed in a different way. If anybody looked at it they wouldn't understand it. But I look at it and I understand this is the whole game. To anyone else it's just a bunch of pictures with color codes: this location represented by this image. Every location is represented by a visual, and every increment of play time is color-coded to tell you what's the overriding feeling we want to get here. For example, this one is intense combat and it's color-coded black. And this one is exploration and that's green. So you can see you're in this location and in this chunk of gameplay and that the overriding feeling is combat.

"The map of the game experience is on a PowerPoint, and I take it with me everywhere so I can refer to it."

---

2 *Splinter Cell 5.*

Flowchart Exercise

Create a flowchart of your game.

- Be sure to indicate direction either with arrows or with a key (as in the Tokyo flow map).
- Make note of any dead ends that show up, so you can fix this in your design documents.
- Make corrections as needed to your game through the flowchart and then update your docs where relevant.

Add your flowchart to your pitch doc.

Flowcharting Checklist

❏ Use flowcharts throughout the design process for:
  - Menu navigation
  - Gameplay
  - Environment flow
  - Story structure/flow
  - Puzzles
  - Prop and story tracking
  - Rube Goldberg devices
  - Character actions
  - Game mechanics
  - Timelines
  - User interface
  - Controller mapping and logic

❏ Use the flowchart to help determine if/how you can add new elements into the game.

❏ Use storyboards to cinematically sketch out and design elements of the game, scene by scene.

Chapter 10
Life is a **Pitch**, and Then They **Buy**

"When you're a small independent developer whose existence is based on what publishers want to buy, you can't just worry about what you sell to the public; you also have to worry about what you can sell to the publisher."

—Matthew Karch, Saber Interactive

How do you get your pitch in order to ensure that you have the best possible chance of conveying your game in a way that's fun, engaging, easy to visualize, and profitable? What does a developer need to have a good pitch? What is the publisher looking for in a game? What should the developer look for in a publisher? What is the publisher looking for in a developer beyond the game? How important are story, art, and game mechanics?

Pitching a AAA title to a major publisher to get a green light and tens of millions of dollars in funding is not one of the easiest tasks in town. Many suggest alternate strategies to success. There is the casual-games route, which has a much lower entry barrier in terms of dollar investment. And there is the serious-games market, where funding can come from a different source than the traditional publisher, and you might have an opportunity to make a positive contribution to the world. A frequent and successful way to get into the industry is doing mods. There are many examples of modders developing relationships that can launch careers and even entire companies.

Whichever route you take, the most important thing is to understand your market, and that means both the publisher and the audience.

In the casual space, which is cited as being the fastest growing market in the games industry, Charles Balas, of Oberon Games, offers the following advice. "I think there are two things that make a game successful in this space. The first thing is you need some sort of emergent gameplay. I would argue that if you're a developer, look at what core game players were playing 10 or 15 years ago and figure out a way to morph the games that were successful then into the paradigm of the casual-game player.

"The other thing that is becoming very, very apparent is we have an enormous number of male programmers making games that they speculate are going to sell to this audience, and I think any team that wants to be successful with this audience needs to include females. Because you have no idea how many games come in to us that are so amazingly offensive to the women on our staff. And yet you can tell the developer tried to figure it out. One company submitted a game that was about coupon clipping, and they brought it to us and sincerely tried to sell it as, 'We spent a lot of time really thinking about what would be interesting to women.' We have another major media company that is pushing us to do a sim-style game where you clean your house."

Know your market. In any arena. Otherwise, neither your gamers, nor the publisher, are going to be interested in you.

The other most important thing is to choose your publisher wisely. Because the relationship you develop with the publisher today is one you're going to be deeply involved with for at least a couple of years, and if all goes well, even longer. If you have problems with commitment, now's the time to get over them.

The publisher/developer relationship requires:

- Honesty
- Flexibility
- Compromise
- Integrity
- Good communication
- Fiscal responsibility

And like all good relationships, a healthy sense of humor helps.

It's also important not to be desperate. It's a lot like choosing a life partner. You want it to be mutually successful, and at the end of the day, or in this case at the end of a multiyear development cycle, you want to know you can get back into bed with each other and look forward to another fun and mutually satisfying experience.

"I have done greenlighting from both sides," says Tracy Fullerton, "and anyone who's been on the side of pitching and getting it greenlit knows the terror. You put everything you can into the presentation, into the demo. I've walked ideas around to more meetings than I can possibly describe. But at some point or another you find there's the person who 'gets it.'

"What I tell my students about this is the objective is not just to get *anyone* to say 'yes' about your idea. The objective is to get the person who *understands* the idea, the best person for that idea. If your objective is to get *anyone* to say 'yes,' you're probably headed for a bad relationship. You want to be doing your game with the person who loves it too, who knows how to market it, and gets it to the players who will love it.

"Also, be honest about what you're pitching, what you can and can't do, what it's going to cost. They want it fast, cheap, and great, and it won't be all of those things. In general, one of the hardest things to do in production is to be honest—be honest with yourself about where you are, what you've got, what you're going to be able to do.

"That green light is that first moment in this relationship. Then you have to go through every deliverable, every milestone, and it doesn't stop there. You have to market it, support it. Everything you do feeds into that product to make sure it's positioned right. You want it to do well, so when it launches everyone has a sense of authorship in it, so everyone says, 'Yeah, this is the thing we did.'"

> "Today, the standard theory for development of an MMO is the 40/40 plan—$40 million in 40 months. To me, that's an insane failure of imagination, where you can't figure out a way to do it for a half or a quarter amount of the money, in a quarter amount of time."
>
> **—Mike Sellers**

And remember Noah Falstein's advice from Chapter 1: persistence is key to success. In the greenlighting process, you're going to get a lot of 'maybe' before you get a definitive 'yes.' Or as Mike Sellers puts it, "it might be a green light, but it's a flashing green light." And it just might be one of the longest lights you'll ever sit through before it turns solid green. Here's a look at the typical time it takes to pass go and collect $10 million:

- From blue sky and brainstorming to developing enough of a vertical slice of the game that you have an awesome demo worthy of showing a publisher: 3–6 months
- Shopping the demo to find a publisher who is (a) interested, (b) a good match, and (c) willing to say yes: 3–12 months (expect closer to 12)
- Negotiating the contract and getting it signed: about 3 months

The "flashing" part of the green light means that at any time the project can be killed. This could be because of misunderstandings about the game, missed milestones, miscommunication, miscalculations on budget or schedule, or flakiness on anybody's part. Or a hundred other things.

Of course, everybody goes into the game wanting it to be a success. But both parties are coming from different points of view, and in order for either to go forward, and keep going forward, they need particular things.

The developer wants a publisher who:

- Gets it
- Loves it
- Supports it

The publisher wants a developer who:

- Has a team of experts in place
- Can take direction
- Has good management
- Can deliver on time and on budget
- Has a good track record
- Works well with others

How this actually plays out well and goes from idea to success is the "secret sauce." To shed light on that secret, let's look at some examples from a leading industry agency, some developers and publishers, and a leading journalist and editor who has his pulse on what's happening and where the industry is going.

Matthew Karch—Greenlighting *TimeShift*

"As a relatively new company, our philosophy was, 'I don't care how good we are, we can't compete with Bungie or *Halo* because we're good but nobody else knows we're good.' We needed to come up with something special. So we said, 'Okay, we're going to stick with a genre we know, which is shooter, but we're gonna come up with something that has an edge.' We were trying to craft innovative gameplay through mechanics.

"We're very strong technically on rendering, and overall technically we have the best minds in Russia working for us. We can do things from a gameplay perspective that other developers can't tackle. We can pull them off and turn them into fun gameplay tools. Our approach was, 'Let's give the player something cool to do.' I don't pooh-pooh story by any means, but I think it's important to have good gameplay first. Look at Nintendo—you just have fun playing it. And that's what our perspective is.

"The mechanic came first. We said, 'Let's come up with something that's cool and compelling from a gameplay standpoint and build everything else around that.'

"Next we defined an art style. We said, 'Let's do something that differentiates us that will look cool.' And we didn't want to go straight sci-fi. When you're a small independent developer whose existence is based on what publishers want to buy, you can't just worry about what you sell to the public, you also have to worry about what you can sell to the publisher. We came up with a unique art style mix of Victorian era sci-fi. That was the original art direction we took. We stuck with it to some degree, but it was toned down.

"Basically, this first-person shooter is about guns, opponents, special effects, and AI. We blocked out environments in low res and started to do gameplay in low res environments; we did some levels, did some prototyping, and built a small but highly polished demo that we shopped around to publishers, and we had a lot of interest. Everyone on the production side thought it was great, but marketing couldn't wrap their arms around it. We kept working and working, and finally Atari bit.

"It took us a year to sell *TimeShift*. Atari picked it up as an opportunistic move, thinking, 'Maybe we'll make some money on it.' The one shining star at Atari, even with their financial troubles, was everyone wanted the game.

"But Atari started to sell off their products, and I was worried personally that they would not be able to pay us for manufacturing the product, or market it correctly. And I heard through the grapevine that one company was interested in purchasing it; it was not the one who did purchase it, by the way. So I went to Atari, and they said they didn't want to sell it but they might have to.

"I traveled to the companies I heard were interested and met with them, and there were multiple offers. And to be honest, the one who bought it is the one I wanted to get it. They're good guys, and I thought they'd be a good company for us to grow with. They picked it up based on my going in and selling it.

"It was in development at Atari for about 20 months before we sold it again. We were closing in on 'done,' and Vivendi said, 'Let's put our own stamp on it,' and within days of being gold they said they wanted to give us more money and make this a franchise. We had been in crunch for 4 months on it. [Laughing] In crunch for 4 years.

"I designed the gameplay mechanic, how I wanted it to work on paper, then the team implemented it in a series of tests to make sure it was viable. It was fun to blow up an opponent so his pieces are lying all over the ground, and then reverse it and have him come all back together. We wanted to make a sandbox style of game in a first-person shooter, and one thing we're refining now is conveying to the player how powerful he really is. We want to show him, 'Look at all the cool s*** you can do.'

"The higher profile you get, the easier it gets to sign up games. In Saber's case, because we're a co-located facility, we do things easily of the quality of the best US games, but in many cases we're half the price. Next-gen games are around $15 million to make, and we can do it for half that. And that has been to our benefit. That's not why we did it. It's just the way we grew."

Tim Willits—id Software

"One of the advantages we have, we're very unique, is that at id we can self-fund, and the previous success of our titles gives us the advantage of not having to wow the publishers. But it always helps if we have a good demo because we can get more money for the game.

"Once we have a demo, we call Activision, EA, Vivendi, Take-Two, Microsoft, the major publishers, and we have a month in which we schedule time to demo the game, and they send someone down to take a look. We show them the game, talk about what the vision is, let them play it if it's playable, state and talk about our goals, what we want to do for marketing, and how we want to position the title. We give them a rough timeframe of when we'll have it done, and then we start to receive bids. For the last eight years we've worked with Activision on our titles, and they haven't always come back with the largest bid. But the devil you know is better than the devil you don't know. But yet we talk to all publishers.

"We're in a unique position because we know the game will always be successful—well, we *don't* know the game will always be successful, but we *do* know the game will always be fun. The publishers know they have a pretty good chance of making money with us because they don't have to pay for development. They have to pay for marketing and QA, and they have to give us an advance, but they don't have to pay for development—there's no milestone."

Adrian Wright—Max Gaming

"I talk to a lot of people who are independent developers and they have this big plan for a game they're going to build, and they say they're going to take it to a big publisher and get big money for it, and it just doesn't work like that. We thought the same thing when we started out. We had a great idea and we got pretty far with a big publisher, but when it came to a decision point they said, 'You guys have never made a game, so why should we do this project?'

"My people have a lot of professional experience, but not in the games industry, except for our lead artist. We weren't part of the club. We didn't know the big boys. You don't know the right people when you first get started. Getting into the indie movement when we did, we were early, but we are much better game developers now, and when we go to shows we know people. What I usually try to tell people is you gotta scale your vision. I'm not saying it can't happen. There are ways to do it. But there are too many people in the industry who have talent and try to do things too big, and it never gets done.

"In 2001 we put a pitch together for a game called *Critical Subterfuge* and looking back it was more than we could handle at the time, so the publishers actually knew what they were talking about. Independent developers weren't a big thing back then, and a lot of people didn't believe you could do it. So we scaled down the game we wanted to make, and for two years we worked part-time making a game called *Dark Horizons: Lore*, an online persistent mech game. That opened up a lot of doors for us. And in order for us to all go full-time, we started doing contract work on games.

"You have to do what you need to do to survive. And for us that meant taking contract work, and that was invaluable because now we're building a portfolio, and when you go to a publisher and they say, 'What have you done?' it might not be in our name but we have references for it. So basically, all the experience you would have built going to a game company we're getting in our own company.

"We have a couple of casual games out now that are our own IP, and three completed contract games this year. We definitely have a much thicker portfolio than six years ago. From the onset we always wanted to make persistent worlds, and that's where we're going in the future.

Clyde Grossman and Bob Jacob—ISM

Grossman: The key thing, no matter how great the game design, is you have to be able to sell it to a publisher. You have to be able to communicate it effectively to that first audience.

So helping our clients create an effective game design is really, as an agency, where our focus is. And what we're looking for is the hook, that something that is unique, some unique gameplay. It's not story. It's not art direction. Bob and I think, and this is something we browbeat our clients with, that good story is great, and great art is great—you need those things—but the thing that pushes it over the top is the hook—the unique gameplay mechanic, some fresh approach to something.

Jacob: Let me look at things from a non-agency point of view for a second. With a good developer, it's almost like love. The developers who make it have chemistry. I'm not sure there's any way to quantify that, but there's a certain magic that happens when a certain group of people gets together.

In terms of a hook, a game designer needs to be able to articulate to a publisher why something is going to be fun, and he needs to be able to do it very quickly and succinctly. And it has to be obvious, where a publisher goes, "I get it. This is cool. I understand it." You really need to be able to do that because games are so expensive and the risks are so high. The publisher needs to be able to feel the game is going to bring something new, something innovative.

Grossman: At the same time, one of the strengths we have is that many, in fact most, developers really have no idea what publishers are looking for and the process publishers have to acquire a game. Usually what happens is the developers come up with an idea they like, and they go out and pitch it without even knowing if it has a shot. Because we're in constant contact with publishers, we have an idea of what's sellable, so we tend to get involved very early with our clients in how they focus their energies so their game has a chance to get sold. This is not an exercise—we've been doing this for ten years, and I think over that time our clients have been able to see that works and have an appreciation for what the keys are to being successful.

The market has moved away from platformer games—you can have a great concept for a platformer game, but there's just no market. And I don't care how great your concept for a western is, it ain't gonna sell. There are certain concepts that aren't going to go anywhere.

So what's the secret to designing a great game? The secret is in the doing it—not in knowing it.

Jacob: You have to have a great concept and you need to be able to communicate it, and most of our effort is, "How do you communicate it?" Game designers tend to get involved with storylines and write large documents. You have to be able to communicate the essence of your concept in a minute—if you can't communicate that in an effective way that sounds exciting and interesting in a minute, you're not going to be able to sell your concept. And there's an important reason for it—people have short attention spans.

Since I got in the business, one of the basic differences is games took $20,000 to $60,000 to make 20 years ago, so the product-development group inside a publisher could make the decision to go with a game on their own. But now with eight-digit budgets, you're not going to get a green light unless marketing can say yes they can sell the product. And marketing people typically are not

"You have to be able to communicate the essence of your concept in a minute—if you can't communicate that in an effective way that sounds exciting and interesting in a minute, you're not going to be able to sell your concept."

—Bob Jacob

really strong gamers. They need a message they can understand quickly.

Grossman: Beyond marketing, more people get involved in these decisions. Every publisher has an executive committee that will greenlight—this includes finance, legal, product development, marketing, sales, operations, whoever sits on that executive board. For the most part, they're not going to read a 150-page design document and know all the weaponry and the various enemies and the levels and whatever. These are the people you need to communicate with. And you will most likely not be sitting in on the marketing meetings. And you have to prepare documents and visual aids that can communicate that. That's why it's so important to be able to communicate it within a minute, because the people who present that idea to the executive committee need to have that sound bite—this is the essence of the game, and this is why we do it.

Jacob: Some of the best advice I can give the readers is don't get hung up on the story, don't get hooked up on the graphics.

Grossman: Uh, yes, the art direction does not sell a concept.

Jacob: It's almost meaningless. Fifteen to twenty years ago you could barely do anything on the computer. Now everybody can do good art. And good stories don't sell games. What sells games is fun. What's special? What kind of feedback does this give me? We can bring in writers and artists later.

Grossman: But if you want to know what sells a game not just into the publisher but what makes it a hit product, it's having something unique and fun. It has to be fun. But you want to have something that has a sense that the game player hasn't seen before, hasn't done before.

Jacob: To my way of thinking, there are two ways of innovating gameplay: (1) You come up with something out of the blue. Those are great, but that doesn't happen that often. It's almost like trying to regulate a lightning storm—when it happens, it happens. Tetris came out of the blue. No one had seen it before. (2) With most publishers, you see something that has been successful and you try to improve it, add some scope to it, trying to do successful games that try to quantify the process. For example, with first-person shooters like *Medal of Honor*, every product ups the ante. Another classic example is EA SPORTS titles—you have *Madden 4, 5, 6, 7.* They keep trying to modify it and change it year after year, but they know what they have, and they know what works.

Grossman: One of the things we tell our clients is if you're trying to identify the hook, which is a marketing term by the way, one of the things about the hook is that it's never something you apply some sort of adjective to. It's not something you say more, better, faster—that's not a hook—you're improving something, which is okay, but that's not a fresh way of looking at something.

Jacob: "Unique" isn't something that's never been seen before or never invented before, it's the fresh way of looking at it. If you look at the movie industry, they're still doing the same genre, but what's enjoyable is when it's original—if it's just the same thing over and over again, you're not going to be interested in it very long.

Grossman: It's difficult for me to conceive of someone who hasn't played games before coming up with something that's a hit. If you design games, you play games. A lot of games are synthesized out of frustration. Bob is a good example of what we're trying to communicate—at Cinemaware, people took an original and unique approach to sports and to action adventure games.

Jacob: What Clyde's referring to was a series of games we made called *TV Sports*—we emulated TV broadcast. We had announcers, half-time shows, other sport scores going on at the same time—no one had done anything like that before. That was the hook. At that time, that was unique. It wasn't something that was more or better or faster. It was a fresh approach.

Coming back to the idea of frustration, I bought an IBM PC in 1982—I bought some games, and I hated every game I bought. I hated them all. Most of the games were adventure games where you input text and get a response. The whole idea of the game was to figure out what some programmer had in mind, whether it made sense or not in the game.

That same level of frustration goes on today in that game designers will buy a new game and play it and say, "Man, this is really frustrating, why didn't they do this, why didn't they do that? Gee, I want to play something better." And great game ideas can be born out of that frustration.

> *"So a lot of what we do is to get people to understand ways to pitch to mitigate the risks."*
>
> **—Clyde Grossman**

What Publishers are Looking For...

Grossman: Publishers are looking for magic. Sometimes they say, "Oh, we need an action game" or "We need a first-person shooter" but that doesn't happen that often—they're looking for magic. I wish there was something more specific. It would make our job easier. But they want to believe. They want to believe that this, whatever "this" is that you're presenting to them, is going to be a hit. That's what they want—no one starts off wanting to do a mediocre game like no one starts off wanting to do an also-ran movie—whatever category it's in, you want it to sell; you want the lightning to strike.

Jacob: The point is, at the very core of this business, it's indefinable because if it could be defined it would have been. It's magic that sells.

Grossman: Half a dozen key people comprise the greenlighting team, and these are heads of the various depts. Most publishers are publicly traded companies—they're going to be committing millions of dollars, and that's a decision that requires a buy-in from a bunch of different departments.

Jacob: Ultimately, the decision makers who pull the trigger can be a small group.

Grossman: At one major publisher, they're called "the ultimates," the guys who pull the trigger. This includes the heads of product development, marketing, sales, and finance. You need those four people, the president of the company or division, often you'll have legal, PR may be there, depending on how the company itself is organized—it's a half a dozen people plus or minus two—that generally is what it takes. It's hard because people are committed to spending millions of dollars.

Jacob: The fact is the risk is high. There are a couple of things to think about when millions of dollars are spent developing a title and it fails. People can actually lose their jobs if a title fails, so they need to feel comfortable.

Grossman: So a lot of what we do is to get people to understand ways to pitch to mitigate the risks.

Jacob: Is the developer a sound business? Are they going to be around? Are they a successfully run company? What about technology? Does the developer have the technology necessary to actually complete this project? Do they have all the people in place to do this project? If not, how many people are they going to have to hire, and what is the risk of having to staff up the project?

Grossman: And the same thing is true of the art department. Do they have the artistic sensibilities and the people to do that in-house, or are they going to have to find these resources elsewhere?

Jacob: There are a million ways a project can fail, and the publishers are looking at all of them.

Grossman: The key to minimize the risk is—do we have the solution? Do we have these resources in-house all right now? This includes audio, game design, management. This business is so big now. When titles cost under $100,000 to make, the teams were small. Now when you have teams of 50 to 60 people or more, management of the teams itself is a risk. The publishers see that the project can fail for a lack of proper internal development. You have to address each of these risks and say you either have a solution, or you have a plan for how you're going to get the solution. You may not have a team of 100 people, but you have a plan on how to get them.

The proper way to do it is to address every area of concern and provide the answers. Publishers want to believe. Publishers are looking to developers for answers, not questions. Philosophically this is important. Over the years developers will say "I can do this or that, and if they want me to do it this way I can do it this way." No, no, no. They're looking for answers, not a lot of questions. You have to be decisive.

Jacob: On the other hand, they also want you to be flexible—there's that fine balance between having a clear vision and being able to communicate it, and not coming across as arrogant where you're closed to suggestions from a publishing partner.

Grossman: Different companies at different times look at different things in terms of greenlighting. You talk about what is going to be the magic, why it's a great game, why it's a great studio. Then you get practical—when is it scheduled to be released? Is that a good time for the publisher? Do they have too many products releasing at the same time? Is there a hole in their cycle? What's the genre? What is it competing against?

This is something a well-run studio will present in its presentation. For example, if you're presenting a first-person shooter, don't ignore the competition. Talk about how it's going to fare against other similar products in the time frame, talk about how your product is going to be differentiated and how it will compare against the others. The studios will address this with or without your input, so you might as well address these issues up front.

A game made today, a game that's meant to be a front-line AAA product in the marketplace is going to take two years to develop. It takes 60 to 100 people and costs more than $10 million to make. That doesn't include the marketing costs, which could be equal to that. So someone with a great idea has to convince someone to spend $20 million dollars—well, you don't do that with three pieces of paper and waving your hands around. There aren't companies, especially publicly traded companies, who'll sign a check and say "We hope you'll build something for us." So you have to approach it very realistically. You have to provide them with good reasons to do it.

Jacob: That's why there are two aspects—one is selling the magic and effectively communicating that, and one is addressing the risks.

Grossman: It's a business.

The Pitch

Grossman: There are effective ways of communicating with people and groups of people, no matter what industry you're in. For the pitch, you take in a one- to two-page executive summary. This has lots of white space, not a lot of words. With lots of white on the paper it can easily be read in a minute or two. Then there's a longer document, usually five to ten pages that fleshes it out in more detail—why it's a great product, why you're a great studio to do this product. The third document, that is as big as it needs to be, is to be read by the game producers, and it's only for the people who are interested in the details.

You need graphics, concept art, sketches hopefully in color, and some sort of prototype—a proof of concept, an animatic—there are a lot of different names and it depends on the product or the studio and where they are in the whole pre-production process, but something that's on screen is really, really helpful.

And one last caveat: I've seen developers make the mistake of creating such an onscreen demo, or a little AVI, which is a visualization of what they want to build, and every once in a while somebody will build something like that but they won't add sound effects. And it is really boring, and really bad. There's nothing that will lose their interest faster than a demo without sound.

Jacob: One thing I would add is that a lot of developers go wrong by making it too elaborate, too big. The prototype should be as small as possible, and it illustrates the core concept and it should look good. As small as practicable, but still illustrate the point you want to make with the game.

Grossman: The fact that you have all of these levels and this big world is great, but you don't show all that. If you come up with something that's a flabby and mediocre demo, the publisher will think "If I give them money, they'll do a lot more flabby and mediocre." You'd be amazed at how many people do these big demos and they're empty and they're boring. It's counterproductive. And it's funny because the designers will write in the docs how exciting it's going to be, and then they create this demo that is just boring—you're not trying to show it's big, you're trying to show it's fun!

Jacob: Some people think if they create this big demo it'll show the scope of the game. It has to be fun—it has to be fun! It can be incredibly small.

Grossman: It has to be small, tight, and intense. For a long time I used the analogy of a little chocolate truffle—the thing about a truffle is it's not a pound of chocolate, it's just a really intense experience of chocolate. And that's the key, to demonstrate the intensity.

It's like doing a movie trailer. It doesn't show two hours of a movie, it shows really intense action. So that's what you want to do. You want to create a trailer of your games. Well, a trailer of a game doesn't show the hero walking though a landscape. What you want to show is something really intense—the hero fighting a boss or doing something really cool, a move that has never been done in a video game.

Jacob: One of the implications is it's virtually impossible to sell a game as innovative because of the scope. Nobody wants to hear that. You can't show it, and it's not sellable. "We have twice as many weapons and three times as many enemies." Ho, hum, yawn. You're not going to sell it. Figure out what the essence of the game is, and then concentrate on it.

Grossman: We touched on story a bit, and one of the things developers do— it's one of my pet peeves—is they go in and say, "We have this great story," and they tell you about the story and then they say, "But what you don't know is there's a secret and *you* don't know what it is."

And I'm thinking, "You're trying to sell this to me, and you're treating me like the consumer and you're not going to tell me what it is?" You don't want to leave the publisher out in the cold. You want to bring them in on the secret.

Think about *The Crying Game*, which had this big twist at the end. Believe me, when they were pitching this to the studios they didn't tell them, "There's this big twist at the end, and we're not going to tell you." I know this is a very practical matter, but it's something I see over and over again from clients and developers, and it's not effective.

The Numbers

Grossman: It's a huge business. Our clients employ several hundreds of employees. It's not a garage-shop hobbyist activity.

Jacob: If you look at the last ten years, we've done over $350 million in business with our clients, with over $65 million in royalties earned by our clients.

Grossman: In this industry, some products see millions of dollars in royalties, and most see none.

Jacob: It's really a question of a number of factors. Like in the book industry, most games are advance-against-royalties. There is a wide disparity in terms of platforms—for example, PS3 or Xbox has certain licensing fees paid for the platforms. As opposed to PCs where there are no fees. Whether it's Microsoft, Sony, or Nintendo, they collect a fee for every disk you manufacture for the system, so that's a cost the publisher has to bear. That's deducted from gross receipts.

So if a game has a retail price, let's say it is $49.95, wholesale is around $36—so what happens to that money—perhaps $10 off the top for platform license fees, now it's $26. Now you've got $2 to $3 in manufacturing costs. Normally there are certain marketing dollars—marketing-development fees or coop advertising—and those are around $2 to $3. Plus there's an allowance for returns, usually a 10–15% holdback. These are all things that are done before the royalties are calculated for the developers.

The fact is that games are so expensive right now, any project we're doing on next-gen platforms the absolutely bottom bottom is $9–15 million for a normal range for a title like that. Say the developer is getting a $5 unit royalty, which is high, actually. It's a budget of $10 million, and so you have to sell 2 million copies just to make back your advance. Let's consider there are no PS3s in the marketplace yet, so the installed base of the next-gen platforms is very small. There's no way you'll sell those kinds of units yet. There may be in two to three years, but not now.

We're in a platform transition right now. Every platform transition we've gone through, every platform change has gotten bigger and more expensive, and the teams necessary to create those games have gotten bigger and bigger.

Grossman: A lot of our discussion has been about business. And it is a business. But ultimately, at the end of the day, it's all about passion. It's about having a creative burning desire that you have to do this. And you really *have* to do it. If you believe strongly enough in it, and you can rally the troops behind you, you can get this stuff done. We do it every day.

Chris Ferriter—Ubisoft

"In a developer-publisher relationship, I can see how my take is very different from the developer's. In a way, the publisher is the client. We're paying the developer to execute our vision of the product in 90% of the cases, so there's probably a lot of compromise that takes place on the developer's part to make us happy.

"When you're working with licensed products, your considerations and concerns as a publisher are definitely different because you have a number of additional stakeholders that you would not have on an original product. So with *CSI*, not only is it an established brand that people have set expectations from, but there are a number of people involved in the process, like CBS, the *CSI* producer and creator, *CSI* actors who care how they're portrayed in the game. So my number-one priority is not only to please the audience, but all of these stakeholders as well.

"My primary concern is that we are authentic to this license. Well, my *primary* concern is that we sell as many units as possible. That is my job, and this is a business, and what we really want is a successful game. And in order to achieve that, we need to be authentic to the license, and I have to ensure that anything we do is going to ring true not only to the audience, but to the stakeholders in this game and this franchise.

"A common misconception is that publishers are spending more money to develop a title than they are to manufacture and market and distribute. And that's rarely true. I would say that in the majority of cases, development costs are fairly low next to manufacturing costs, marketing costs, and overhead."

—Chris Ferriter

"I have a secondary goal when it comes to game design, and that is that I have to ensure that the design we're attempting to execute is realistic. Because part of my job is to ensure the product is complete at a certain time. So we want to review the game design to make sure that not only is it desirable to do from a content point of view, but that it's also realistic to do.

"A lot of people don't know what a producer does. At a developer, when you say 'producer,' that's typically a project manager, and that's easy to qualify. It's hard to explain what a producer does, not just in this industry but anywhere in the entire entertainment industry—we facilitate. We have to make sure that all of the pieces come together, that everybody responsible for working on this project works together to meet our common goal.

"There are a lot of groups that work on a production on the outside, and all of the information from all of these groups typically flows through the publisher, through the producer, who needs to ensure that PR has the assets they need and marketing is working off of a schedule that works with the developer's schedule. We also need to communicate high-level goals for the game so that marketing understands

Image courtesy of Christopher Ferriter.

exactly how they're positioning this product, you have an editorial website that needs to go up, finance for milestones that need to be paid in a timely manner so the developer doesn't get their power cut off because they can't pay their bills, legal to ensure that we're not violating any terms of the contract—a lot of things that need to come together at the same time. It's very interesting to hear misconceptions about what we do, and often it's very hard for a producer to explain what they do.

"I feel very strongly about documents. Honestly, I think there's a big problem with the way game designs are created in the industry on average. It's unfortunate, but in a lot of situations with third-party development publisher relationships, a game-design doc is generated very early to fulfill requirements of a milestone, and it's often treated as something that *has* to be done—it's a line item in the contract. It's not treated as the document that serves its purpose of conveying exactly what needs to be built.

"A lot of times you end up with these big unwieldy documents that don't accurately explain everything about the game. When I think about the game-design document, I want a blueprint of what's going to be built, and that's rarely what's created. Instead you get a rough overview of features of the game and core concept of what's going to be built. Obviously that's not true in all situations, but in a lot of situations it is, and it's not only the fault of the developer but the fault of the publisher as well.

"We typically lead the charge when it comes to the scheduling of the milestones, and when you're in negotiation the developer has input into this.

And this'll be back and forth to come to an agreement. But a game-design document is something that's typically created early in the project cycle, and it's a lot of times looked at as a starting point. And I don't think it's a starting point at all. Much in the way when a real-estate developer decides they're going to develop townhomes, they don't start on day one with blueprints. There's research that goes into it. You have to answer questions. And you certainly don't break ground before you have blueprints. But we do that in this industry a lot. It's not uncommon to see a game that has an evolving design.

A lot of times publishers and developers look at preproduction as a waste of time. 'Why should we spend time thinking about what we're going to be building? We should just be building it.' We're one of the few industries that thinks like that.

"As an industry, we need to embrace the idea that pre-production is important, that there's a certain amount of time in the schedule that very few tangible playable items are delivered. It's a time when we need to figure out what exactly it is that we're going to build. This is when you do your brainstorming, your focus testing, your prototyping. And at the end of the day when assignments are handed out, you're creating artwork, programmers are programming, and we're all working toward a common goal that we all agree on, rather than, 'We'll tough through it together.'

"There are a lot of reasons why a project gets killed. You say, 'We've invested $500,000 on this,' but that's a lot less than fulfilling the milestones and paying the manufacturing and distributing the product. A common misconception is that publishers are spending more money to develop a title than they are to manufacture and market and distribute. And that's rarely true.

"The goals for a demo or a prototype differ based on the game, but there's a core promise that you want to get across in that prototype, and you can easily do that with less than a minute of gameplay. And that says to the publisher, 'This is a proof of concept, and we feel that we can deliver on this times 100.'"

—Chris Ferriter

"I would say that in the majority of cases, development costs are fairly low next to manufacturing costs, marketing costs, overhead. It certainly depends on the platform. You're going to have much, much higher manufacturing costs for a cartridge-based system than a PC game, but with console products, manufacturing can be very expensive, distribution can be expensive, marketing can be expensive, and you certainly don't want to incur those costs if what you have doesn't show any promise. A lot of times people will say, 'The game was almost developed, why not finish and ship?' but it's not that simple."

CSI

"The opportunity to work on a license like *CSI* is very cool, and I'm very intrigued by the fact that this game doesn't necessarily skew toward gamers, the 18-to-34 male audience. The *CSI* target audience is women 25 to 50, which is very different from the majority of games out there. It's a very unique challenge to appeal to this group that is very difficult to reach using the traditional methods. And it is one of the fastest growing segments in the market right now. It is really a phenomenon, especially when you compare it to the growth rate of the traditional games console and PC market.

"We signed a deal with CBS to publish a number of *CSI* games for *CSI* and *CSI: Miami* and went out to find developers to build the game that we wanted to build. Originally it was developed by 369, a division of Radical, which did *CSI: Dark Motives* and *CSI: Miami* for us. These were all 2D Macromedia Flash–based PC

> *"We have a business-development department that actively seeks out and meets with developers."*
>
> **—Chris Ferriter**

games, and the primary reason was we wanted them to be able to run on very low-spec systems. Like I said, our market is very different for *CSI*, so at the time it was our belief, and we still believe this to be true, that the majority of people interested in purchasing this game would not necessarily be the people who have invested in high-end, high-tech systems.

"After *CSI: Dark Motives*, we thought that things are changing, technology is changing, and people have been upgrading their computers, and we decided to see if we could make a 3D game because 3D really allows for a lot more immersion in this license. The 2D games are interesting, but because they're done in 2D they're very flat, and at the same time we were limited by the technology in what we do. In 3D you can do a lot more, and the *CSI* license is really at its core about how things that are so small can be so important. With 3D we can focus on those things that are small, and we give the player the ability to investigate and think about everything in their environment, where they want to go and what they focus on. The 2D games for their time were very good, but the 3D could obviously open up a lot of goals for us, so our goal was to find a developer to deliver our vision.

"We have a business-development department that actively seeks out and meets with developers. When we're starting a project, we work closely with business development to determine who the best developers are to deliver on our primary goals of that project. Typical goals we'll have at the onsite [meeting] are general creative thoughts you have on the license, a budget, and the time frame you have in mind. At that point we'll meet with several developers and start a dialog and determine who is the best for that project. We will evaluate games the developer has worked on in the past, have them submit a proposal to us if they're interested, and we will look at their proprietary technology, their staffing, their overhead—obviously cost is an important part of this.

"With *CSI 3* it worked a little bit different. We did go through this process, but we were approached by Telltale, who was a very young developer at the time, and they said, 'We feel like we can do justice to this game.' Telltale gave us a demo of what they thought they could deliver, and the demo was very impressive, and we decided to go with them.

"The demo was a very, very short demo. It was one room using existing assets that we had created for the previous games. And the purpose of the demo was to show what *CSI* could be in 3D. It was very simple, with the ablity to look around the room, move around the room a bit and converse with one or two characters. The goals for a demo or a prototype differ based on the game, but there's a core promise that you want to get across in that prototype, and you can easily do that with less than a minute of gameplay. And that says to the publisher, 'This is a proof of concept, and we feel that we can deliver on this times 100.'

"We are heavily involved in this product. The more important the product is in terms of potential to generate revenue, the more involved the publisher will typically be. Publishers have to balance their costs and budgets

"I created this Visio file to communicate how the camera system should work within the environments in *CSI 3*. It was based on the first prototype delivery we received from Telltale, and the original file contained hyperlinks on all the objects and rails so you could click on any object or area and it would take you to the page that related to that object, so you could essentially navigate through the environment at a rudimentary level just as the player would navigate through the game." —**Chris Ferriter**

See Appendix E for full document. Image courtesy of Ubisoft. (See color plates.)

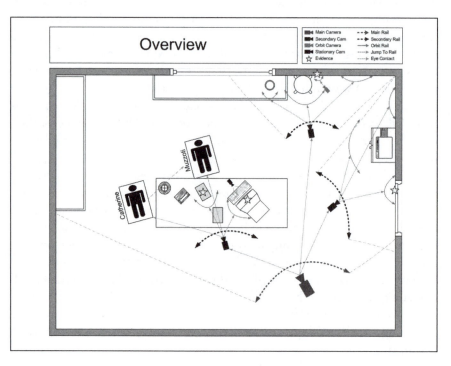

as well, so every time you assign a resource to a product, you are in essence billing a portion of that resource's time to that product. So if you have two products, one that has the ability to generate a great deal of revenue and one that's not expected to generate much revenue, it doesn't make sense to have 80% of someone's salary attached to the product that doesn't have the potential to see returns on that.

"It's fairly typical for a publishing group to be fairly involved in any project that's developed by a third party. Certainly there's the evaluation of milestones, but you're constantly making sure that this group you've contracted is tracking toward the ultimate goal or promise you've agreed upon. It's similar in a way to bringing in a contractor to put an addition on your home. You wouldn't just hire somebody and let them go at it. You'd want to see plans, be involved, know what the finished product is going to look like and when it will be done. You want to track that and know it's going to be done on time to spec. It's similar with a developer-publisher relationship. There's constant dialog to ensure everyone's goals are being met.

"The milestones you set completely depend on the project. When I set up milestones, the overall purpose is to ensure that we are tracking accurately towards our goal. Certainly you'd want to highlight what the biggest risks of the project are, and you would want to see proof that those milestones are accounted for in those deliveries.

"For *CSI 3* this is a very good example. We didn't want to compromise the game with respect to 3D, and we didn't want to significantly raise the specs—we still wanted to run on low-spec systems—so our big concern was are we going to be able to make this look as good as 2D—because 2D art can look phenomenal. The characters can't emote, but it'll look beautiful. With 3D it was completely different. Every time you add polys or a bump map or high-res textures, you can negatively affect the performance of your target system. So we want to be able to see if that would be able to hit our visual targets with milestones. We wanted to see proof of concept early on to make sure that when we get close to final in this game, we would have a very good idea of what the rest of the rooms would look like, and we wanted to know what the characters would look like. So you use the milestones as a tool to ensure that you would meet your goals.

"Our development cycle is approximately one year. We absolutely check in more during certain times; usually as the game progresses and we start nearing that completion date things tend to become a lot more frantic. You really want to make sure everything is coming together. The two times when they're more frantic are at the start of a project at pre-production, and at post-production when you're trying to close a project. Aside from those times, when you may speak many, many times a day, I typically communicate via email or phone with Telltale on a daily basis.

"There are a lot of dependencies that the publisher is responsible for as well. I don't want to give the impression that I'm calling to check on them. Often it's a dialog of what's going on with, for instance, voice recording, because we use the cast of *CSI* as the voices for the characters in the game. There'll be a lot of things we work closely together on.

"Certainly, the game needs to be at a stage where we can start producing voice recording, so I'm responsible for facilitating voice recording, securing the talent and making sure they're available, securing studio, making sure all of the scripts are ready for the talent.

"This is just one example, but there are a number of things throughout the development cycle that we work on together."

Mark Lamia—Treyarch and Activision

"Each publisher has its own process, but for most publishers looking at a new game, a new developer is a high-risk venture. The cost of developing premium or AAA games is a high-risk venture. You put the two together, and that's a *very* high-risk venture. From a AAA game-development perspective, if you're new, the publisher is looking to limit the areas of risk as much as possible.

> *"If you get involved with the wrong publisher, and in the middle you have issues and they stop supporting you in a way you thought you were going to get supported, that's probably a couple of years in your company's life. And as an early startup, sure you can afford to take some risks, but if you've been at it for a little while and you haven't quite had that hit, your publisher choice is going to be very critical."*
>
> **—Mark Lamia**

"Following are some of the factors we look at and how we evaluate the risk when looking at a project when somebody says, 'I got this great idea for a game; how do I get it made?' And the answer for myself and for many people is, 'Before we get into what that idea is, who are you working with?' Because there are tons of great ideas out there and so few teams who can execute on them. Unless you're a AAA-established game developer like id who can come to the table and say, 'I've got the next great game,' publishers are going to be a little wary to take anything for granted.

"You need to identify the genre or subject matter so that the publisher can see there's a demonstrable track record and it's popular. So if someone comes to me and talks about a genre that is no longer hot, it would be harder for someone to get their premiere flight sim done than other things, for example. First-person shooters are obviously popular, so that has a better chance than a flight simulation right now.

"Finding out what publishers want is the best route for people who aren't already AAA established. Sometimes they want games made out of properties they've spent money licensing or developed expertise on. You can sometimes collaborate with a publisher that way. Once you have a reputation, then things open up more for you. Finding a marketable concept is critical. Not every idea flies. But the more successful you are, the more your ideas can stray from the norm and the more ability you have to do original work.

"On the idea of the concept, having a concept that's extensible is more important than ever, especially with the cost of premium games. You can see if it's franchisable. Or is it already part of a franchise? If so, that's valuable from a creative perspective because you can build on an established world. But really from a PR or marketing side there are a lot of benefits there, and it reduces some of the risk for the publisher in terms of gaining exposure for the game. Also, the publisher is already vested in leveraging its value.

"The team is the most important aspect for the greenlight process. AAA well-run and experienced development teams will have a much better chance. For startups, unless they're a startup of a new company with experienced leads in management, design, programming, and art in the genre they're proposing, it's very hard for startups to get premium products greenlit. There are very few entirely self-funded startups that have people who don't have track records behind them. So if that is the case, you need to surround yourself with leads and talent that do have that experience, otherwise the publisher will be concerned with investing.

"This next point is obvious, but there are a lot of people coming out of school who think they'll get a development company started, but it doesn't happen. This is very rare. My advice is do apprenticing, associating with established companies, or get a contract working with experienced developers. Spending time learning the craft and getting experience with an established developer is a great way to gain experience, and it also helps you establish a relationship with a publisher that you could leverage some day.

"This worked with Splash Damage. They started out as modders and went pro! After id software's *Return to Castle Wolfenstein* released, they brought Splash Damage to Activision to work on a multiplayer expansion. They added some cool gameplay elements to *Wolfenstein* multiplayer working with id. Before working with us, they had experience modding the id online game *Quake 3*. They worked in their craft, in their community, and pulled themselves together as a team and got recognized by a leading developer. After they did the mod on *Wolfenstein: Enemy Territory*, they helped id on the *DOOM 3* multiplayer. Then id and Splash Damage came to Activision after that and got their own gig. With the *Enemy Territory* style of gameplay, now

Biodome and Goliath shots from *Enemy Territory: Quake Wars*.
Images courtesy of id Software, Inc.

they have their own full premium game they are developing with id called *Enemy Territory: Quake Wars*.

"Not only did they establish themselves and learn their craft among the best in the industry, they were also establishing a relationship with us. Since they were all from the mod community, when we started working with them, the team quit their 'jobs' to become game developers.

"You need experience to start a team. You need a track record in place, with discipline in management. A publisher likes to look at companies and their track record of how they're managed, how they've grown, their financial health; and those companies that are more healthy are looked at as a better risk than those that aren't. If there's anything that can impact them financially, that can have a dramatic impact on the developer, and if you're a publisher, you don't want to see your developer run on hard times. It can seriously affect them and the project.

"Solid technology and tools are music to a publisher's ears. Only a few are going to go down a path and successfully get a greenlight making their own technology the first time out with their own game concept. Unless they're a AAA developer, to be able to get a green light with a new concept on new technology is about the riskiest thing a publisher can do. New developers entering the market and developing games are very likely to have technology and scheduling issues, and if on new technology likely to have financial disasters that follow. There are plenty of examples of those on the market.

"Unless you want to be a technology company, my advice would be for startups or people if you can self-finance it, if it's really important to get your game made, find a reliable set of technology and tools. There'll still be a ton of work and risk, but you won't get drowned in core technical risk.

"On the side of the person who's trying to get the gig, it really is important to pick a publisher who already has a solid track record in the business that you're trying to get into or the genre. You need to have the stability of knowing your people are going to get paid, this publisher is an established publisher, and they're financially stable.

"It's also hard for publishers to stay in business, and some are not as stable as others. The ability of the publisher to maintain its strength affects how their marketing and sales organizations can support you, and if they cut checks to you when you need them. There are publishers now that were once mighty who have run into hard times, and that trickles down to the developer.

"If the publisher has a solid track record in, say, first-person shooters, for example Activision makes a lot of these, they'll talk the same language as the developer. But also inside their organization that means that the publishing studio is organized to help you, and QA who's going to test for you knows how to test those games, marketing knows the demographic, the PR group knows them inside out—who to target, how to target them, who to work with, how to establish buzz in this area, and sales knows how to sell your product. They get it. They're enthusiastic, and they can get above the noise that's out there, and there's a lot of noise in the commercial space for games these days. If you do a good job, you can capitalize on it in the future—sequels or acquisition as part of the business plan down the line.

"You can get involved with a publisher not in the business, but you need to believe they're strategically aligned to move in that direction. If they're not in the business and it looks opportunistic of them, and they can't tell you their strategy of how they're going to move this genre, you may find you won't get support, and titles that don't get the support in the market have little chance of succeeding.

"Publishers have to evaluate their P & L[1]. They have to make money as well, and you need to be competitive on costs. As a new company or startup, if you're going to offer up a game-development budget you have to pay yourself like a new company. If you're really good, then great, you can negotiate an upside benefit. But you can't expect to make a lot of money and have huge profit margins when you're starting up. The more experienced you are, the more you bring to the table, the more you can try to negotiate for yourself up front. But just because you want to get a deal, don't sign up for it if you're not sure that you can afford it. If you're desperate and you want a deal so bad that you'll sign up for a deal even if you don't think you can get it done, then you shouldn't, because it puts a horrible strain on the development cycle, on you, your team, and on your publisher. If you can negotiate what you think you need with contingencies, that's ideal, but you have to be realistic about how much contingency you are negotiating for.

---

1 Profit and loss statement.

"*Call of Duty 3* from a greenlight perspective is one of the less risky titles we could have greenlit. The developer is not a new company. The concept is marketable within a major franchise. Conceptually what they came up with for *Call of Duty 3* passed the litmus test: it's a very popular established franchise that Activision needed a developer to make, the team is part of an established subsidiary of Activision, and Treyarch, who did a great job developing *Call of Duty 2: Big Red One* the prior year, is an established developer. While they did rebuild their technology for next gen, a lot of tools and tech were built out of technology we had here. That's about as easy as it gets for a publisher to greenlight a game. As an example, that's why a *Call of Duty 3* could get a greenlight at Treyarch. It would be very hard to get a new company in the *Call of Duty* franchise unless they had solid technology with a strong existing team and a track record in the genre.

"The length of time it takes to close a contract depends on the complexity of the deal, but it's a couple of weeks to months. If you're a new team, plan for months to do a deal. That's once you find the publisher. For a publisher search, I wouldn't put a time limit on it.

"I know more projects that never have gotten made. With the exception of the top developers, almost every developer I know has a game they've been trying to get made for years. Once they do something that catapults them into the low-risk category to a publisher, their time to get a deal made is less than a year. This has more to do with when the team is available.

"From a publisher's perspective, there aren't that many low-risk opportunities out there. So until you're an established developer, getting an idea made is going to be very difficult, and a long and hard process, and to the extent it's not, you need to be careful with who you're dealing with.

"If you get involved with the wrong publisher, and in the middle you have issues and they stop supporting you in a way you thought you were going to get supported, that's probably a couple of years in your company's life. As an early startup, sure you can afford to take some risks, but if you've been a developer for a little while and you haven't quite had that hit, your publisher choice is going to be very critical.

"It becomes actually harder after a while, if you've produced what should be premium games and you haven't actually had that hit, that can become an issue for you in trying to get a big publisher. If you've had attempts to do that, and have a solid team, a contributing factor could be the amount of financing and support they gave you, or it might not have gotten the attention and exposure you'd hope it would get. So you need to know, 'This publisher is committed to my business, and our goals are aligned.' That's the optimal situation. Be careful what choice you are making. To think that you're involved in a game for the long term and have a publisher drop support could be devastating for your company."

Charles Balas—Oberon

"I have a feeling the casual-games industry for the last five years is like first graders playing soccer. They're all on the field playing with the ball, and not having had a lot of forward thinking. The nice thing about the download space is, at this point, distribution has become a commodity, so it's the IP that has the value. To develop a downloadable game is around $50,000 to $120,000, so it's not a lot of money. Everything else is $5 million and above. With digital distribution, because it eliminates putting boxes on the shelves, the casual-games space is a way to break into the industry right now.

"Part of why I was interested in getting into this space was that 2003 was the tipping point for this industry—it was the first year we outperformed Hollywood. So it fell into the business culture that the video-game industry is a serious industry.

"One of the things that's going to need to change in our industry, and no one's been able

> *"To develop a downloadable game is around $50,000 to $120,000, so it's not a lot of money. Everything else is $5 million and above. With digital distribution, because it eliminates putting boxes on the shelves, the casual-games space is a way to break into the industry right now."*
>
> **—Charles Balas**

to tackle it, is nobody's thinking about creative plays[2] and what we can do to change how it's being promoted. The almighty sacred cow is the conversion rate—what percentage of people that download and play your one-hour demo are willing to pull out their credit card and pay for it? And so that's the big thing about game design in this space. It's all about creating a compelling game experience. It's a completely different proposition creating a game that'll get reviewers excited and have cool packaging and word of mouth and get the game off the shelf. This is an industry that lives and dies on demos. You have an industry average of .7 percent conversion rates. So anything that converts at a 1.0 percent rate or above is considered a huge success. I think there's something flawed with the model, because you have 99% of the audience telling you they don't want to buy your product.

"So the challenge becomes what you can do when you put promotional dollars behind it. You can definitely increase the download velocity, but you can't increase the conversion rate. And in fact, you may corrupt the conversion rate because you have unqualified people downloading your game—in other words, people who are never going to buy your game.

---

2 Promotional and advertising mechanisms that would allow us to put marketing dollars behind something and turn it into a hit.

"We don't know yet in this industry how to be king makers. The crazy part about the whole thing is the $19.95 price point and the 60-minute demo was a totally random decision made by RealNetworks, and it has again become another sacred cow in the industry. What is interesting is the studies done on consumers show us the purchasing decision on the game takes place in the first five minutes. So you're giving away 55 minutes of gameplay. So what you've trained your consumers to do is they can get an hour of play at Yahoo!, AOL, and any of the myriad of Oberon sites. So you have an audience of people who can probably play 20 or 30 hours of your game and never have to pay for it.

"What makes a successful hit in our industry? We have a strong belief that it's true but we have no way to quantify it, that a vast majority of people who buy games are either category busters or category makers. These are people who have never bought games before. So if you have a game like *Mystery Case Files*, you have a bunch of people who are swimming and never chose to buy. When you have a break-out hit, you've resonated with people who have never plopped down their card.

"Honestly, the probability of the first-time or startup game developer to get a deal with a major publisher at this point is about as good a chance as you or I are going to be in *MI4*. Because I know these people, and I now how they are and what they do.

"*Far Cry* was a first-person shooter from Crytek in Croatia. They shopped it to every major publisher and got no traction. They finally sold it to Ubisoft for $250,000—they just sold it so they could get out of the debt they were in. And it was the Game of the Year for *PC Gamer* magazine. It was a critical delight in 2004; it did what most first-person shooters were unable to do prior to that. It was bleeding edge in terms of graphics, including *Unreal* or *Doom 3*, and they were able to create seamless open outdoor environments where you could see for miles, and no indie had been able to do that. It was a hard-core game. Here's a group of people who are extraordinarily talented and basically through blood, sweat, and tears made an amazing game, but they basically sold the game just to pay off their debts. And it was a fantastic game. And first-person shooter is one of the most successful genres of all. So, you can be incredibly different and you're still not going to make it in the PC console world today. It was different ten years ago.

"Cut your teeth first on the casual-games space.

"So, when a developer submits a game, there is a scheduled review process that assesses the interest in the game. Depending on the level of interest, there are a variety of tools at our disposal to decide what type of relationship we might want to have with the game. That relationship can be as low-touch as simply distributing the product, to a purchase of the IP.

"If there is interest, our producers will often give the developer feedback on some improvements, as a way of seeing how easy they are to work with and how open to help that developer might be. We can also run the game through user testing, beta testing and limited-market releases to measure the potential success of the game. These mechanisms help us in better predicting how a game will do in the market and what relationship we wish to have with that developer.

"If you want to make it, do it in casual games."

James Brightman of *GameDaily Biz*—A Pulse on the Industry

"It's a bit strange right now because there's sort of almost a battle for input versus continuing graphics technology. On the one hand you have Nintendo, with the launching of the Wii, and they're going a completely different direction—they're focusing on input and trying to get people who have not played a game before because the controllers are too complex. That's a very critical part of game design right now because the developers have to really seriously think about how to use the new controls. And even on the PS3 they're incorporating motion sensing, and they're inviting developers to incorporate it.

> *"…There's a war going on with the companies that are trying to take over control of your living room…"*
>
> **James Brightman**

"The Wii is the premise of that entire system—those controls—so there's a war going on with the companies that are trying to take over control of your living room, the digital entertainment hub—Microsoft is getting into the video distribution of high-definition movies, and Sony is going to be emphasizing their online capability, and they're getting behind because Microsoft has a big mind share. But I really see developers trying to balance these different aspects because the cost of games is constantly rising. Games are costing $15–20 million, and as a publisher you really have to ask, 'Is it worth that investment?' because you have to make a profit.

"The Wii might be appealing for developers because the cost of development will be lower, because you don't have to pump tons of money into art assets and animations. The Wii graphics won't look ugly, but it won't look like a PS3 or Xbox, either. It'll be interesting to see over the next five or six years because the cost of development is a very big problem and can hinder creativity. The pubs decide what's going to get published, and devs would rather create more original titles. Then there's the whole other side of marketing, and you have to decide how much to put into marketing—it's an enormous, enormous investment."

Sequels vs. Original IP

"Once a game is successful, it gets into that sequelitis trap. But at some point you have to have an original property, otherwise you can't make a franchise. *Halo* was an original property, and they didn't know how it was going to do. At the first E3 it showed, it was really poorly received. So they took that and came back with a hit. *Halo 2* sold $124 million in one day when it first went on sale and set a new record for any entertainment property. It was a huge success for Microsoft and Bungie Studios. So, you have a franchise like that developed, and gamers want to see more of that. One of the most anticipated games is *Halo 3*. The so-called problem with franchises isn't that bad, because gamers want them.

> *"...the cost of development is a very big problem and can hinder creativity."*
>
> **James Brightman**

"The problem is when publishers want to make a cash cow out of something. You have a franchise that goes on and on and on, and all they care about is the money, and creativity suffers. They nearly killed *Tomb Raider*. That's a perfect example. Every couple of years they put out a *Tomb Raider* that declined and declined in quality, and eventually they realized they were killing it—and they switched developers and they ended up starting at ground zero and came out with a good game that did well. The problem is when publishers exploit a property and try to make a cash cow out of it and the creativity gets out of the way because they're focusing just on money. Eventually the trust of the public fades away and the quality goes down.

"In terms of the whole money equation and isolating creativity, a new trend is creating new IP not just for video games, but you're able to offset the risk by creating IP just for the sake of IP. That IP could be used not just for a video game, but a book, comic book, toys, movies. Oddworld Inhabitants started as an animation company and went to being a video-game company, and now they've gone over to creating IP in this model. *Death Jr.* has comic books, games, and Foundation 9 is very much into that philosophy of creating IP. Chair Entertainment is creating an IP called *Empire*—it's a comic book, video game, a movie. So it minimizes risk when you have a property that can branch out into all those things at once and not just have to invest in only a video game that might or might not be a hit."

Hollywood and Games

"There's convergence and the cross-pollination between the two industries where you have games that become movies and movies that become games, licensing going back and forth with game-based movies and movie-based games. And a lot of convergence of talent where the same people might work on an animation movie and those skills can work in the video-game industry and vice-versa. And so I think there are a lot of tie-ins between Hollywood and the game industry. In some ways it's beneficial, in some not. There are many in the industry who don't like it. They say the industry is trying to be too much like Hollywood and it shouldn't and it should strive to define the industry on its own terms—not everything has to be cinematic.

"That's what gets back to the Wii philosophy that there's nothing more important than controls—you don't have to have a game look like a movie as long as you're having fun playing it. Obviously the first games were not about story; they were about having fun. In some ways maybe Nintendo is looking at that. To be fair to Microsoft and Sony, Microsoft has the Xbox Live Arcade on the 360 where you can download old classic arcade and new arcade games, and Sony will have something very similar on its PS3 online network, so that's a whole other way of making money for these smaller developers."

Serious Games, Casual Games, Mobile Games, MMOs, and Portables

"Regarding serious games, I did an interview with Henry Jenkins, a professor at MIT who is a proponent of serious games, and I asked, 'When do these games stop being serious games and just become games? Or maybe they're just software applications? How do you define what a video game is?' And he thinks whether you call them serious games or not, they're still games.

"There are various teaching applications for teaching, military, doctors for surgery, flying—there are a lot of applications. You don't see that much on PS3 or Xbox; Nintendo has had a little of that on the DS. Something like *Brain Age* that tests your mental acuity for an age for your brain based on math tests, reading tests, recognizing patterns. I don't think people would consider that a serious game, but it is similar. And the army with its video game *America's Army*. They use that as a recruitment tool, and it's based on real infantry tactics the army would use. So you do get a cross over in the traditional market.

"On the casual-game side, there are a number of portals—websites that allow you to download games on the PC. Those are very, very simple games for a few dollars or free (ad-supported) and those games are very appealing to older women—it's a large percentage of that audience, and there is some crossover with Xbox Live Arcade where you might have some casual games.

"Then you have mobile games, which is gaming on your cell phone. You see some growth there—it's a huge opportunity for the video-game industry, because what has a larger installed base? Everybody has a cell phone. The trick is to figure out how do we get people who have these cell phones who are actually subscribers to pay a little bit to download games. Right now the number who are downloading these games is relatively small.

"On the business side you have in-game advertising that could help offset costs we talked about. You're already seeing billboards, for example, in racing and sports games that mimic real life. They have to be very careful about how they implement advertising in other games, though—you wouldn't want to see a billboard for Coke in the middle of an RPG unless it made sense for it to be there.

"The MMO business is huge, especially *World of Warcraft*—it has 7.5 million subscribers worldwide. It's a big contributor to Vivendi Games quarterly.

"And then you have micro-transactions—where you can buy extra characters, items, new weapons, swords, armor, some special item that gives you powers. That becomes very attractive to some of the gamers out there who want to have more. In some of these MMOs, there's an obsessive quality to have the best characters and they spend hours and hours leveling up—it's almost like a social status. There are stories, especially in Asia, there are people that have become so addicted to these MMOs they've literally gotten ill because they've not taken breaks to eat or sleep, and there have even been fatalities.

"In Asia they have Internet cafes—it's very popular because of piracy of physical games. The online gaming is huge, and people go into Internet cafes and play endlessly—they've even opened up clinics to fight this. That's becoming a big thing on consoles where you have extra downloadable content with games that are sold, and that's potentially another huge opportunity. These can bring incremental revenue to publishers.

"The portable market has grown. It used to be just GB[3] and GBA[4], and with the introduction of Sony's PSP, you have another viable competitor out there on the portable side. And the portable market in general has helped the industry grow. In these console transition years, you typically see sales dip a little because consumers are waiting for the next consoles to come out.

"But the portables, especially the Nintendo DS, have become a huge success for Nintendo both in Japan and the US. I don't think Microsoft is ready to get into the portable sector, although there have been some rumors about that. Nintendo owns that sector; there's no doubt about it. The PSP is the first real contender that Nintendo has seen. The Game Boy dates back a long time. The portable market is getting back to design and cost, and the portable sector could help in that regard because developers can create games for portables for a lot less cost."

---

3 Game Boy.

4 Game Boy Advance.

Online Game Downloads

"In five or ten years, the thinking is that everything will be online and it's like you're shopping at Amazon. And by then, broadband will be more pervasive, and there's a lot of thinking out there that the industry is heading in that direction. GameStop has finally started, on their website, a digital-download service that could be the start of a business-model switch. There's a lot of stuff going on, on all sides.

"There are a number of people who think it's going in that direction, including Bill Gates. Take HD DVD and Blu-ray—that format war is starting in earnest, but that war might not even matter because by the time people are ready to make the switch from DVD to HD DVD and Blu-ray, it may not matter with everything online. Some top Sony executives have said, 'I'd be surprised if the PS4 had an optical drive at all.' That was Phil Harrison, the head of Sony Computer Entertainment Worldwide Studios— so there is definitely that thinking out there that the industry could be going that way.

"The music industry is struggling with this with CDs. How many people buy CDs versus download from iTunes or other services? The game industry might be going that same way in five years. Maybe the retail sector will still be there, but its market share will be reduced. It's definitely going to happen. When this takes over from retail, I don't know."

Industry Growth and Public Perception

"The NPD Group, the market research firm that tracks all POS[5] data for the industry in the US, recorded that [2005] saw $10.5 billion in sales, and we are on pace to probably beat that. We could have upwards of $13 billion in the US alone [in 2006], and on a worldwide scale it's growing.

"The industry is getting bigger, and more players are trying to get involved. Look at the big media companies—they see covering the industry as a big part of their business. IGN and its affiliated sites were bought by News Corp.: you know, Rupert Murdoch, FOX, and all that. MTV, Viacom, also purchased GameTrailers.com not that long ago. GameSpot is owned by CNET, which is another huge media company.

"The public perception is changing, and that deals with gaming as a hobby and entertainment for adults. Because a lot of people have the idea, and this is where there's the generational gap, where people in their 50s and 60s think of gaming as a kid's hobby. And that's where the controversy pops

---

5 Point of sale.

up with violence in games like *Grand Theft Auto*. Everybody always points to *Grand Theft Auto*. That game is designed for adults, not for kids. If it says 'M for Mature,' you're not supposed to give it to your 12-year-old.

"But perception is changing, because of the people who grew up with games, and decisions about the industry are being made by these people. And because of that, laws facing the industry won't be a problem anymore because the generation that's getting older already has an understanding of video games. Rock and roll went through the same thing. Comic books went through the same things. When they had violence and sexual imagery in comic books, people started freaking out. It happens in an industry just about every generation."

Greenlighting Exercise

You now have a high-level pitch doc (Chapter 8) and flowchart (Chapter 9) of your game. Generally, in the greenlighting process, you would absolutely need a demo that captures the essence of your game. If you have the ability to do a vertical slice of your game, then by all means do it.

1. Define your game in one sentence.
2. Define your elevator pitch—in 60 seconds, give the essence of what your game is all about and make it exciting.
3. In the pitch process, once you give your 60-second elevator pitch, you need to be able to respond with punch when the publisher says "Tell me more."

    (a) Expand your 60-second pitch into a paragraph's worth of information. If they are still interested, they'll want to know even more.

    (b) Expand that pitch into a page. If they're hooked, you have your pitch document (and demo) ready to go.

4. Practice your pitch out loud, until you have it nailed and can rattle it off to anyone who says, "So, what are you working on?"
5. Now you are prepared with your:

    (a) 60-second pitch

    (b) One-paragraph pitch

    (c) One-page pitch

    (d) Entire pitch document (and demo)

Pitch your game to someone. With enthusiasm.

Greenlighting Checklist

- ❏ Your game needs to be fun.
- ❏ Your game needs to have a great hook.
- ❏ You need to be able to communicate what your game is all about in 60 seconds.
- ❏ Know what publishers want—for example, don't pitch a game to a publisher who has decided they're not doing that genre anymore.
- ❏ The greenlighting process marks the beginning of a long and intimate relationship—choose your publisher wisely.
- ❏ Know who's on your greenlighting committee—marketing, finance, legal, sales, operations, product development.
- ❏ Be aware of the risks publishers perceive and be able to mitigate them—they want to see:
  - Good business and management practices
  - Solid technology in place
  - Staff and resources available
  - Artistic capabilities
  - Capable development staff
  - Decisiveness
  - Flexibility
  - Fun/cool game
  - Good gameplay mechanics
  - Hot genre
  - Marketing
- ❏ Pitch requirements include:
  - One- to two-page executive summary
  - Approximately 10- to 15-page pitch doc
  - Sketches, concept art, graphics (in color is preferable)
  - Short fun prototype/demo showing the core concept of the game—with sound

Appendix A

CSI Case **Treatment**

Rough Cut
Case 4 Treatment

Updates
8/5/05 - Minor Updates mostly to evidence -GL
8/8/05 - Trinity updated - GL
8/9/05 – Rewrote Crime Recons & Added Forensic Recons – GL

Overview

The son of a politically connected real estate developer is found dead in a remote desert area. Poison is the cause of death and everyone in his life has a motive for the killing. Evidence points to a contractor owed a large sum of money and the victim's hard edged mother, who is currently embroiled in a tight primary race for a nomination to the state senate and is upset over negative publicity stemming from her son's public life. Eventually the evidence proves the victim's wife killed her husband to cash in on a life insurance policy and begin life anew with another man.

Characters, Line Counts & Relationships
(names needed for CBS for name clearance, lines needed for sound budgeting, relationships needed for art comp/voice casting)

- ?
- ?
- Brass
- Robbins

- VICTIM
- WIFE
- MOTHER
- CONTRACTOR
- CONTRACTOR'S SHOP

- **Victim** –30's male – Father was a somewhat prominent physician, who died of a heart attack while the Victim was in high school and left him a sizeable trust fund. Fueled by easy money, he was a cruel, narcissistic playboy found irresistibly charming by women. Throughout college he loved to drink, dabbled in recreational drugs, loved to gamble, sleep around a lot, treat women like crap and not study much- all of which helped dwindle said trust fund considerably. After college he moved back to Las Vegas, where, separated by the lackies and hangers-on at school he cleaned up his act somewhat and got married. It wasn't long however, before the Victim fell off the wagon and began living life on the wild side "Vegas-style". While alive his reputation did his mother's political ambitions little good when she decided to compete for a Republican nomination to the state senate, though the Victim's Mom received an outpouring of sympathy from voters after his death.

- **Mom** – late 50's Female – A hard-nosed, tough-as-nails politically connected real estate developer known for being as intelligent as she is aggressive. A woman quick to burn bridges both personal and professional. Upon graduating from college she married the victim's father, an older man who was already a successful physician. She went to law school, entered the real estate development business and found success, despite her penchant to litigate at the drop of the hat. Her husband passed away several years ago leaving their only son with a somewhat hefty trust fund she suspects is not quite so hefty anymore. A recent bitter political campaign for the republican nomination to a seat in the state senate, along with several lawsuits hint at financial trouble for this suspect. Her son's conduct was also damaging to her campaign, and he refused to contribute much in the way of financial support to the effort. She is openly hostile to CSI and feels they are beneath her. Tight-lipped, not real emotional about her son's death though there is some affection there.
  - o Mom hates her daughter-in-law (Wife), and will blame her for the killing.

- **Wife** – Late 20s Female – Hard-nosed, ambitious workaholic, (shades of Mom). She hails from humble origins, an only child raised by a submissive mother and an abusive, alcoholic father. Over the years she's worked incredibly hard to put as much distance as possible between then and now and prides herself on what she's been able to accomplish. Had few serious relationships before meeting the Victim, who was tending bar at a watering hole near her firm and seemed serious about cleaning up his act. Deciding she was "good for him" they eventually married, but soon afterwards the marriage started to crumble. The Victim began drinking a lot, gambling, and racking up debts all over town. Silently outraged at this betrayal the Wife eventually found solace with a young lawyer at her firm. Fearing her marriage will become an echo of the one her mother suffered under, and seeing an opportunity to free herself from her husband's financial entanglements, she had the Victim increase his life insurance and poisoned him.
  - o Wife will blame the Contractor.

- **Contractor** – Late 40s Male – Slightly crooked contractor with mob ties. Has done work for the victim's mother for years and more recently for the Victim. Got to know the Victim when he was in high school and at varying times has acted as his bookie and drug pusher. More recently he invited him to sit in on some high stakes poker games he runs out of his shop. The Contractor acts as "the house" during these games, and has some mob friends who bring in heavy hitters to participate. Soon the Contractor got greedy- he and his mob pals fixed a game and managed to bilk the victim out of A LOT of money. Afterwards however, the Victim became suspicious at his run of "bad luck" and cut off all contact with the Contractor and refused to send payment. The mob started leaning on the Contractor for the money, making him desperate. He acts saddened and is cooperative but is cagey and lies a lot.
    - o Will blame the Mother.

Relationships
- Victim is Mom's only child. Never close, the two had a rocky, tempestuous relationship compounded by the fact that his outlandish lifestyle hurt her political ambitions.
- Victim and his wife were married three years. She was originally a calming influence on him but he eventually regressed and began partying hard, drinking a lot, sleeping around, and racking up serious gambling debts.
- Contractor has worked for the Victim's mother for years. Their business relationship has been rocky at times due to her demanding and aggressive nature.
- Contractor has known the Vctim since he was a young man. They recently had a falling out over a "fixed" poker game which left the Victim owing the Contractor's mob friends a large sum of money.

(Two mob stories – here and 5 – too many. Remove from here.)
- Mom hates the Wife, blames her for the Victim's outlandish behavior.
- Wife is not fond of the Contractor. She blames him for her husband's gambling problem.
- Wife is carrying on an affair at work with an unmarried man. The affair has turned serious; she sees it as her last shot at real happiness (love?).

Forensic Tool, Lab System & Mini Game Count

Detection Tools	# of times used in case
Object Manipulation (Reveals items)	2
Magnifying Scope	6
Fingerprint Powder	3
Magnetic Fingerprint Powder	
Ninhydrin	1
Luminol	
Leuko Crystal Violet (LCV)	
Flashlight	2
UV Light	
USB Data Drive	2
Collection Tools	# of times used in case
Given by Character (GIFT)	8
Camera	1
Glove	14
Tweezers	4
Swab	1
Adhesive Lifting Tape (used with FP Powder)	
Adhesive Specimen Mount	
Electrostatic Dust Print Lifter	
Mikrosil	1
Plaster Cast & Frame	2
Lab System	# of times used in case
Microscope Match	2
Computer Fingerprint Search/Match	7
Computer DNA Search/Match	3
Computer Footprint/TireTread Search/Match	3
Computer Special Search/Match	3
Computer Audio/Visual Search/Match	
Mass Spectrometer (TBD – or computer as alternate)	
Mini Games	
MINI GAME - 2D PUZZLE ASSEMBLY	
MINI GAME – Chemical Litmus test	4
MINI GAME – 3D Assemble/Disassemble	1

Evidence for Trinity

Criteria: firm evidence, or clear circumstantial that supports weaker evidence.

(Walkthrough Phase)

- VICTIM
    - o (Victim – Crime Scene)
        - ▪ Bruise on Forehead Photo
        - ▪ Rolled Cigarette
        - ▪ Salt Particles
- MOM
    - o (Suspect – Crime Scene)
        - ▪ Boot Print (hypo only)
        - ▪ Testimony – Saw him pick up Camping Gear from Garage
        - ▪
    - o (Suspect – Victim)
        - ▪ Salt Particles on Jar = Poison (hypo)
        - ▪ Jar with Fingerprint

- CONTRACTOR
    - o (Suspect – Crime Scene)
        - ▪ Boot Print (hypo only)
        - ▪ Rake (hypo only)
        - ▪ Victim's Cell phone
    - o (Suspect – Victim)
        - ▪ Bruise on Forehead Photo (hypo)
        - ▪ Salt Particles on Lid = Poison

- WIFE
    - o (Suspect – Crime Scene)
        - ▪ Boot Print (hypo only)
        - ▪ Humidor
        - ▪ Fingerprint from jar at House matches wife
    - o (Suspect – Victim)
        - ▪ Tobacco matches
        - ▪ Salt = Poison

Crime Reconstruction Cutscenes

NOTE: Labels (ABC, etc.) are to facilitate searches, and do not indicate appearance order.

Short

CRIME RECONSTRUCTION 010
CONDITIONS: Bruise on Forehead + Boot Print
SUGGESTS: Victim hit on head, left to die?

CRIME RECONSTRUCTION 020
CONDITIONS: Salt-like particles CS01 + blow to head not a killing blow + Consistent with poison
SUGGESTS: Victim takes a drag while sleeping under the stars, begins to cough violently, passes out, stops breathing?

CRIME RECONSTRUCTION 030
CONDITIONS: Pesticide Matches Salt + Robbins Tox Report Confirms Poisoned
EVIDENCE SUGGESTS: Victim definitely poisoned by Pesticide - but who did it?

CRIME RECONSTRUCTION 040
CONDITIONS: Salt Particles in Shop Match + Vic Fingerprints Match
EVIDENCE SUGGESTS: Victim in Contractor shop, contractor possibly poisoned victim?

Medium

CRIME RECONSTRUCTION 050
CONDITIONS: Vic DNA matches + DNA of hair from Shop + Pesticide from Shop Matches Murder Weapon
EVIDENCE SUGGESTS: Victim and Contractor fought inside Shop. Shaken, but angry, Contractor quickly grabbed pesticide, sprinkled it on Victim's tobacco

CRIME RECONSTRUCTION 060
CONDITIONS: Mom Testimony of Marriage in trouble and Wife Having Affair + Insurance policy
EVIDENCE SUGGESTS: Wife not telling truth, has motive to kill husband

CRIME RECONSTRUCTION 070
CONDITIONS: Testimony says Vic hurt Mom's Campaign SHOP 04 and
CONDO 06 + Papers show bad relationship
SUGGESTS: Mom not telling truth, has motive to kill son

CRIME RECONSTRUCTION 080
CONDITIONS: Campaign problems + Pesticide in House + Camping gear in
House
EVIDENCE SUGGESTS: Victim and Mom argue. Victim heads to garage to get
everything ready for camping trip. Mom goes into garage, picks up bottle of
pesticide, and sprinkles some on tobacco.

FINAL

CRIME RECONSTRUCTION 100
CONDITIONS: Fingerprint from jar match Wife's fingerprint + Salt-like particles
CONDO15 match sodium monofluoroacetate + Oven Mitt + Insurance Policy +
Affair Photo
EVIDENCE SUGGESTS: Wife upped their life-insurance policy, then she
poisons his tobacco with pesticide, using oven mitt with small burn hole.

Case Flow

VERY LINEAR

Crime Scene 01 (Victim)

An anonymous tip brings the CSI team to a remote corner of a state park where the Victim's body lay just outside his small tent. He appears to have been the victim of a robbery: there is no wallet nor backpack nor anything that might identify him and the victim has a deep bruise on his forehead.
(any way to make this a gruesome death on top of the poisoning? Extreme dyhydration? Scarfiaction? Facial changes like that political figure a while back?)

Evidence Player interacts with:
- Footprints (CASTING PLASTER and FRAME) ➔ Boot print from crime scene CS01
- Tire tracks (CASTING PLASTER and FRAME) ➔ Tire tracks from crime scene CS01
- Victim (Not Collected)
  - Deep bruise on Victim's forehead (Photo)
  - Watch (GLOVE)
    - Markings on back (Evidence Viewer) ➔
  - Note (GLOVE) ➔ Handwritten note CS01
    - Wadded up in Victim's pocket.
    - Message is vague, no signature ("Pay up or else", etc.)
- Sleeping Bag (Not Collected)
  - Hand rolled cigarette butt (TWEEZERS)
    - Salt on backside of Butt (ADHESIVE SPECIMEN MOUNT)
      ➔ Salt-like particles CS01
- Roll box (GLOVE)
  - Knocked over, tobacco swept away by the elements.

CRIME RECONSTRUCTION 010
CONDITIONS: Bruise on Forehead + Boot Print + Photo of Crime Scene
SUGGESTS: Victim hit on head, rolled, left to die?

LAB 02
Player processes items:

COMPUTER
REQUIRES: Boot print CS01
- Boot print is from high end hiking boot, male model, size 11

REQUIRES: Tire tracks CS01
- No match found in database (why? Bad print? If not, there should be SOME match to a tire, which would list a number of trucks, but nothing else.)

MICROSCOPE
REQUIRES: Handwritten note CS01
- Handwriting analysis dragged to microscope for future comparison.

CHEMICAL ANALYZER
REQUIRES: Salt-like particles CS01
- Chemical not found in database.

Analyze tobacco – anything interesting?

MORGUE 02

REQUIRES: Photo of Vic Body Position CS01
REQUIRES: Crime Photos Taken
- Body Recovered
- Vic Fingerprints (GIFT by Robbins) ➔ Vic Fingerprints MORGUE02
- Vic DNA (GIFT by Robbins) ➔Vic DNA MORGUE02
- Vic Boot Print (GIFT by Robbins) ➔ Vic Boot Print MORGUE02
(Player should gather this with transparent tape)
- Blow to head not a killing blow.
- Body moved post-mortem.
- Coughing bit needs to be pulled out here, as his lungs/throat could give it away

REQUIRES: Salt-like particles CS01
- Cause of death consistent with poisoning, could be overdose.
Need more details... is this a gruesome death?

- Can't test for it unless it is identified.

CRIME RECONSTRUCTION 020
CONDITIONS: Salt-like particles CS01 + blow to head not a killing blow +
Consistent with poison
SUGGESTS: Victim takes a drag while sleeping under the stars, begins to cough
violently, passes out, stops breathing?

BRASS 02
REQUIRES: Mold CSO01
REQUIRES: "Bruhler-Bouchant Geneva Switzerland No. 63445"
Brass does search of theft identification program using 63445.
- Victim registered watch with homeowner's insurance.
- Suspect Unlocked: Wife

LAB 03
Player processes items:

FINGERPRINT - CODIS
REQUIRES: Vic Fingerprints MORGUE02
- No match found in database
- Fingerprints added to computer as well for future comparison.

DNA
REQUIRES: Vic DNA MORGUE02
- No match found in database
- DNA added to computer as well for future comparison.

CONDO 03

Wife conversation:
- Shocked and saddened at death of her husband.
- Says Victim often liked to camp on his own.
- Last time she saw the Victim was when he left for Mom's house to pick up
  camping gear and head out to desert. "He only just told me that morning
  he was leaving." There was no bruise on his head.
- Yes, Victim preferred hand rolled cigarettes, was a connoisseur, found it
  "chic".

- Yes our marriage had some rocky times, but Victim was "wholly and completely" committed to turning things around, part of the reason he went camping: to get his "head right". He stopped drinking and doing drugs and had looked into checking himself into a treatment facility.
- Enemies? I think something happened between the Victim and the Contractor. He's a sleazy guy; think he was mad at my husband for something. Contractor quit remodeling kitchen as a result of squabble.
    - o Suspect/Location unlocked: Contractor
- This is going to sound suspicious, but the Victim and I upped our life insurance recently to $500,000 each. We both felt it was important, especially after buying the condo and given the fact we plan to have children soon that we have more coverage.
- Does not consent to search "I need some privacy right now, I'm very upset".

(Find tobacco to match to hand rolled cig tobacco – validates it is the vic's cig – though COULD be someone elses!)

SHOP04

Contractor interrogation:
- Is shocked to hear of Victim's death, feigns sadness. Asks how he died
- Denies there was any beef between him and the Victim. Says he stopped working on the Victim's kitchen because she fired him.
- Last time he saw the Victim was at the condo about a week ago.
- He was supposed to return tomorrow, so he wasn't missing.
- Won't give prints. (why?)
- Wouldn't be surprised if Mom had something to do with it. She was very angry with the Victim for the negative publicity he caused her campaign. Also, her son has a bit of money linked to his father's passing. He had promised to contribute some money to the campaign and then reneged. I overhead her talking to him about it on the phone.
    - o Suspect/Location unlocked: Mom
- Consents to search of shop floor, but not my office. Don't want things messed up in there.
- Wears boots.
    - o Won't give boot print. (why?)

REQUIRES: Tire tracks from crime scene CS01

- Claims he lent truck to friend, has no idea where it could be now.

REQUIRES: Handwritten note CS01

- Denies writing the note.
- Refuses to give handwriting sample (why)

Evidence Player interacts with:

- Cardboard box of odds & ends (Not collectible)
    - Salt (MAGNIFYING SCOPE, ADHESIVE SPECIMEN MOUNT) ➔ Salt-like particles SHOP04
        - Plastic lid (GLOVE)
            - No identifying markings.
        - Fingerprints on Lid (FINGERPRINT POWDER) ➔ partial fingerprint SHOP04
        - Contractor claims not to know what lid was for or what salt is. "Could be anything."
- Table (Not Collected)
    - Poker chip wedged under table leg (GLOVE)
        - Fingerprint (FINGERPRINT POWDER) ➔ Fingerprint from poker chip SHOP04
    - Bottle of Mr. Clean on table (Not Collected)
        - Contractor claims he felt need to clean the place up recently, and that Mr. Clean is the toughest on grease and stains.

LAB 05
Player processes items:

COMPUTER
REQUIRES: Fingerprint from poker chip SHOP04
REQUIRES: Vic Fingerprints MORGUE02

- Match found

CHEMICAL ANALYZER
REQUIRES: Salt-like particles SHOP04

- Chemical not found in database.
- …but it is the exact same Substance as the other one!

CRIME RECONSTRUCTION 040
CONDITIONS: Salt Particles in Shop Match + Vic Fingerprints Match
EVIDENCE SUGGESTS: Victim in Contractor shop, contractor possibly
poisoned victim.

CONDO06

(what is the condition that triggers this?)
Wife conversation:

- Victim may have gambled at the shop, which might explain what the rift is
  about: money

SHOP06

Contractor interrogation:

- Victim has never been to his shop, has no idea how that fingerprint got on
  that poker chip but he's been to their condo plenty of times, it could have
  easily got mixed in with some things he brought back to the shop from
  there recently.

Need to discuss the match with the salt at this time. Need to put some suspicion
on the contractor, or cast suspicion off. Trinity is not complete enough to go to
the next level, and this should flag the player of this.

HOUSE05

Mom interrogation

- Seems a bit shaken at the news, then hardens.
- Supposes it was only a matter of time, with his "lifestyle". Asks if it was an
  overdose.
  - Son partied hard, dabbled in drugs.
- Last time she saw her son he picked up his camping gear out of her
  garage and headed out to the desert. She didn't notice any bruise.
- Blames Wife, says she was having an affair and that their marriage was in
  trouble. (this should be hinted, CSI should uncover this via investiagation
  to bring to light)
- Denies her campaign is in financial trouble.
- Denies Victim's conduct was causing her campaign any problems.

- Denies an argument about money took place between her and the Vicitm.
- Won't give prints.
- Won't consent to search.

CRIME RECONSTRUCTION 060
CONDITIONS: Mom Testimony of Marriage in trouble and Wife Having Affair +
Insurance policy
EVIDENCE SUGGESTS: Wife not telling truth, has motive to kill husband
(Bad recon – based on motive, not evidence, not how CSIs work)

CONDO06

Wife interrogation
- Vehemently denies affair. The Mom has always hated me, always been jealous, has always blamed me for the Victim's very public behavior. (OK,good for hint of affair, let CSI find something now or later to help prove there is something going on)
- Agrees with testimony that Mom was furious about public behavior hurting her campaign

BRASS06
REQUIRES: finished conv. With Mom in House 05
CSI gets call from Brass summoning them to his office.
- This story is all over the papers, we have to tread carefully.

Newspaper (GIFT by Brass) ➔ Newspaper BRASS06
- Brass gives them a newspaper, story is front page news.
- Investigative article reveals strife within Mom's campaign. Staffers have quit over not being paid. Victim's lifestyle hurting her in the polls, though pollsters showing Mom is starting to get some sympathy from voters upon the media's announcement of Victim's death.
(Is there SOMETHING the player can do with the paper to solve the case? Compare a picture/drawing of item/symbol with something else? Some reason to give the player this item?)
- CSI suggests they talk to Mom again.

HOUSE07
REQUIRES: Newspaper

Mom interrogation
- Denies media accounts. (what does this mean? Are we really saying "you killed your son for sympathy votes" with no evidence?)
- CSI notes a handwriting sample would go a long ways towards eliminated her as a suspect. (why isn't this asked before, since it was valid? There needs to be a reason it waits until now. Assume will be ultimately be gated on Brass 6 paper, but needs logical reason to not ask sooner.)
  - Mom to copy what's on the note, but grabs the first piece of paper she can find, a hand-written estimate given to her by the Contractor, on which she's written an angry addendum or two. Then she throws CSI out.
  - Handwriting samples (GIFT by Mom) ➜ Handwriting samples HOUSE07

CRIME RECONSTRUCTION 070
CONDITIONS: Testimony says Vic hurt Mom's Campaign SHOP 04 and
CONDO 06 + Papers show bad relationship
SUGGESTS: Mom not telling truth, has motive to kill son
(again, MOTIVE, not reconstructing the crime!)

LAB 08
Player processes items:

MICROSCOPE
REQUIRES: Handwriting samples HOUSE07
REQUIRES: Handwritten note CS01
- No match found with Mom's handwriting.
- Match found with Contractor's handwriting.

BRASS09

REQUIRES: Contractor's handwriting matches that found on note.
REQUIRES: Victim's fingerprints found on poker chip in shop.
- Warrant for Search (SHOP)

SHOP10
Contractor interrogation
- Contractor not happy with warrant.
- Clams up, won't say anything more.

Evidence Player interacts with:

- Pesticide Safety: A Consumer's Handbook (OPEN WITH OBJECT MANIPULATION)
    - Page on sodium monofluoroacetate is dog-eared.
        - Fingerprint (NINHYDRIN, CAMERA) ➔ Fingerprint from book SHOP10
        - Talks about poison being odorless, tasteless. Very deadly.

Ask Contractor for a sample of pesticide, and he gives you a jar of it:
    - Pesticide (GIFT)
    - Who else has access to your shop? (Mom or wife?) Both have been there.
- Cell phone (FLASHLIGHT, GLOVE) ➔ phone from SHOP10
    - Phone underneath piece of furniture, hidden from view.
- Garbage can (Not collected)
    - Broken rake handle (GLOVE) ➔ rake handle SHOP10
        - HAIR (MAGNIFYING SCOPE, TWEEZERS) ➔ hair from SHOP10
- Ledger (GLOVE) ➔ Ledger sheet SHOP10.
    - CSI notes this doesn't look like any normal small business balance sheet.

LAB11

Player processes items:

- Regarding the phone, Sanders directs CSI to Brass, who can track down the owner and gain access to voicemail faster by working with cell phone provider.

COMPUTER
REQUIRES: Vic DNA MORGUE02
REQUIRES: Hair from SHOP10
- Match found

COMPUTER (OR BRASS OFFICE)
REQUIRES: Ledger sheet SHOP10
- Gambling operation, most likely poker. Show's large, debt outstanding.

FINGERPRINT - AFIS
REQUIRES: Fingerprint from book SHOP10

- Positive ID on Contractor
- Has criminal record: fraud, extortion, illegal gambling operations

CHEMICAL ANALYZER
REQUIRES: Pesticide from Contractor
- Pesticide is a match to salt, we should check with Robbins
  - Salt-like particles SHOP04 are sodium monofluoroacetate
  - Salt-like particles CS01 are sodium monofluoroacetate

MORGUE12

REQUIRES: Pesticide is a match to salt found in CS01
- Cause of death is sodium monofluoroacetate poisoning. (needs a reason to NOT know about this… is it rare, does it not have obvious signs, what about conditions that can mask it?)

(note: Al should have a much bigger part here, especially with a mystery poison. There should be some more red herrings, and perhaps a few "circumstances" to help him determine the cause of death, even IF he finds out the chemical.)

CRIME RECONSTRUCTION 030
CONDITIONS: Pesticide Matches Salt + Robbins Tox Report Confirms Poisoned
EVIDENCE SUGGESTS: Victim poisoned by Pesticide - but who did it?

BRASS12

REQUIRES: Positive fingerprint ID on Contractor found in book.
REQUIRES: Pesticide matches Crime Scene
REQUIRES: Hair found on handle is that of Victim's.
- Warrant for Questioning (Contractor)

REQUIRES: Phone from SHOP10
- Brass able to quickly gain cooperation of phone provider. The phone is registered to the Victim.
- Gives 3 VOICE MAIL MESSAGES (GIFT)

LAB 12.5

AUDIO/VISUAL PROCESSING

- There are a few voice mails:
    - Angry voice mail from Contractor.
    - Voice mail from stripper thanking him for gift.
    - Angry voice mail from mother about promised campaign contribution that never materialized.

BRASS 12.75

We'll need to strengthen this Search Warrant.

REQUIRES: Mom Denies an argument about money took place between her and the Vicitm.

REQUIRES: Angry voice mail from mother about promised campaign contribution that never materialized.

- Warrant for Search (HOUSE)

INTERROGATION ROOM13 (Suspect: Contactor)

- I didn't kill him!
- Okay, okay, I wrote the note. He owed me money, but it was no big deal, just a friendly game of poker and he wouldn't pay up. I wrote it in a moment of anger because he was dodging my calls. I left it for him in his mother's garage; she told me he was going to pick up some camping gear there and I knew he'd see it.
- I lied when you asked me about the sodium monofluoroacetate pesticide because I'm not licensed to carry it. A "friend" got me a large quantity at a discount rate.
    - Of course I read up on the stuff, it's dangerous, I gotta make sure no one gets hurt!
- Poisoned! Hey man I've very careful with this stuff. I wear gloves when I handle it and I always let people know what it is I'm spreading around.
- The jar that belongs to the lid? I'm not sure, really. I use the stuff on a lot of jobs. Works real good killing pests you find in homes when you're remodeling. I know I had some at the Victim's home. The Wife asked me all kinds of questions about it, told me she was worried their cat might get sick. Funny, don't remember seeing any cat around.
- Bootprint (GIFT from Contractor) ➔ Contractor's bootprint INTR13
- Alright, alright! Yes, we got into it before he went camping. He saw my note and drove to my shop in a rage. He went after me and I popped him in the head with the rake handle to protect myself. He stormed out,

threatening to see me killed. I was scared! But that's all that happened. What happened after he left, I don't know.

CRIME RECONSTRUCTION 050
CONDITIONS: Vic DNA matches + DNA of hair from Shop + Pesticide from Shop Matches Murder Weapon
EVIDENCE SUGGESTS: Victim and Contractor fought inside Shop. Shaken, but angry, Contractor quickly grabbed pesticide, sprinkled it on Victim's tobacco

HOUSE13
Evidence Player interacts with:
- Salt on jar (MAGNIFYING SCOPE, ADHESIVE SPECIMEN MOUNT) ➔ Salt-like particles HOUSE13
  - Plastic jar (GLOVE)
    - No identifying markings.
    - Fingerprints on Jar (FINGERPRINT POWDER) Fingerprint on Jar HOUSE13
- Computer (Not collectible)
  - Encrypted Email → Encrypted Email HOUSE13
  - Digital pictures (USB MEMORY STICK) ➔ Digital pictures HOUSE13
    - Show wife hugging young man in a romantic fashion.
- Memos (GLOVE) ➔ Memos HOUSE13
  - Back and forth memos from Mom to her campaign manager about the effect Victim is having on her campaign. Talk about solutions to "problem".

LAB 13.5
Player processes items:

COMPUTER
  - Email is from P.I.
    - Indicates Wife was having an affair recently.
COMPUTER- AFIS
REQUIRES: Fingerprint on Jar HOUSE13
- No match found in database

COMPUTER
REQUIRES: Fingerprint from jar HOUSE13
REQUIRES: Fingerprint from book SHOP10
- Not a match

CHEMICAL ANALYZER
REQUIRES: Salt-like particles HOUSE13
- Salt-like particles HOUSE13 are sodium monofluoroacetate

COMPUTER
REQUIRES: Contractor's bootprint (INTR13)
REQUIRES: Boot print from crime scene CS01
- Are not a match.
- CSI notes it may belong to their anonymous caller.

CONDO13.5
Wife interrogation
- The man in those pictures is a friend! A friend!
- Get out!

BRASS14

REQUIRES: Memos HOUSE13
REQUIRES: Salt-like particles HOUSE13 are sodium monofluoroacetate
- Warrant for Questioning (Mom)

REQUIRES: Email HOUSE13
REQUIRES: Digital pictures HOUSE13
Will need more here
- Warrant for Search (CONDO)

INTERROGATION ROOM15 (Suspect: Mom)
- Yes, the Victim was causing me to lose ground in the polls. Why would you expect me to acknowledge it publicly?
- He promised he'd contribute some money to my campaign. After all I'd done for him it was only fair. When he reneged I had to consider putting a 2nd mortgage on my home.

- I told him to get his camping gear out of the garage so the Contractor could hang drywall in there. He picked it up and left. So what?
- Jar of pesticide? No idea, ask the Contractor.
- Wife has been cheating on Victim for months. That's the proof, THAT'S your killer.
- Fingerprint (GIFT from Mom) ➔ Mom's fingerprint (INTR15)

CRIME RECONSTRUCTION 080
CONDITIONS: Campaign problems + Pesticide in House + Camping gear in House
EVIDENCE SUGGESTS: Victim and Mom argue. Victim heads to garage to get everything ready for camping trip. Mom goes into garage, picks up bottle of pesticide, and sprinkles some on tobacco.

CONDO15
Evidence Player interacts with:
- Humidification device (GLOVE)
    o Has been thoroughly cleaned inside and out. Mr. Clean again?
- Dead Ant Near Tobacco (TWEEZERS) ➔ Ant CONDO15
- Tobacco w/salt-like particles (MAGNIFYING SCOPE, ADHESIVE SPECIMEN MOUNT) ➔ Tobacco w/salt-like particles CONDO15
- Men's bikini briefs (NOT COLLECTED)
    o Semen (UV LIGHT, SWAB) ➔ Semen CONDO15
    o Wife is sure they belong to her husband.
- Oven mitt (GLOVE)
    o Has a small hole in one of the finger areas.

LAB16
Player processes items:

COMPUTER
REQUIRES: Fingerprint from jar HOUSE13
REQUIRES: Mom's fingerprint (INTR15)
- Not a match

REQUIRES: Semen CONDO15
REQUIRES: Vic DNA MORGUE02
- Not a match

CHEMICAL ANALYZER
REQUIRES: Tobacco w/salt-like particles CONDO15
- salt-like particles CONDO15 are sodium monofluoroacetate

BRASS17

REQUIRES: Salt-like particles CONDO15 are sodium monofluoroacetate
REQUIRES: Semen CONDO15 and Vic DNA MORGUE02 do not match
REQUIRES: This is going to sound suspicious, but the Victim and I upped our life insurance recently…
- Warrant for Questioning (Wife)

INTERROGATION ROOM18 (Suspect: Wife)
- I was going to end the affair. It was difficult before the Victim turned his life around; I felt alone, I was very unhappy.
- I never asked the Contractor about his pesticide, he's lying because he probably did it.
- No, I never touched any jar belonging to him. Why would I?
- I have no idea how pesticide might have gotten into my husband's tobacco. Ask the Contractor.
- Fingerprint (GIFT from Wife) ➔ Wife's fingerprint (INTR17)

LAB19
Player processes items:

COMPUTER
REQUIRES: Fingerprint from jar HOUSE13
REQUIRES: Wife's fingerprint (INTR17)
- Match

INTERROGATION ROOM20 (Suspect: Wife)
- Yes, I did it! I wasn't going to spend the next forty years of my life being miserable like my mother. I wasn't going to allow him to embarrass me in public, destroy everything I worked for with his gambling- giving away our hard earned cash to strippers. I deserve to be happy! I deserve to be happy!

CRIME RECONSTRUCTION 100
CONDITIONS: Fingerprint from jar match Wife's fingerprint + Salt-like particles
CONDO15 match sodium monofluoroacetate + Oven Mitt + Insurance Policy +
Affair Photo
EVIDENCE SUGGESTS: Wife having affair, Upped their life-insurance policy,
then she poisons his tobacco with pesticide, using oven mitt with small burn hole.

Brief Timeline of Events Surrounding the Crime

- Mom demands Victim take his belongings out of her garage so the Contractor can hang drywall; camping gear is among the items in question.
- Victim decides he'll take the gear then head out to the desert - alone.
- Victim informs Mom of his plans, "I'll come get that crap tomorrow."
- Mom informs Contractor of his plans, "That stuff will be out of the garage tomorrow so you can finish your work in there."
- Contractor leaves note for Victim.
- Victim informs wife of his plans that morning.
- Wife hurriedly poisons Victim's tobacco.
- Victim arrives at Mom's house, takes gear, finds note.
- Victim heads to Contractor's shop in a rage and gets into an altercation with Contractor.
- Victim heads out to desert.
- Wife demands Contractor get his crap out of their kitchen.
- Contractor stops by condo to retrieve tools and things, including canister of pesticide.
- Wife has lover over for tryst.
- Contractor brings canister of pesticide to Mom's garage. Forgetting lid at shop.
- Victim smokes a cigarette and dies.
- An anonymous hiker discovers the Victim's body and calls the police from a pay phone. Moves victim out of sleeping bag and steals his wallet.

Appendix B

Nihilistic **Documents**

#	Item Type	Location	Description	Gating Method	Reward	Special Features Desc.
		General				Unique Features
1	Combat	Campfire near City Walls	Small group of soldiers around a campfire spot player and advance	Chase Player	Placed Treasure	Campfire can be attacked causing sparks which can ignite nearby enemies, spikes
2	Combat	Outside Main Gate	Small group of guards around the front gate spot player and advance	Door Opening		Torches on wall can be picked up, spikes
3	Combat	Outside Dock	Group of Footmen standing on dock attack player if he approaches	Chase Player	Placed Treasure	Can throw enemies into water
4	Combat Wave	Outside Dock	2 Footmen and a Veteran attack player if he picks up treasure	Chase Player		Can throw enemies into water
5	World Interaction	Front Gate	Standard door opening for front gate	World Interaction		
6	Combat Wave	Inside First Courtyard	First wave of placed enemies	World Interaction		Spikes
7	Combat Wave	Inside First Courtyard		World Interaction		Spikes
8	Combat Wave	Inside First Courtyard		World Interaction		Spikes
9	World Interaction	Inside First Courtyard	Push Over Column	World Interaction		
10	Combat	Middle plateau	Wyvern Attacks player on raised path	Mantling	Placed Treasure	Wyvern will attack player if they attempt to mantle while still alive
11	Combat	Middle plateau	Group of soldiers follow player up cliff	Mantling		
12	Puzzle	First mantling run	Mantling run to reach main level of keep	Mantling		
13	Combat	Hidden mantle area	Area to side of mantling path with more wyverns	Mantling	Placed Treasure	
14	Combat	Outside of Keep	Small group of Footmen with Captain attack player if he approaches	Chase Player		Torches on wall can be picked up
15	World Interaction	Outside of Keep	Door opening for "hidden" room	World Interaction	Placed Treasure	
16	Combat Wave	Bridge	Group of Footmen and Veterans attack as player climbs up	Door Opening		Torches on wall can be picked up
17	Combat Wave	Bridge	Archers defend bridge	Door Opening		Can throw enemies off bridge, spikes
18	Combat Wave	Bridge	Captain and more Veterans defend Keep entrance	Door Opening		Torches on wall
19	Combat Wave	Bridge	Group of soldiers chase player down bridge	Door Opening		
20	World Interaction	Keep Entrance	Standard door opening for Keep entrance	World Interaction		Torches on wall can be picked up
21	Combat	Tower Entryway	Small group of Veterans confront player	Gate		Lots of breakable/throwable props
22	Combat	"T" Intersection	Small group of Veterans confront player	Door Opening		Breakable columns
23	World Interaction	"T" Intersection	Standard door opening to storeroom	World Interaction		
24	Combat	Storage Room	Single Captain attacks player	Chase Player	Placed Treasure	
25	World Interaction	"T" Intersection	Standard door opening to Barracks	World Interaction		
26	Combat Wave	Barracks 1	Small group of guards attack player as they enter room	Door Opening	Placed Treasure	
27	Combat Wave	Barracks 1		Door Opening		
28	World Interaction	Barracks 1	Standard door opening for Torture Room	World Interaction		
29	Combat	Torture Room	Small group of Veterans confront player(playing cards as per design doc?)			
30	Combat	Barracks 2	Medium group of soliders attack as player enters room.	Door Opening		
31	World Interaction	Barracks 2	Standard door opening for Upper Plaza	World Interaction		
32	Combat Wave	Upper Plaza	Large group of soliders attack player when entering Upper Plaza	World Interaction	Placed Treasure	Braziers can be picked up and thrown or destroyed
33	Combat Wave	Upper Plaza	Group of Veterans comes out of sealed door	World Interaction		
34	World Interaction	Upper Plaza	Push Over Column	World Interaction		
35	Combat Wave	Tower Stairs	Several Veterans are along staircase	World Interaction	Placed Treasure	
36	Combat Wave	Tower Stairs	Captain and more at first landing	World Interaction		
37	World Interaction	Tower Stairs	Push Snake Head Block	World Interaction		
38	Cinematic	Tower Stairs	Snake column rises			
39	Puzzle	Tower Stairs	Mantling sequence to top of snake tower	Mantling		
40	World Interaction	Tower Arena	Get Legedary Sword	World Interaction	Legendary Sword	
	Combat	Tower Arena	Large group of Veterans			
41	Cinematic	Tower Arena	Sorceress Queen			
42	Combat	Tower Arena	Sorceress Queen		Level Completion	

NIHILISTIC

MISSION ART/LD PIPELINE CHECKLIST

Mission : _____

Initials	Phase 1	Est. Time	Department
_____	Location Doc		LDs
_____	"Establishing Look" location concepts (2-4 wide shots to establish general Atmosphere and look)		Artists
_____	LD Mission Layout Pass		LDs
_____	Rough block in		
_____	Add in 1-3 encounters		
_____	Create references: master file and tile files		
	LDs need to adhere to the naming converntions laid out in http://ns-srv1/nsiwiki/moin.cgi/LostKingLevelNamingConventions		
_____	Mesh name in tile file should match MB filename		
_____	Reference updates in LD hands		
_____	Establish cameras		LDs
_____	Kick Off Meeting		LDs/Artists
_____	LD runs through mission with Artist:		LDs/Artists
_____	what is each room/space		
_____	camera run through		
_____	chance for artist input/ideas for room concept		
_____	LD to create overview screen capture with rooms,		LDs/Artists
	major areas/arenas, and "render arcs" (what degree and where skyline/backdrops will be viewable; does not have to be a contiguous arc) spec'd out		
_____	Spec out mission establishing shot: camera pan, etc		LDs/Artists
_____	Add over-view screen cap to mission doc/e-mail		LDs/Artists
_____	Continue to block/refine cameras		LDs
_____	Create prop lists and some placeholders (for size,functionality ref only)		LDs
	Use correct naming convention.		
_____	Preliminary FX request		Artists
_____	LD Review and Approval		LDs
_____	LD Handoff to Art		LDs

Initials	Phase 2	Est. Time	Department
_____	Preliminary lighting pass: very basic, 1 day pass. Separate layer for later import		Artists
_____	Set default F-STOP/HDR parameters		
_____	Modelers begin 1st pass geo work on relevent tiles: rough Uvs, Default Grid texture, tessellation into approximately 4 meter grid lengths at the minimum (auto UV layout OK). Note: LDs consider their tile geo to be the collision geo)		Artists
_____	Art/LD Review		
_____	LD feedback on first pass art		
_____	Art feedback on camera framing		
_____	Money shot discussions		
_____	Camera cleanup pass		LDs

Initials	Phase 3	Est. Time	Department
_____	Detail Concepts based on screen captures		Artists
	lighting ideas		
	What do the rooms/building interiors look like		
	What objects would we like to see in there (aside from what is required for game play) to "sell" the space's purpose (ie barracks, armory)		
_____	Start creating "filler" mattes and identify rough placement based on overview screen		
_____	Append set piece list to Prop Doc		Artists
_____	Prop descriptions and trauma requirements list		LDs/Artists

1/10/2007/3:36 PM

NIHILISTIC

MISSION ART/LD PIPELINE CHECKLIST

Phase 4

____ Preliminary Character lighting pass (set regions, set defaults)	Artists
____ Mission Artists block in mission:	Artists
____ Add placeholder skybox at minimum (use day or night sky from other missions)	
Place filler mattes (matte paintings needed to fill vista camera angles): borrow from other missions at minimum.	
____ Terrain pass/rough UV:first pass texture/shader, unstiched UVs and Unblended shaders at minimum.	
____ Water pass (both LD established (gameplay) and for looks only): place water volume markers (LDs can help here) add rough pass reflections (artists)	
____ Set color palettes oh Photoshop for texture artists	
Rough Texture pass: general textures/colors and UVs, uniform UVs at 256/meter, unstiched (seams OK) and unblended (eg. alpha blended terrain) shaders at minimum.	
____ Begin modeling set pieces (based on generated art list in phase 1): include first pass texture	Artists
Prop building and trauma set up: UV layout and generic color ("wireframe texture") at max (in anticipation of changes)	Artists
____ Trauma set up	LDs
____ Additional/remaining FX requests lists	LDs
____ Reference updates in Artists' hands as first pass geo goes in	Artists
____ LD/Artist meet to select geo to be converted into larger tiles: LDs convert tiles	Artists
____ Art review and approval	Artists
Framerate sanity check (with [as close to possible] as many props, enemies, FXs, Fullscreen FX, and texture mem footprint in place)	
____ Art hand off to LDs	Artists

Phase 5

____ Final game camera and layout tweaks	LDs
____ Final object placement pass	LDs
____ Final environmental fx placement/triggering	LDs
____ Final tweaking of enemy encounters	LDs
Any additional custom scripts fro enemy attack sequences (triggering fx, forcing trauma breaks on objects during cinematics, etc.)	LDs
____ Final interactivity on script objects (trauma, interactable props, puzzle objects)	LDs
____ Any additional sectoring/visibility/streaming control custom scripts	LDs
____ Add placeholder cinematic and cutscene triggers.	LDs
____ Playthroughs and reviews until internal approval	LDs
____ Submit to THQ for review	LDs

Phase 6

____ Final lighting pass (Mission and Character)	Artists
____ Final details on Models: final texture and UV work; skew/twist geo	Artists
____ Final shader work	Artists
____ Finalize FX	Artists
____ Final HDR/Bloom settings	Artists
____ Final F-STOP pass	LDs
____ Establish story cutscenes.	LDs
____ Final cinematic triggering	LDs
____ Optimizations	Artists
____ Weld verts	
____ remove UV seams	
____ Backface culling	
____ LDs tweak with final assets	LDs
____ Final internal review	LDs/Artists
____ Submit to THQ for approval	

N/A = Not Applicable
IP = In Progress

1/10/2007/3:36 PM

Unlockable Moves by Mission

Count	Mission	Combo Name	Tree	Description	Button Sequence (XB360)	Special Features	Starting Move	Combo Total Damage	# of Hits	Damage per Hit
	0 (AUTO)	1H Light Combo	1H Sword	Add description	X+X+X+X	None	Light	18	4	4.5
	0 (AUTO)	DW Light Combo	Dual Wield	Stopping the momentum of his previous swing, Kalden reverses the momentum and strings from the left back to the right	X+X+X+X+X	None	Light	20	5	4.0
	0 (AUTO)	1H Heavy Combo	1H Sword	Add description	Y+Y+Y	None	Heavy	30	3	10.0
	0 (AUTO)	DW Heavy Combo	Dual Wield	Kalden does a quick flip with his blades close together for massive overhead smash	Y+Y+Y+Y	None	Heavy	36	4	9.0
	0 (AUTO)	Quick Grapple	Grapple	Player grabs a grunt-sized enemy and drives them head-first into the ground	B	None	Grapple	20	1	20.0
2	1 (SP_01)	Fast Stun	1H Sword	Player lunges forward with his left arm/shoulder to knock an opponent off-balance	X+Y	Stun	Light	7	2	3.5
	1 (SP_01)	Grapple Pile Driver	Grapple	Player grabs a grunt-sized enemy and drives them head-first into the ground	B+L	None	Grapple	35	2	17.5
	0 (AUTO)	2H Light Combo	2H Heavy	Lower-Right to upper-left uppercut	X+X+X	None	Light	19	3	6.3
	0 (AUTO)	2H Heavy Combo	2H Heavy	Add description	Y+Y+Y+Y	None	Heavy	36	4	9.0
4	2 (BI_03)	Baseball Hit	Dual Wield	After a fast1 attack, the player sends a fierce upward sideway blow to the target causing him to go catwheeling ragdoll into the environment	X+Y	Radgoll Reaction	Light	8	2	4.0
	2 (BI_03)	Grapple Slam	Grapple	Player grabs a weaker enemy, flips him around to grab his arms, and slams him repeatedly against the ground flat on his back	B+B	Repeatable x 3	Grapple	50	4	12.5
	2 (BI_05)	Head Butt	1H Sword	Player grabs enemy with his free hand to pull him closer, then violently head-butts the enemy	Y+B	Stun	Heavy	19	2	9.5
	2 (BI_03)	Uppercut	2H Heavy	After first opening attack, a quick uppercut sends the enemy flying into the air.	X+Y	Chain to air attacks	Light	16	2	8.0
4	3 (BI_04)	Kick	Dual Wield	Player stops using the blades briefly and extends his leg in a powerful kick to the midsection	X+B	Ragdoll Reaction	Light	10	2	5.0
	3 (BI_04)	Grapple BackBreaker	Grapple	Player grabs a grunt and smashes him back first over his bended knee	B+Y	None	Grapple	60	2	30.0
	3 (BI_04)	Disarm	1H Sword	After landing two heavy attacks, the player does a quick upward flick with his sword against the unbalanced enemy which disarms his primary weapon and sends it into the air in a head-height arc	Y+Y+X	Disarm	Heavy	30	3	10.0
	3 (BI_04)	Double Spin Attack	Dual Wield	Player does a quick spin move with both blades extended which is intended to damage all players in close radius and knock them back a moderate amount	X+X+(HOLD X)	Multiple Enemies	Light	23	4	5.8
3	5 (SP_04)	Groin Kick	2H Heavy	Kalden does a surprise kick to the twig and berries after a single heavy strike	Y+X	Stun	Heavy	23	2	11.5
	5 (SP_04)	SOD Fast Combo	1H Sword	Repeatable Cool move that replaces the normal combo-ender	X+X+X+X (Repeatable)	Repeatable	Light	20	3	6.7
	5 (SP_04)	SOD Fast Combo	Dual Wield	Repeatable Cool move that replaces the normal combo-ender	X+X+X+X+X	Repeatable	Light	20	5	4.0
4	6 (SM_02)	Decapitation Attack	Dual Wield	Kalden reels back in preparation to scissor the enemy with both weapons; he brings them together from either side of the enemy with a loud clap of force at neck level; the weapons bounce from the impact.	X+X+X+Y	Decapitation	Light	35	4	8.8
	6 (SM_02)	Quick Punch	1H Sword	Kalden performs a very fast Punch with his left hand against an unsuspecting enemy	X+B	Stun	Light	7	2	3.5
	6 (SM_02)	Hook Move	2H Heavy	After the second fast attack, player plunges the axe into the enemy dead ahead, and uses it to pull / swing them around and fling them into the crowd	X+X+Y	Enemy Throw	Light	32	3	10.7
	6 (SM_02)	SOD Fast Combo	2H Heavy	Repeatable Cool move that replaces the normal combo-ender	X + X + X + X	Repeatable	Light	15	4	3.8
3	7 (SP_05)	Blade Charge	1H Sword	Blade reversed his blade hold and charges forward leading with a back-handed blade slash	X+X+Y	Shield Breaking	Light	33	3	11.0
	7 (SP_05)	SOD Heavy Combo	1H Sword	Chargeable cool move that replaces the heavy combo ender	Y+Y+Y	Chargeable	Heavy	30	4	7.5
	7 (SP_05)	SOD Heavy Combo	Dual Wield	Chargeable cool move that replaces the heavy combo ender	Y+Y+Y+Y	Chargeable	Heavy	50	4	12.5
	0 (AUTO)	Shield Uppercut	1H Sword	Player uses the shield in his secondary hand to bash the enemy in an uppercut manueuver	X+X+Y (With Shield)	Uppercut	Light	37	3	12.3
6	8 (KS_01)	Windmill Attack	Dual Wield	The player swings both arms in a windmill fashion with blades extended intended to land multiple blows on a single enemy in range causing higher damage.	X+X+Y	Rapid strikes on single target	Light	21	3	7.0
	8 (KS_01)	SOD Heavy Combo	2H Heavy	Inserted during a combo to give player a smooth turn-around	Y+Y+Y+Y	Chargeable	Heavy	20	3	6.7
	8 (KS_01)	Charge-Up Sweep	2H Heavy	The player presses and holds the Y button to charge up a limited 180-degree arc sweep attack with a quick forward dash. Variable damage/size of sweep radius.	(Hold Y)	Charge-Up Mechanic Multiple Enemies	Heavy	25	2	12.5
	8 (KS_01)	Grab Weapon	1H Sword	After stunning the victim via a combo, the player uses his free hand to grab the weapon from the right hand of the enemy and take it into his own left hand	X+Y+B	Weapon Grab	Light	7	3	2.3

	8 (KS_01)	Grab Weapon Stab	1H Sword	After disarming the enemy, Kalden uses his primary weapon to deliver a quick slash	X+Y+B+X	Unblockable	Light	27	4	6.8
	8 (KS_01)	Grab Weapon Stab 2	1H Sword	After disarming the enemy, Kalden stabs with the grabbed weapon and leaves it in the enemy	X+Y+B+X+X	Unblockable	Light	52	5	10.4
	8 (KS_01)	Hilt Smash	2H Heavy	Player knocks his hilt onto enemies head.	X+X+B	Stun	Light	22	3	7.3
5	9 (KS_05)	Windmill Attack 2	Dual Wield	The player swings both arms in a windmill fashion with blades extended intended to land multiple blows on a single enemy in range causing higher damage.	X+X+Y+Y		Light	41	4	10.3
	9 (KS_05)	Suplex	1H Sword	Player uses his empty left hand to grab the victim around the neck and drops backward into a suplex fall, WWE-style.	X+X+B	Works on Captains (and peons)	Light	35	3	11.7
	9 (KS_05)	Shockwave	Dual Wield	Kalden plants both swords into the crowd and triggers a massive shockwave 360-degrees which send each guy backward in a unique ragdoll contortion	Y+Y+(HOLD Y)	Area of Effect Attack	Heavy	36	3	12.0
	9 (KS_05)	Forward Shockwave	2H Heavy	After two heavy attacks, player smashes his blade onto the ground causing a shockwave to radiate forward in a 90-degree arc causing reactions against multiple enemies to a range of about 3m	Y+Y+(HoldY)	Ranged Attack	Heavy	31	3	10.3
	9 (KS_05)	Boomerang Throw	2H Heavy	Player throws the weapon in an arc that returns to the players hands (boomerang)	X+B	Ranged Attack	Light	25	2	12.5
2	10 (SP_02)	Shield Decap	1H Sword	After the Head Butt move, if the player is holding a shield, he uses it to cut the head off the victim (rather than doing the Shield Arm Grab)	Y+B+B	Beheading	Heavy	54	3	18.0
	0 (AUTO)	Shield Arm Grab	1H Sword	After the head-butt move, the player quickly grabs the enemies left hand and pulls it violently toward Kalden, which simultaneously removes the guy's shield, and sends him ragdolling in some direction	Y+B+B	Disarm Shield	Heavy	29	3	9.7
	10 (SP_02)	Steerable Spin	Dual Wield	Similar to the "Body Swing", but using blades. The player can optionally repeat several rotations & steer/move in a limited way	X+X+X+(HOLD X)	Massive Crowd Control	Light	36	4	9.0
3	11 (ST_01)	Skewer	Dual Wield	Kalden stabs the enemy with both swords, then (unless combo'ed into Body Fling) retracs the blades	Y+Y+B	Stun	Heavy	40	3	13.3
	11 (ST_01)	Neck Grab & Drop	1H Sword	Kalden grabs the enemy with his emtpy hand after two heavy hits and holds him a choke-hold in the air, facing Kalden. This position is held for a long time (approx 2 seconds) after which Kalden drops him to the ground if not comboed	Y+Y+B	Enemy Grab	Heavy	30	3	10.0
	11 (ST_01)	Log Splitter	2H Heavy	Player lands a vicious attack directly through the middle of the enemies head, sometimes resulting in a cleave in two reaction	X+X+B+Y	Brutal Kill	Light	62	4	15.5
3	13 (ST_02)	Leg Chop	Dual Wield	The player croches slightly and extends both arms and performs a fast spin move at leg-level. intending to cut legs of any opponents in range.	X+X+X+X+Y	Multi-target Dismemberment	Light	52	5	10.4
	13 (ST_02)	Execution Kill	2H Heavy	After an initial leg breaking kick. Kalden uses a slow but heavy blow from his 2H weapon to behead the player	Y+X+Y	Instant Kill for Grunt or Captain Sized	Heavy	58	3	19.3
	13 (ST_02)	Neck Throw	1H Sword	During the neck hold, the player can press "B" to throw the enemy backward into other enemies or environmental hazards	Y+Y+B+B	Throw Enemy	Heavy	50	4	12.5
1	14 (AR_03)	Body Swing & Release	1H Sword	During a neck hold, Kalden tosses the enemy in the air to grab hold of his leg or legs, then swings him in repeated 360 degree arcs to clear space around the player.	Y+Y+B+(Hold B)	Multiple Enemies	Heavy	35	4	8.8
2	16 (AR_04)	All Limb	Dual Wield	If the player presses "B" during the impalement move, the blades are ripped apart with such force that the victim is "quartered" (all limbs are removed)	Y+Y+B+Y	Dismemberment	Heavy	508	4	127.0
	16 (AR_04)	Coprse on a Stick	2H Heavy	After performing the Skewer Knockdown, the player picks up his weapon with the body still attached, and uses it as a club to do a 360 spin move, knocking down multiple enemies and then flinging the body	X+X+Y+(Hold Y)	360 Knockdowns	Light	30	2	15.0
1	17 (SM_03)	Charge-Up Smash	2H Heavy	Player holds the blade above his head while charging the move for a variable length of time, then releases a heavy blow against a single targeted enemy at close range	Y+(Hold Y)	Charge-Up Mechanic	Heavy	58	2	29.0

Corsair Conscript

Offensive Theme	Fodder
Defensive Theme	No defenses
Difficulty (1-10)	1
Avg. Group Size	3-8
Health	15
Status	Tuning

Primary Purpose	Allow the player to learn the basic combat mechanics
Purpose #2	Teach the player to pay attention to incoming attacks during his attack combos
Purpose #3	Teach the player to use "quick grapples"
Purpose #4	Allow the player to enjoy killing dudes easily without much threat

AI Action

AI Tactic	Description	When AI performs?	Player Response							Damage	QA Verification/Comments	Status	Purpose
			Block	Parry	Dodge	Counter Attack	Jump	Throw	Grapple				
1-Hit "Heavy" Combo	AI gets into near range to do a single overhand attack	50% of time when blessed	10	10	5	10	5	5	2	10		Not working	General Harassment
1-Hit "Light" Combo	AI gets into medium range to do a single overhand attack	50% of time when blessed	10	10	5	5	5	5	2	10		Working	General Harassment

Player Action

Player Action	Result
Light Combo	Killed at end
Heavy Combo	Killed during combo
Sweep Attack	N/A
Grapple Attack	Killed by any grapple
Knockdown Attack	Killed
Knockback Attack	Killed
Thrown Weapon	Killed
Jump Attack	Killed
Disarm Attack	N/A
Flee	Aggressively chase & attack
World Puzzle	Aggressively chase & attack

QA Verification/Comments

Corsair Veteran

Offensive Theme	First enemy with combo attacks
Defensive Theme	First blocking enemy, Blocks short seuqences only
Difficulty (1-10)	3
Avg. Group Size	4-8
Health	36

Status	Tuning

		QA Verification/Comments
Primary Purpose	Teach the player how to use longer combos to defeat AI blocking	
Purpose #2	Teach the player to defend against combos using their block	
Purpose #3	Provide a relatively easy/safe opponent to practice moves in early part of game	
Purpose #4		

AI Action

AI Tactic	Description	When AI performs?	Player Response								Purpose	Status	QA Verification/Comments
			Block	Parry	Dodge	Counter Attack	Jump	Throw	Grapple	Damage			
3-Hit Fast Combo	AI performs 3 quick slashes	50% of time when blessed	10	5	5	5	5	5	2	20	General Harassment	**Working**	
2-Hit Fierce Combo	AI performs 2 slashes	50% of time when blessed	10	5	5	5	5	5	2	2	General Harassment	Interrupts if not blocked	

Player Action

Player Action	Result	QA Verification/Comments
Light Combo	AI will block first 2 hits of combo if not initiated during a downtime. Will kill in 3 combos if blocked, 2 if not blocked	Blocking is lasting for more attacks than designed, bug opened
Heavy Combo	AI will attempt to block the heavy, but will be block-broken and die during the second heavy combo	
Sweep Attack	N/A	
Quick Grapple	Vulnerable, killed with anything beyond a basic throw	
Unblockable Attack	Hit	
Instant Kill Attack	Killed	
Knockdown Attack	Knockdown	
Knockback Attack	Killed	
Thrown Weapon	Killed	
Jump Attack	N/A	
Disarm Attack	Flee	
Flee	Aggressively chase & attack	
World Puzzle	Aggressively chase & attack	
Gruesome Event	AI goes into Stunned state 50% of the time, 10% of the time if Captain is present	

Corsair Captain

Offensive Theme	Long Fast/Heavy Combos
Defensive Theme	Blocks with shield and dodges
Difficulty (1-10)	5
Avg. Group Size	1
Health	225
Status	In Progress

Primary Purpose	Teach the player to read long combos and counter with special grab moves
Purpose #2	Engages in combat immediately unlike other Captains
Purpose #3	Demonstrate the group behaviors (battle cry, impact of death on group morale)
Purpose #4	Forces the player to dodge an unblockable Shield Combo

AI Action

Progress	AI Tactic	Description	When AI performs?	Player Response							Damage	Purpose	QA Verification/Comments
				Block	Parry	Dodge	Counter Attack	Jump	Throw	Grapple			
	Fast Combo	AI performs 2-hit fast combo	50% When Blessed	10	8	5	5	5	5	2	20	General Harassment	
	Heavy combo	AI performs Heavy Light combo to break block	25% When Blessed/25% When player is blocking	10	5	8	5	5	5	2	30	Punishes player for staying in block	
	Fierce Combo	AI performs A 4 Hit Fierce combo	25% When Blessed/50% When player is blocking/50% when less than 2 grunts under his command	10	8	5	5	2	2	2	40	Teach player to dodge or block final hit of combo	
	Shield Combo	AI performs an unblockable uppercut shield attack H+H that sends Conan into the air flying backwards	25% of time when player is blocking/ 50% when less than 2 grunts under his command	2	2	10	2	5	5	2	40	Punishes player for staying in block	
	Dodge	AI performs a dodge to avoid heavy attacks	Before and after heavy attacks and certain actions.	0	0	0	10	0	0	2	N/A	Teach player to use fast attacks before landing a heavy attack	
	Rally Cry	AI executes a special animation & audio cue which if completed temporarily makes veterans more aggressive	First use approx 20 seconds into battle, subsequently approximately every 45 seconds.	0	0	0	10	0	0	2	N/A	Teach group mechanics, encourage player to attack to interrupt	

Player Action	Result	QA Verification/Comments
Light Combo	Blocks with shield, follows up with counter attack	
Heavy Combo	Blocks with shield, follows up with counter attack	
Sweep Attack	Knockdown	
Grapple Attack	Grappled	
Unblockable Attack	Hit	
Instant Kill Attack	Killed	
Knockdown Attack	Knockdown	
Knockback Attack	Knockback	
Thrown Weapon	Blocks with shield	
Jump Attack	N/A	
Disarm Attack	Flee	
Flee	Aggressively chase & attack	
World Puzzle	Aggressively chase & attack	

Corsair Archer

Offensive Theme	Teach player that arrows must be countered with shields or parries
Defensive Theme	Use of cover
Difficulty (1-10)	4
Avg. Group Size	6
Health	25
Status	First Pass

Primary Purpose	Teach the player to time a weapon throw when archer is exposed
Purpose #2	
Purpose #3	

AI Action

Progress	AI Tactic	Description	When Performed?	Player Response							Damage	Purpose	QA Verification/Comments
				Block	Parry	Dodge	Counter Attack	Jump	Throw Object	Grapple			
	Fire Ranged	Archer fires a basic bow shot	100% of the time when blessed	10	8	8	2	2	2	2	10	Teach player how to block arrows properly	
	Dodge	AI performs a dodge into cover	100% of the time after firing arrow	0	0	0	2	0	5	0	N/A	Teach player to time attack when AI is exposed	

Player Action	Result	QA Verification/Comments
Light Combo	Knockdown at end of combo, kill after 2 full combos	
Heavy Combo	Kill during combo	
Sweep Attack	Hit	
Grapple Attack	Hit	
Unblockable Attack	Hit	
Instant Kill Attack	Hit	
Knockdown Attack	Hit	
Knockback Attack	Killed	
Thrown Weapon	Killed	
Jump Attack	Hit	
Disarmed	Flee	
Flee	Aggressively chase & attack	
World Puzzle	Aggressively chase & attack	
Gruesome Event	AI goes into Stunned state 90% of the time, or 50% of the time if Captain is present.	
On Fire	AI goes into Stunned state 90% of the time, or 50% of the time if Captain is present.	

Combat Effectiveness Chart

Legend	
Unavailable	
Ineffective	
Low	
Medium	
High (•)	
Overkill	
Special Weakness	

!	Primary Strategy
X	Player Punishment
?	Teach Skill

Enemies in order of Introduction

Column headers (enemies): Corsair Veteran, Corsair Captain, Corsair Archer, Corsair Kamikaze, Bone Cleaver #1, Stygian Footman, Stygian Veteran, Big Cat, Sand Dragon, Kush Footman, Kush Warrior, Kush Archer, Cave Ape, Cave Ape Sorcerer, Elephant Demon, Stygian Archer, Stygian Captain, Wyvern, Sorceress Queen, Argosian Veteran, Argosian Archer, Argosian Captain, Bone Cleaver #2, Sea Serpent, Guardian, Guardian Executioner, Giant Squid, Ghostly Warrior, Nemesis, Nemesis Phase 2

Combo String
X+X+X+X

Basic Combos
- 1H Light Combo
- 1H Heavy Combo
- DW Light Combo
- DW Heavy Combo
- 2H Light Combo
- 2H Heavy Combo

1H Special Moves
- Torch Attack
- Shield Bash
- 1H Fast Stun
- Blade Charge
- Neck Grab
- Torch Sweep
- Quick Punch
- Disarm
- Head Butt
- Neck Throw
- Grab Weapon
- Shield Grab
- Body Swing
- Suplex
- Shield Decap

DW Special Moves
- Windmill
- Baseball Hit
- Skewer
- Kick
- Double Spin
- Shockwave
- Decap-a-clap
- Leg Chop
- All Limb
- Steerable Spin

2H Special Moves
- Uppercut
- Hook Move
- Forward Shockwave
- Hilt Smash
- Flatten
- Shatter Weapon
- Groin Kick
- Fast Throw
- Log Splitter
- Corpse on a stick
- Execution Kill

Parry Counter Moves
- 1H Parry Counter
- DW Parry Counter
- 2H Parry Counter

Air Moves
- Air Attack
- Air Descending Attack

Special Strategies
- Lure To Attack
- Post-Attack Window (!)
- Hit Onto Spike
- Lure To Position/Fall
- Attack Environment Object
- Burn Environment Object

Special Moves
- Prone Kill
- Throw (Overhand)
- Throw (Sidearm)
- Throw (Spear)
- Throw (Prop)

Magic Powers
- Song of Death
- Earthquake
- Fire Blade
- Wormhole
- Raise Dead
- Spirits of the Ancestors

Column Tuned Percentage: 25%

Appendix C

Death Jr. II **Documents**

This document was confidential while *Death Jr. II: Root of Evil* was being developed. Since the game is published, this document is no longer confidential. Used with permission.

Game Design Document v5.0
CONFIDENTIAL

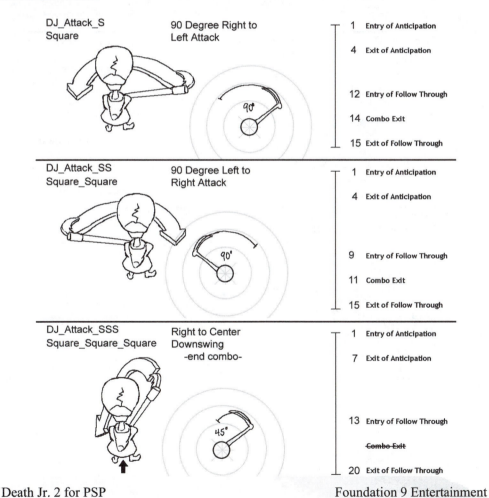

DJ_Attack_S
Square

90 Degree Right to
Left Attack

1	Entry of Anticipation
4	Exit of Anticipation
12	Entry of Follow Through
14	Combo Exit
15	Exit of Follow Through

DJ_Attack_SS
Square_Square

90 Degree Left to
Right Attack

1	Entry of Anticipation
4	Exit of Anticipation
9	Entry of Follow Through
11	Combo Exit
15	Exit of Follow Through

DJ_Attack_SSS
Square_Square_Square

Right to Center
Downswing
-end combo-

1	Entry of Anticipation
7	Exit of Anticipation
13	Entry of Follow Through
	~~Combo Exit~~
20	Exit of Follow Through

90°   90°   45°

Game Design Document v5.0
CONFIDENTIAL

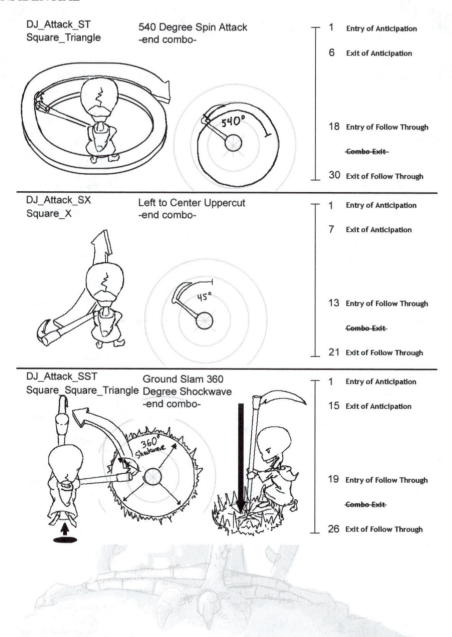

DJ_Attack_ST
Square_Triangle

540 Degree Spin Attack
-end combo-

540°

1	Entry of Anticipation
6	Exit of Anticipation
18	Entry of Follow Through
~~Combo Exit~~	
30	Exit of Follow Through

DJ_Attack_SX
Square_X

Left to Center Uppercut
-end combo-

45°

1	Entry of Anticipation
7	Exit of Anticipation
13	Entry of Follow Through
~~Combo Exit~~	
21	Exit of Follow Through

DJ_Attack_SST
Square_Square_Triangle

Ground Slam 360
Degree Shockwave
-end combo-

360°
Shockwave

1	Entry of Anticipation
15	Exit of Anticipation
19	Entry of Follow Through
~~Combo Exit~~	
26	Exit of Follow Through

Game Design Document v5.0
CONFIDENTIAL

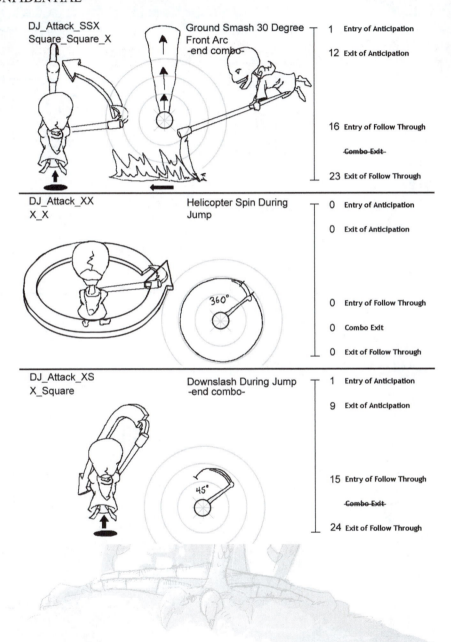

DJ_Attack_SSX
Square_Square_X

Ground Smash 30 Degree
Front Arc
-end combo-

1	Entry of Anticipation
12	Exit of Anticipation
16	Entry of Follow Through
	Combo Exit
23	Exit of Follow Through

DJ_Attack_XX
X_X

Helicopter Spin During
Jump

360°

0	Entry of Anticipation
0	Exit of Anticipation
0	Entry of Follow Through
0	Combo Exit
0	Exit of Follow Through

DJ_Attack_XS
X_Square

Downslash During Jump
-end combo-

45°

1	Entry of Anticipation
9	Exit of Anticipation
15	Entry of Follow Through
	Combo Exit
24	Exit of Follow Through

Death Jr. 2 for PSP   Foundation 9 Entertainment

DJ2 – Level Flow Diagram – 02.06.06

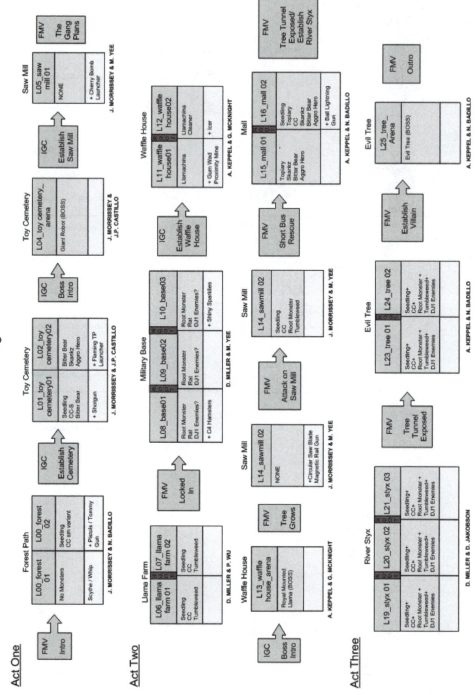

Game Design Document v5.0
CONFIDENTIAL

Military Base

🎬 **MOVIE:** As DJ / Pandora enter the base, roots come up from the ground, blocking the exit and knocking over a number of barrels marked with various biohazard/dangerous chemical warnings. The chemicals leak from the barrels and begin to mix, producing gases that enter the ventilation ducts.

▬**GAME:** The fumes from the chemicals cause DJ / Pandora to hallucinate. Crazy things come to life from out of nowhere. A running battle ensues with the kids trying to find a way out through the maze-like facility.

Game Design Document v5.0
CONFIDENTIAL

Waffle House

MOVIE: DJ / Pandora exit the Military Base through a tunnel that leads right into the basement of the Golden Llama Waffle House. DJ / Pandora are still hallucinating so the whole scene is very twisted and nonsensical – perhaps everything appears gigantic as if DJ / Pandora had shrunk to the size of lab rats?

GAME: The military base opens up to the local Golden Llama Waffle House. DJ / Pandora are still hallucinating and so they're faced with very strange breakfast foods and dangerous waffle irons. After defeating these challenges DJ / Pandora emerge into the parking lot where they must now face…

Game Design Document v5.0
CONFIDENTIAL

🎬 **MOVIE:** The Royal Mounted Llama on the roof of the waffle house comes to life (think Bob's Big Boy, only angry). The waffle house itself is surrounded by roots, (so that the player can not get onto the building in order to attack the Llama Boss.)

🎞 **GAME:** There are several trucks bearing drums of Agent Orange parked around the waffle house. The player must trigger catapults to launch these drums at the waffle house to defeat the Llama Boss.

🎬 **MOVIE:** The *Agent Orange* is used on the plants/trees. DJ / Pandora thinks it works because the tree roots go away, but the player sees the tree grow stronger and more powerful. The tree begins to go Godzilla on the surrounding area. DJ / Pandora head back to the Saw Mill.

Appendix D

Guitar Hero II Weekly **Status Report**

GH2: Last Week 5-1-06	
COMPLETED TASKS	
Completed Tasks	**Notes**
Production	
Tracy/Daniel/Helen/Elena • Text pass/revisions • Updated Rockabilly blurb • Final outsource plan in schedule • Continued scheduling • E3 optimization plan Kendall • Kickoff call with RedOctane • Send remaining materials for MS1 to ROI and Liquid • Resume filtering • Hammer out poster artist contracts • Work with ROI to begin production • Set up Hickenbottom outsource	
Design	
Chris C • E3 revisions/monitoring • Rock store improvements (first pass) • New Save flow (360) – first pass	
Code	
James • Synchronized moves • Look into gem creation bug • Debug Christine • Complete: solo character select screen support (simplified E3 version) • Complete: E3 guitar select screen • Debug Ethan • Debug/Elliot support Moss • 360 build process Dogles • Optimization support for artists • Debug	

1

Art		
Dare		
• Art direction		
Pete McD		
• Debug/E3 optimization		
Steve		
• E3 polish/optimization/debug		
Moore		
• New Fest (Graveyard): PS2 revision • E3 demo polish		
Gayle		
• Ramp up - lighting/Milo/Reference for preset genres		
Gibson		
• E3 Debug/Revision		
Dave Bog		
• Fest FX optimization		
Aaron		
• E3 debug/optimization		
Adolph		
• Set up dummy milo files for outsourcers • **Add Axel and Judy to 360 Build** • E3 Debug & Support		
Booth		
• E3 Optimization		
Warburg		
• E3 Optimization		
Gilpin		
• E3 optimization and revisions • Review ROI 360 Izzy 1 final revisions - compile feedback • Review ROI PS2 Izzy 1, compile feedback • Review ROI PS2 Clive, compile feedback		

Jenn:

- Finish tweaking Judy model for E3
- Debug/Revisions

Matt P.:

- Complete: Xavier ortho package
- Complete: Rock Girl 1 ortho package
- Updates to Johnny reference

Paul:

- Complete: Death Metal 1 ortho package
- Band ortho package
- Crowd outsource package

Reiko:
- Complete: new female singer ortho package

Noah:
- Lip sync song 3 "Arterial Black"
- Lip sync song 4 "Who Was in My Room Last Night?"
- Lip sync song 5 "War Pigs"
- Lip sync song 6 "YYZ" (no lyrics, haha!)
- Lip sync song 7 "John the Fisherman"
- Lip sync revisions

Chris H:
- Implement MOCAP for Band
- Debug/Revision

Jeff C

- Debug/Revision
- Begin: Pandora – Implement MOCAP

Joe K

- Implement: Single Player Guitar Select
- Implement: Pause screen
- Implement: Song Select
- Mock-up: Multiplayer Guitar/bass select
- Implement venue select screen
- Implement: Multiplayer Guitar/Bass select
- Debug/Revisions

Elliot

- Co-op revisions
- Revisions: New Track tattoo: Judy

▪ Revisions: New Track tattoo: Rockabilly ▪ Debug	
Audio	
Eric B	
▪ Continue revisions	
Izzy/Jeff	
▪ Author War Pigs ▪ Author Who Was in My Room Last Night ▪ Author Arterial Black ▪ Author YYZ ▪ Author John the Fisherman ▪ Continue tweaks/revisions	
QA	
Luke/Bill/Arthur	
▪ QA awesomeness ▪ Bug count and updates in Freq Pit ▪ Bug DB pass with Helen/Elena for E3 ▪ Framerate testing in Fest for E3 ▪ Full camera pass with new testing tools ▪ Ship build testing ▪ Investigate swap errors	

INCOMPLETE TASKS		
Task	**Reason for Slippage**	**Solution to Slippage**
Production		
(Helen) Complete metagame scheduling	-Continued progress; more info needed	-Will revisit upon updated spec from Canfield after E3
Art		
Code		
(Moss) Begin: Bone Palettes (Moss) Complete: 360 performance characterization	- Getting 360 build running and bug fixes took up Moss's week	-Adjusted schedule
(Ethan) Bank Report readout in Milo	-E3 optimization/coop revisions were priority	- Adjusted schedule

4

GH2: The Week Ahead
5-8-06

Highlights

- **E3 MILESTONE BUILD WAS A SUCCESS!**
- **Monday – final tweaks to build before Daniel gets on a plane Tuesday morning**
- GH2 testing room (5th flr) & build in pit: everyone should try out practice mode and multi-coop

Weekly Overview

- **Production**
  - Daniel/Tracy/Elena/Helen
    - Final list of tweaks for E3 build
    - Analyze design schedule
    - Update venue schedule per venue
    - Schedule Warburg as art tech
  - Kendall
    - Contact new poster artists
    - Filename tracker
    - Define remaining guitars and get approval from RedOctane
    - Ongoing outsource implementation
    - Resume filtering
- **Design**
  - Chris C
    - Update venue specs with encore FX
    - co-op streak spec
    - co-op tour plan/spec
    - char select screen spec revisions
    - complete: sync offset spec
    - guitar select screen spec revisions
- **Code**
  - James
    - Monday: Final tweaks to E3 build (if necessary)
    - Investigate DVD emulation for 360 w/ Luke/360 build stuff
    - Figure out why Exporter can't include Synth
    - Investigate where new twist bones are for emulating in code
  - Christine
    - Rip out E3 flow/go back to normal flow
    - Port localization fixes to system
    - Multi pro face off - game
    - Complete: Port Tutorial
    - Remaining placeholder screens
  - Ethan
    - BankReport Updates + bank readout in milo
    - HUD/track for multi pro face off
    - PS2 sample loader
    - Inline samples
  - Moss
    - Complete: 360 performance characterization
    - Bone Palettes
  - Dogles
    - Basic lip sync for strutter (KISS song)
    - Monday: Final tweaks to E3 build (if necessary)
    - FaceFX 1.5 Integration

5

- Updates to skin rendering
- Begin: RO venue - Volumetric Spotlight 360

- **Art**
    - Dare
        - Art Direction
    - Pete McD
        - Monday: Final tweaks to E3 build
        - New Large Club (RedOctane): 360 modeling/textures/maps revision
    - Steve
        - Battle of the Bands: Multiplayer venue revisions
        - Stonehenge: Block out
    - Matt Perlot
        - Vacation
    - Moore
        - Battle of the Bands: PS2 Lighting scripts
    - Gayle
        - Ramp up - lighting/Milo/Reference for preset genres
    - Gibson
        - Complete: Battle of the Bands: PS2 FX (pt2) and hookup
    - Dave Bog
        - Complete: Spider club: PS2 FX- thrown bottles
        - Spider club: PS2 FX- televisions
        - Begin: Spider club: PS2 FX revisions
    - Aaron
        - Monday: Final tweaks to E3 build
        - Battle of the Bands: camera revisions
        - New Small Club 1 (Spider): camera revisions
    - Adolph
        - New upper arm twisting joints (w/James)
        - Research improved skinning method
        - Define character pipeline for GH2 (w/Booth)
    - Booth
        - Define character pipeline for GH2 (w/Adolph)
    - Warburg
        - Tech art ramp
    - Gilpin
        - Outsource Oversight: Review/Feedback for:
            - Johnny 1 360 progress
            - Rocker Chick 1 360 progress
            - Death Metal 1 360 progress
            - Xavier 360 progress
            - Axel 2 360 progress
            - Izzy 1 360 progress
            - Clive PS2 progress
            - PS2 band chars progress
    - Paul
        - Final concept art: New Grim
        - Orthographic drawing: New Grim
        - Revisions: New Grim
        - Reference material for style, fabrics, etc.: New Grim
        - Revisions: Rockabilly 2 ortho
        - Reference material for style, fabrics, etc.: Rockabilly 2
    - Reiko
        - Reference material for style, fabrics, etc.: Judy 2
        - Final Judy 2 ortho package

6

- o Noah
    - Lip sync song 8
    - Lip sync song 9
- o Chris H
    - Buy MOCAP for Johnny and Clive
    - Begin: Buy MOCAP for Axel and Death Metal
- o Jeff C
    - Complete: New Pandora: Implement MOCAP
    - Begin: Integrate Crowd MOCAP
- o Joe K.
    - Monday: Final tweaks to E3 build (if necessary)
    - Mock-up: Multiplayer Co-op results
    - Mock-up: Single Player Results
    - Mock-up: Multiplayer Character select
    - Implement: Multiplayer Character select
    - Implement new Choose Band screen
- o Elliot
    - Track Tattoos: Characters TBD

Audio

- o Eric B
    - Get new list of stuff to Randy
    - Tweaks to lighting cues
- o Izzy/ Jeff
    - Monday: Final tweaks to E3 build
    - Author new song(s) if they come in

QA

- Luke/Bill/Arthur
    - o Final E3 check
    - o Framerate pass
    - o QA awesomeness

OPEN ISSUES	
Issue	**Game Plan**
• Rock ending design	• Daniel/Canfield- complete design, decide if worth it.
• Need Hardware from Red Octane ASAP	• Daniel send reminder to RO each week, Elena will send email about 360 debugs and we will check that we have sufficient PS2 debugs
• Total list of concept needs?	• Dare & Elena identify specific revisions needed asap and schedules for Paul/Perlot/Reiko revised
• Metagame designs – sanity check needed!	• Based on character select screen, what other screens need clarification/design revisiting?

7

RISK AREAS	
Potential Risk	**Notes**
360 schedule still light	Post E3, major analysis needed
Art staff –HUD artist still open	
Posters not yet scheduled	Helen will work with Kendall to get these into the schedule; once scheduled, will be better equipped to determine potential risk
Liquid schedule & RO India schedules	If Liquid gets behind, RO India gets behind, we could get ourselves into trouble!

MULTI-DISCIPLINE MEETINGS		
Meetings Needed	**Notes**	**Personnel Required**
Audio Scheduling	Meet with Eric to determine approximately how long it takes to author a song with all the new stuff	Helen, Elena, Eric B
Encore FX design follow up	POST E3 (schedule for when Daniel's back from LA)	Daniel, Canfield, Dare, James, Eric B, Elena, Helen
James schedule	Will meet to allocate tasks	James, Elena, Helen
Art schedule w/Dare	Plan a recurring meeting	Dare, Elena, Helen
Stonehenge kickoff		Dare, Elena, Chris, venue team

8

Appendix E
CSI 3 **Camera System**

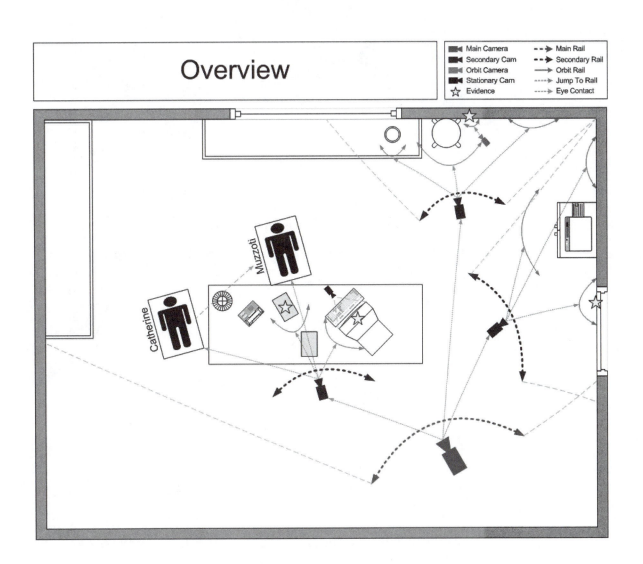

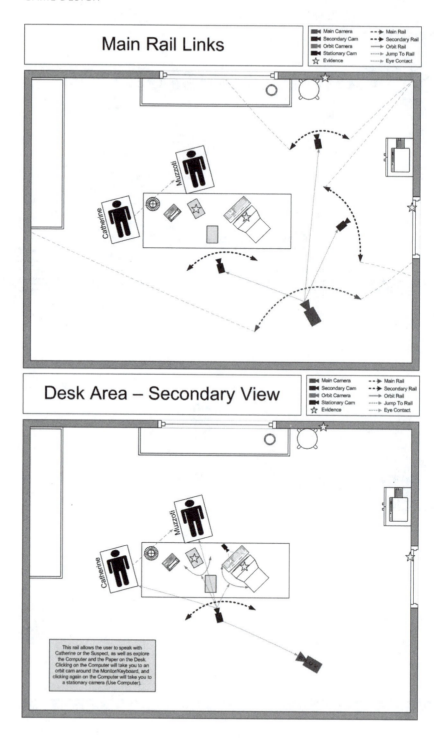

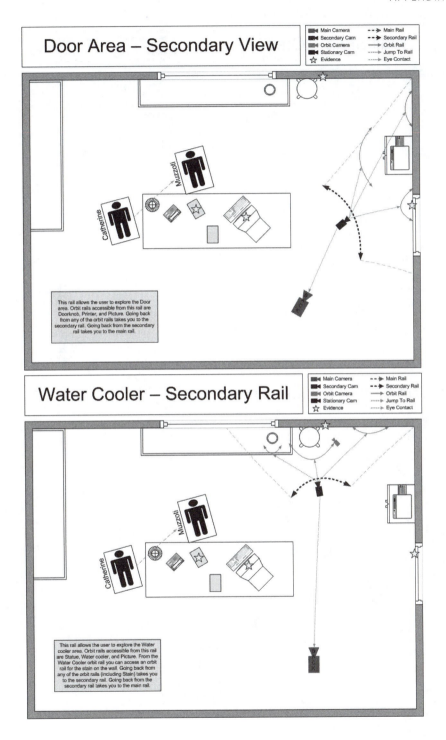

Door Area – Secondary View

▣ Main Camera		- - ▶ Main Rail	
▣ Secondary Cam		- - ▶ Secondary Rail	
▣ Orbit Camera		──▶ Orbit Rail	
▣ Stationary Cam		···▶ Jump To Rail	
☆ Evidence		···▶ Eye Contact	

Muzzoli

Catherine

This rail allows the user to explore the Door area. Orbit rails accessible from this rail are Doorknob, Printer, and Picture. Going back from any of the orbit rails takes you to the secondary rail. Going back from the secondary rail takes you to the main rail.

Water Cooler – Secondary Rail

▣ Main Camera		- - ▶ Main Rail	
▣ Secondary Cam		- - ▶ Secondary Rail	
▣ Orbit Camera		──▶ Orbit Rail	
▣ Stationary Cam		···▶ Jump To Rail	
☆ Evidence		···▶ Eye Contact	

Muzzoli

Catherine

This rail allows the user to explore the Water cooler area. Orbit rails accessible from this rail are Statue, Water cooler, and Picture. From the Water Cooler orbit rail you can access an orbit rail for the stain on the wall. Going back from any of the orbit rails (including Stain) takes you to the secondary rail. Going back from the secondary rail takes you to the main rail.

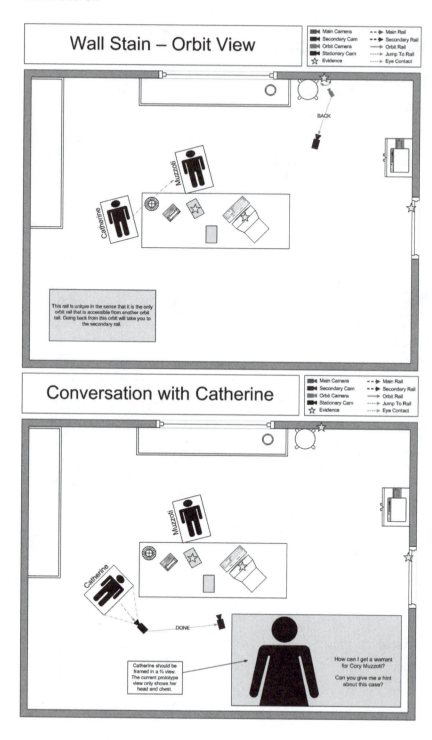

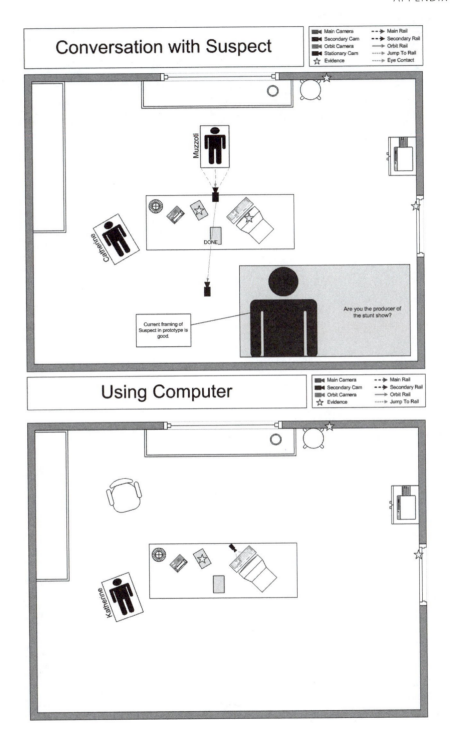

Biographies

Charles Balas is marketing manager at Oberon Games in Seattle, Washington. He began his career in 1997 at Sierra in sales and business development and in 2000 became brand manager and director of marketing for Cool Media Group. He has worked at Monolith and launched Zango Games with 180Solutions before joining Oberon in 2005. Balas has also founded his own company, Brand X Games, in Washington, with a small team focusing on developing original IP.

Hal Barwood is an icon in the games industry whose first professional gig was in 1990 when Noah Falstein and David Fox called him about a new project at Lucas. Barwood's professional background prior to joining Lucas was in Hollywood, resulting in six produced movies, and uncredited writing on *Close Encounters of the Third Kind*. Barwood was designer, writer, and project lead on many titles at Lucas during his thirteen-and-a-half-year tenure, including *Indiana Jones and the Fate of Atlantis*, *Big Sky Trooper*, *Indiana Jones and his Desktop Adventures*, *Star Wars Yoda Stories*, *Indiana Jones and the Infernal Machine*, and *RTX Red Rock*; he directed the full-motion video sequences on the shooter *Star Wars Rebel Assault II*. Barwood has been a consultant since 2003, as president of Finite Arts, and has partnered with Falstein on The 400 Project, which deals with rules in game design.

Corey Bridges has been in the industry "in stealth mode" since 2003, as co-founder of Multiverse. A self-proclaimed "computer geek" with a degree in English from UC Berkeley, Bridges was the project manager of the communication browser for Netscape, from pre-IPO to just before the AOL acquisition, and went on to become employee number eight at Netflix, before starting his own production company making not-run-of-the-mill corporate training videos with *NASCAR*, *Batman*, and *Flash Gordon* themes. Bridges joined Bill Turpin, Rafhael Cedeno, and Robin McCollum, all Netscape veterans, and started The Multiverse Network in 2003, which has created a comprehensive MMOG platform for independent developers.

James Brightman is the lead business editor (editor-in-chief) of *GameDaily Biz*, a leading industry newsletter that is part of GameDaily.com, founded in 1995 in San Francisco, California, by Gigex. Brightman started covering the industry in 2001 as a volunteer with Gamerfeed, which supplied editorial content that was used by Gigex. Brightman joined GameDaily in 2002 and has been the main editor since 2004. GameDaily, which consists of the consumer website GameDaily.com and the industry newsletter *GameDaily Biz*, was purchased in August 2006 by AOL and is part of AOL Games.

Chris Charla is executive producer of development at Foundation 9 in Emeryville, California. Charla began his career in 1995 as associate editor of *Next-Generation* magazine, launched ign.com for the publisher, then returned to the magazine to become editor-in-chief while at the same time moonlighting on his first professional game, *Klax*. Charla left in 1991 to join Digital Eclipse, which merged with Imagine Engine to form Backbone Entertainment. He has worked on many Atari and Midway anthologies, as well as *Alienators*, *Spyro the Dragon* for GBA, and the original IPs *Brooktown* and *Death Jr.* at Backbone.

Riley Cooper is a principal designer for Crystal Dynamics in Menlo Park, California, where he began his career in 1995 as a tester. Prior to joining Crystal Dynamics, Cooper studied rhetoric at UC Berkeley, which he says is "sort of applicable writing and critical thinking." His first project as a designer was *Solar Eclipse*, in which he did level design. He has worked on many prototypes over the years, as well as design on *Legacy of Kain: Soul Reaver*, *Legacy of Kain: Soul Reaver 2*, *Legacy of Kain: Defiance*, and as lead designer on *Lara Croft Tomb Raider: Legend*.

Matt Costello began in the industry as a games journalist for a number of publications, including the *LA Times*, *Sports Illustrated*, and *Playboy*, then became a novelist and started designing RPGs and board games such as *Dungeons & Dragons*, *Call of Cthulhu*, and *Batman*. Costello wrote the industry-changing hit title *The 7th Guest*, the first full-motion video CD-ROM puzzle game, released in 1992 by Virgin Games, which sold millions of copies. Projects since have included many more novels, three of which have been optioned for movies, and one of which, *Beneath Still Waters*, was produced and released by Lions Gate on DVD in March 2007, and such games as *The 11th Hour*, *Aladdin's MathQuest*, *The Cartoon History of the Universe*, *Zoog Disney*, *Hercules*, *Clifford the Big Red Dog Reading Adventure*, *Barbie Riding Club*, *Shellshock: Nam '67*, *Just Cause*, *The Italian Job*, *DOOM 3*, and *Pirates of the Caribbean 3*. Costello is currently working on two new unannounced games for id Software and Eidos.

Mary DeMarle is a narrative designer for Ubisoft, Montreal, currently working on *Splinter Cell 5*. DeMarle began her career in 1997 at Presto Studios on *The Jour-*

neyman Project 4 for Activision, and when that project was cancelled, she became designer on *Myst III: Exile*. She worked on *Homeworld 2* with Relic Entertainment and *Myst IV: Revelation* with Ubisoft before taking the role of narrative designer on *Splinter Cell 5*.

Denis Dyack is co-founder and president of Silicon Knights, which opened in 1991 in St. Catharines, Ontario, Canada. Dyack's first game, *Cyber Empires*, began development in 1988 and was published before the company became incorporated. The company's first three games were real-time action/strategy hybrid games for the PC, and they now do only console games. Their titles include *Metal Gear Solid: The Twin Snakes*, *Eternal Darkness: Sanity's Requiem*, *Blood Omen: Legacy of Kain*, *Dark Legions*, *Fantasy Empires*, and the *Too Human* trilogy. They are currently working on an unannounced game with Sega.

Noah Falstein began his career one week after graduating from college in 1980, with Milton Bradley. Falstein worked on the first team to reverse engineer the Atari VCS, then in 1982 went to Williams Electronics, now part of Midway, where he tested *Joust* to become familiar with the system and then became project lead and co-designer on the cult-classic *Sinister*. In February 1984 he joined Lucasfilm Games as employee number seven, then in 1991 became employee number nine at 3DO. With "one more start-up fever in me," Falstein joined DreamWorks Interactive as the third employee. In 1996, Falstein became president of his own design consulting company, The Inspiracy, based in Marin County, California. He has worked "on every type of project except sports games," and the majority of his work today is in serious games. Falstein writes the column "Better by Design" for *Game Developer* magazine.

Chris Ferriter is a producer at Ubisoft in San Francisco, California. Ferriter began his career in 1994 doing optical special effects, then digital special effects as the industry moved to CGI, and worked on ride films such as *Honey I Shrunk the Audience*, specializing in 3D and large-format IMAX films. In 1998 he went to work for THQ as lead tester then became producer on the *Motocross* franchise. He has worked for Midway, Atari, and EA Canada, and his credits include *Mortal Kombat* for the GBA and *Super Duper Sumos*, among many others. Ferriter joined Ubisoft in 2005 to manage the *CSI* franchise.

Annie Fox and her husband, David, opened the world's first public-access microcomputer facility in 1977 in San Rafael, California. In 1981, they turned this educational nonprofit over to clients to run, and in 1983 Fox's book, *Armchair BASIC: An Absolute Beginner's Guide to Microcomputers and Programming in BASIC*, was published by Osborne/McGraw-Hill. Fox wrote screenplays for the next seven years and began her games career in 1990, when she and her writing partner wrote *Sherlock Holmes Consulting Detective*, the first CD-ROM to use digitized video. Fox started writing and designing junior graphic adventure games and quickly became revered in the industry. Among her many credits are *Putt-Putt* adventures, *Madeline, Get Ready for School, Charlie Brown!, Mr. Potato Head Saves Veggie Valley, SFPD Homicide Case File: The Body in the Bay*, and *Fatty Bear's Birthday Surprise*. She currently presents workshops for teens and works on her Internet project *Hey Terra*, on which she has written two books.

David Fox and his wife, Annie, opened the world's first microcomputer center in 1977 in San Rafael, California. In 1981, they turned this educational nonprofit over to clients to run. Fox finished writing his manuscript for the book *Computer Animation Primer* in the spring of 1982, on using the Atari 800 to create computer animations, and discovered that Atari had funded Lucasfilm (now LucasArts) with $1 million to start a games group. Fox was hired by Loren Carpenter as employee number one and worked there for ten years as a designer, project lead, and one of the programmers on several projects, including *Rescue on Fractalus!, Labyrinth, Zak McKracken and the Alien Mindbenders, Indiana Jones and the Last Crusade: The Graphic Adventure*, and was primary script programmer on *Maniac Mansion*. Fox has since worked with Rocket Science Games, TalkCity, and Xulu Entertainment, and he has done a variety of production, design, and consulting projects.

Tracy Fullerton is assistant professor at the USC School of Cinematic Arts, Interactive Media Division, and co-director of the Electronic Arts Game Innovation Lab in Los Angeles, California. Fullerton's career spans designing some of the earliest online games for Microsoft and Sony, including *Jeopardy! Online* and *Wheel of Fortune Online*, as well as vocation-based games, educational titles, and interactive television for MTV, the History Channel, and TBS, among others. Fullerton began teaching part-time in 1995 and has been full-time staff since 2004 at USC. She is co-author of the book *Game Design Workshop: Designing, Prototyping, & Playtesting Games.*

Clyde Grossman is co-founder of Interactive Studio Management (ISM), founded in 1996 with business partner Bob Jacob. Grossman began his career in the industry in 1980 as a programmer at Atari, shifted into management, and eventually served as VP of product development for Sony Computer Entertainment of America, VP of publishing for Microprose, and executive director of software development for Sega of America. He has been responsible for the release of more than 100 games during his career, with sales of over $600 million in revenue.

Dave Grossman is a senior designer at Telltale Games in San Rafael, California. Grossman started his career in 1989 at LucasArts, where he worked for five years, apprenticing on two *Monkey Island* titles with Ron Gilbert, then becoming one of two project leads on *Maniac Mansion: Day of the Tentacle*. Grossman left Lucas for a freelance career and worked on the *Pajama Sam* series, *Freddie Fish, Winnie the Pooh,*

SpongeBob, *Total Annihilation*, and *Full Throttle*, among many other titles. He joined Telltale in the summer of 2005 as a senior designer, where he leads design on projects and mentors other designers. At Telltale, he has been lead designer on *Bone: The Great Cow Race*, *Sam & Max: Season 1*, and *Telltale Texas Hold'em*.

Justin Hayward is an artist at Bungie Studios, part of Microsoft Game Studios. Hayward's previous experience in games was as a modder, doing computer artwork mods for the games community, primarily model building and texturing, to modify the *Quake 3* engine. Hayward began his career in the industry in 2001, in Microsoft's paid internship program on Bungie's single-player version of *Halo 2*. Hayward currently works on the multiplayer version of *Halo 3* doing art and level design.

Rob Huebner is co-founder and CEO of Nihilistic Software in Novato, California. Huebner began his career in the industry in 1990 as a network programmer at Interplay for two and a half years, doing the online features for *Descent*. He worked for the next two and a half years as senior programmer on LucasArts' big FPS *Star Wars Jedi Knight: Dark Forces II*, and then went to Blizzard South in Irvine, California, as senior programmer on *StarCraft*, before starting Nihilistic with a group of 12 artists, programmers, and designers who had been the team on *Jedi Knight*. Huebner is on the board of IGDA and the advisory board for GDC. Nihilistic develops AAA titles and has developed *Vampire: The Masquerade*, *Marvel: Nemesis*, and *StarCraft: Ghost*. Their current project, *Conan* (working title), will be released in 2007 on the PS3 and Xbox 360.

Roger Holzberg is vice president of creative at WDPRO (Walt Disney Parks and Resorts Online) in Los Angeles, California. Holzberg began his career in 1992 when he acquired digital publishing rights to make interactive IMAX movies on CD-ROM. He worked for Knowledge Adventure developing adventure, entertainment, and edutainment products, including *Steven Spielberg's Director's Chair* and *Virtual Pyramid*, consulted for DreamWorks and Disney, and then worked for Disney Interactive on adventure games. He was creative lead of Disney World's Millennium Celebration and became creative director of WDPRO when it was founded in 2002.

Bob Jacob is co-founder of Interactive Studio Management (ISM), founded in 1996 with business partner Clyde Grossman. Jacob started in the industry in 1984 when he founded Cinemaware, producing games based on movie themes. Jacob also founded Acme Interactive, which merged with Malibu Graphics to form Malibu Comic Entertainment. Jacob is responsible for the design, management, and development of more than 25 hit games, including *Defender of the Crown*, *Evander Holyfield Boxing*, *Rocket Ranger*, *TV Sports Basketball*, *TV Sports Football*, and *Wings*. ISM has closed more than 150 publishing deals for its clients, negotiating contracts that have produced $275 million in development revenue and $75 million in royalties.

Matthew Karch is co-founder of Saber Interactive, a co-located company in St. Petersburg, Russia, and Cranford, New Jersey. Prior to starting Saber in 2000, Karch, who speaks fluent Russian, had his own law firm doing legal work for technology companies, helping with personnel transfers for computer programmers, which is how he met his partners, who came to him for help with a project. Their first title, *Will Rock*, was placed with Ubisoft by Jacob and Grossman at ISM. Saber has since worked on a *Sopranos* game with HBO and is currently doing a big-budget, large-scale undisclosed title. Their AAA project, *TimeShift*, is expected in the second half of 2007 from Vivendi.

Mark Lamia is VP and chief operating officer of Activision studio Treyarch. Lamia joined Activision in 1995, rising through the ranks to become vice president of North American Studios in 2000, with experience in a multitude of roles, and has handled some of the most high-profile and successful titles in the video-game industry. In 2006, he moved into the role at Treyarch, the developer of *Call of Duty 2: Big Red One* and *Call of Duty 3*.

Greg Land is lead designer and lead writer of *CSI* games at Telltale Games in San Rafael, California. Land started his career in 1996 in the test department "playing games" at LucasArts, moved into level design in 1998, then became a lead level designer, working on such titles as *Star Wars Jedi Starfighter*, *Star Wars Republic Commando*, *Star Wars Force Commander*, *Star Wars Starfighter*, and *Star Wars Bounty Hunter*. Land worked at Lucas for eight and a half years before joining Telltale in 2004 to take the lead on *CSI: 3 Dimensions of Murder* and ultimately the fourth title in the franchise, *CSI: Hard Evidence*, both published by Ubisoft.

Greg LoPiccolo is VP of product development at Harmonix in Cambridge, Massachusetts. LoPiccolo was a bassist in the alternative rock group Tribe and worked as an AV director for Looking Glass Studios, scoring music and audio on games before taking on the role of project director for *Thief: The Dark Project*. In 1998, after five years with Looking Glass, he joing Harmonix and has worked on *Frequency*, *Amplitude*, *Eyetoy: Antigrav*, *Karaoke Revolution*, *Guitar Hero*, and *Guitar Hero II*. Harmonix, founded in 1995, was purchased by MTV Networks in November, 2006.

Mike Mika is studio head at Backbone Entertainment in Emeryville, California. Mika's professional career started in the Game-Boy era, but like many/most of the industry's brightest he had worked on games as a hobby prior to going pro. Mika has worked for Disney, Midway, and Digital Eclipse, among others, with credits on such titles as *NFL Blitz*, *Tarzan*, *Lizzie McGuire*, *Mech Assault*, *Klax*, *Little Nicky*, and Backbone's original IP the *Death Jr.* franchise.

Joe Morrissey is game designer and writer at Backbone Entertainment in Emeryville, California. He came into the industry with a background entirely in English, rather than programming. Morrissey began his career in 1998 at Blizzard North, as a systems administrator, fixing computers and handling networking "across the hall from the lead story guy for all of the quests" on *Diablo*. "He was overworked and I offered to give him a hand, and three or four months into that he went to another company." Morrissey subsequently worked as designer on *Diablo II* and *Diablo II: Lord of Destruction* before joining Backbone to help with their efforts on *Death Jr. II: Root of Evil*.

Mike Sellers marks the games industry as his third career, which he started in 1994, with his brother Steve, when they founded Archetype Interactive to do a graphical online game. On December 15, 1995, they released the early beta of *Meridian 59*, the world's first 3D MMOG. In June 1996, 3DO purchased Architype, and in early 1997 3DO shut down their Internet division except for this game. Sellers started *My Place* in 1997 and sold it to eUniverse in 1999. He then went to work at Maxis as lead designer on the unreleased *Sim City Online* and on *Sims 2* before moving to Austin, Texas, to work on the next revision of *Ultima Online* for EA. A year later, Sellers founded Online Alchemy to do the next gen of MMOGs. Sellers is currently developing character AI and negotiating a license for a well-known existing property that "came to us, and you sit up and go, 'That could be very interesting to make as an MMOG.'"

Rob Swigart, based in Menlo Park, California, created the world's first interactive novel, *Portal*, published by Activision in 1986 and republished two years later as a hard-copy science-fiction novel by St. Martin's Press. Swigart has done projects for the Menlo Park think tank, Institute for the Future, since the late '70s, developing scenarios and vignettes for Fortune 500 companies, as well as co-writing a business book with the institute's executive director. He is the creator and author of *Down Time*, a collection of 21 hypermedia stories, and *Directions*, a "quasi-sentimental pseudo-scientific hyperpoem" based on the father of occupational medicine, Bernardino Ramazzini (1633-1714). He has authored ten novels including *Little America*, *The Time Trip*, *The Book of Revelations*, and *Xibalba Gate*, published in 2006, a science-fiction novel in which the characters interact in an MMOG to explore Central-American archeology.

Tim Willits is co-owner and lead designer at id Software, which employs 32 people in Mesquite, Texas. Willits began his career at id Software in 1995 with the distinction of being the first person hired from the Internet "map-making" community with his work on *DOOM*. His first published title was *The Ultimate DOOM*. He then worked as a level designer on the hugely popular *Quake* and *Wolfenstein* franchises. In 2000, the role of lead designer fell onto Tim as he began work on *DOOM 3*. Tim has also produced projects external to id Software such as *Quake 4* with Raven Software and various mission packs for early id Software titles. He is currently leading the internal team at id Software on a yet undisclosed new franchise.

Dennis Wixon is the user research manager at Microsoft Game Studios in Redmond, Washington. Wixon manages games-user research at Microsoft, the largest user-research team in the industry that works exclusively on games and exclusively in the area of game-design evaluation and improvement. Wixon has worked in testing for 25 years, with large-scale applications and consumer applications, and has been working on games testing since 1999, "because that's really only as long as there's been research in games." Wixon has a Ph.D. in experimental social psychology.

Adrian Wright is president of Max Gaming Technologies, a small independent development firm that opened in 2001 just outside of Cleveland, Ohio. Their first project, *Dark Horizons: Lore*, was released through GarageGames in 2004. Wright started in the industry in the early '90s running leagues and ladders for several games, including an eight-year run for *Mech Warrior*. Max Gaming has created the original IP casual games *Kachinko* and *Twin Distress*, has many established credits in contract development, is working on a multiplayer FPS educational title, and is developing an MMOG using the Multiverse platform.

Game List

Game Design: From Blue Sky to Green Light draws on more than 450 years of experience designing, greenlighting, and publishing games. Our experts have been involved in that capacity on the following collection of nearly 350 published titles:

101 Dalmatians: Escape from DeVil Manor

The 11th Hour

3D Table Sports

The 7th Guest

Adventurers Club

Air Power: WWI

Aladdin's MathQuest

Alice in Wonderland

Alienators

Amplitude

Anastasia

AOL News Quiz

Arcade's Greatest Hits

Atlas Shrugged

Attention Trainer

BackYard Wrestling 2: There Goes the Neighborhood

BackYard Wrestling: Don't Try This at Home

Bad Boys II

Baghdad Central: Desert Gunner

Barbie Riding Club

Bassmasters 2000

Battlefield 1942

Battlehawks 1942

Battlezone

Big Anthony's Mixed-Up Magic

Big Sky Trooper

Big World

Blackthorne

Blood Omen: Legacy of Kain

Blue's Clues: Blue's 123 Time Activities

Bone: The Great Cow Race

Borderline

Brazil

Brooktown High Senior Year

BugRiders

A Bug's Life

Buzz Lightyear Astro Blasters

Cadillacs and Dinosaurs: The Second Cataclysm

Call of Duty

Call of Duty 2

Call of Duty 2: Big Red One

Call of Duty 3

Call of Duty: Finest Hour

Call of Duty: United Offensive

Call to Power II

Championship Motocross 2001

Chaos Island: The Lost World Jurassic Park

The Cartoon History of the Universe

Chase

Civilization: Call to Power

Clifford the Big Red Dog Reading Adventure

Cloud

Clue Chronicles: Fatal Illusion

Columbus: Encounter, Discovery and Beyond

Commander

Commander Keen

Counting on Frank

Cryo Acquisition

CSI: 3 Dimensions of Murder

CSI: Hard Evidence

Curious George Comes Home

Cyber Bond

Cyberchase: Carnival Chaos

Cyberchase: Casablanca Quest

The D Show

Danger Girl

The Dark Half

Dark Horizons: Lore

Dark Legions

Dark Reign 2

Dark Reign: The Future of War

Dark Ride

Day of Defeat

Death Jr.

Death Jr. II: Root of Evil

Derelict

Descent

Diablo

Diablo II

Diablo II: Lord of Destruction

Die Hard Trilogy 2: Viva Las Vegas

The Dig

Dimension

The Discoverers

Disney's Goofy's Fun House

Disney's Magical Moment Pins

Disney's Mission: SPACE Race, EPCOT

Disney's Villains' Revenge

Disney's Virtual Magic Kingdom

DOOM

DOOM 3

DOOM 3: Resurrection of Evil

DOOM II

DRU

Duke Nukem: Land of the Babes

Duke Nukem: Time To Kill

Ellie's Enchanted Garden

Empires: Dawn of the Modern World

ESPN National Hockey Night

Eternal Darkness: Sanity's Requiem

Evolution/Revolution: The World 1890–1930

EyeToy: Antigrav

Fantasy Empires

Fatal Abyss

Fatty Bear's Birthday Surprise

flOw

Force 21

Freddi Fish 4: The Case of the Hogfish Rustlers of Briny Gulch

Freedom Fighter 56

Frequency

Full Spectrum Warrior

Full Throttle

The Game of LIFE

Geist

Get Ready for School, Charlie Brown!

Grade Builder: Algebra 1

Guitar Hero

Guitar Hero II

Habitat

Halo 2

Halo 3

Heavy Gear

Hercules

History IQ

Homeworld 2

Hooked on Phonics

Hungry Red Planet

I'm Your Man

Imagynasium

Immune Attack

imstar*

Indiana Jones and his Desktop Adventures

Indiana Jones and the Fate of Atlantis

Indiana Jones and the Infernal Machine

Indiana Jones and the Last Crusade: The Graphic Adventure

Inquizition

Interactive Comic Book

Interstate '82

Iron Phoenix

The Italian Job

JabberChat

Jeopardy! Online

Jet Grind Radio

Just Cause

Just Cause 2

Kachinko

Karaoke Revolution

Kids On Site

Klax

Kobe Bryant in NBA Courtside

Koronis Rift

Labyrinth

Lara Croft Tomb Raider: Legend

Legacy of Kain: Defiance

Legacy of Kain: Soul Reaver

Legacy of Kain: Soul Reaver 2

Legend of Kay

Let's Explore the Airport

Let's Explore the Farm

Little Nicky

Lizzie McGuire

Logic Quest

The Lost Vikings

Madeline and the Magnificent Puppet Show

Madeline: European Adventures

Maniac Mansion

Maniac Mansion: Day of the Tentacle

Marvel Nemesis: Rise of the Imperfects

Mary-Kate & Ashley: Crush Course

Mary-Kate & Ashley: Magical Mystery Mall

Mary-Kate & Ashley: Sweet 16: License to Drive

MechAssault

Meridian 59

Metal Arms: Glitch in the System

Metal Gear Solid: The Twin Snakes

Mickey Saves the Day

Midtown Madness 3

Mirage

Monkey Island 2: LeChuck's Revenge

The Monkey Wrench Conspiracy

Monster Garage

Return to Castle Wolfenstein: Tides of War

Ride For Your Life

Risk

Robotron X

Rock N' Roll Racing

RTX Red Rock

Rugrats Studio Tour

Rugrats: Search for Reptar

Sam & Max: Season 1

SeaBlade

The Secret of Monkey Island

Secret Weapons of the Luftwaffe

Secret Weapons of the Luftwaffe Expansion Disks

SFPD Homicide Case File: The Body in the Bay

Shanghai: Dynasty

Shellshock: Nam '67

Sherlock Holmes Consulting Detective Volume 1

Sherlock Holmes Consulting Detective Volume 2

Shrek

Shrek 2

Shrek Super Party

Shrek Treasure Hunt

The Simpsons Skateboarding

The Sims 2

Sinistar

Small Soldiers

Solar Eclipse

Solar Knights

Soldier of Fortune 2

The Sopranos: Road to Respect

SpaceStationSim

Speed

Splinter Cell 5

Spyro the Dragon

Spyro: Enter the Dragonfly

Star Rider

Star Trek: Armada II

Star Trek: Away Team

Star Trek: Bridge Commander

Star Trek: Deep Space Nine: Dominion Wars

Star Trek: Elite Force II

Star Trek: Starfleet Command III

Star Wars Bounty Hunter

Star Wars Empire at War

Star Wars Force Commander

Star Wars Jedi Knight II: Jedi Outcast

Star Wars Jedi Knight: Dark Forces II

Star Wars Jedi Knight: Jedi Academy

Star Wars Jedi Starfighter

Star Wars Rebel Assault II

Star Wars Republic Commando

Star Wars Starfighter

Star Wars Yoda Stories

StarCraft

StarCraft: Ghost

Starsky & Hutch

STEPS

Steven Spielberg's Director's Chair

Strife

Strike Fleet

Super Duper Sumos

Supreme Warrior

Tarzan

TechGen RTS

Their Finest Hour: The Battle of Britain

Thief: The Dark Project

Tiger Shark

Tiger Woods PGA Tour

TimeShift

Too Human

References

American Film Institute. "AFI's 100 Years…100 Heroes & Villains." Available online (http://www.afi.com/tvevents/100years/handv.aspx), 2003

"Amaze Bought by California Company." *Austin Business Journal*, November 15, 2006. Available online (http://austin.bizjournals.com/austin/stories/2006/11/13/daily23.html).

Surette, Tim. "Analyst: Industry to hit $44 billion by 2011." *GameSpot*, September 26, 2006. Available online (http://www.gamespot.com/news/6158664.html).

Dubner, Stephen J. and Levitt, Steven D. "A Star is Made: The Birth-Month Soccer Anomaly." Freakonomics column, *The New York Times*, May 7, 2006.

"'Boom Time' for Video Games Industry." *BBC News World Edition*. June 25, 2002. Available online (http://news.bbc.co.uk/2/hi/entertainment/2064660.stm).

Hill, Jason. "Game Industry at the Crossroads." *The Sydney Morning Herald*. September 7, 2006. Available online (http://www.smh.com.au/news/games/game-industry-at-the-crossroads/2006/09/06/1157222139337.html).

Stokley, Sarah. "Games Development: A Real Career Choice?" *Builder AU*. September 12, 2004. Available online (http://www.builderau.com.au/strategy/futuretech/soa/Games_development_a_real_career_choice_/0,339028285,339169404,00.htm).

Shuster, Loren. "Global Gaming Industry Now a Whopping $35 Billion Market." *Compiler*, July 2003. Available online (http://www.synopsys.com/news/pubs/compiler/art1lead_nokia-jul03.html).

The Myers & Briggs Foundation. "The Myers & Briggs Foundation." Available online (http://www.myersbriggs.org/), 2006.

Senkowsky, Sonya. "The Growing Gaming Industry." Available online (http://www.wkconline.org/index.php/seminar_showcase/entertainment_2005_story/the_growing_gaming_industry/), 2005.

O'Brien, Luke. "Why There Are No Indie Video Games and Why That's Bad For Gamers." *Slate*, May 26, 2006. Available online (http://www.slate.com/id/2142453/).

Wikipedia contributors. "Hannibal Lecter." *Wikipedia, The Free Encyclopedia*, http://en.wikipedia.org/w/index.php?title=Hannibal_Lecter&oldid=93891421 (accessed December 13, 2006).

Wikipedia contributors. "Society of Mind." *Wikipedia, The Free Encyclopedia*, http://en.wikipedia.org/w/index.php?title=Society_of_Mind&oldid=75286347 (accessed December 29, 2006).

Wikipedia contributors. "Extreme Programming." *Wikipedia, The Free Encyclopedia*, http://en.wikipedia.org/w/index.php?title=Extreme_Programming&oldid=93935539 (accessed December 29, 2006).

Index